HEALING FOR FREEDOM

The Institute for the Psychological Sciences Monograph Series

GENERAL EDITOR: *Craig Steven Titus*

The Institute for the Psychological Sciences (IPS) Monograph Series publishes original scholarly works that promote studies in the broad field of the psychological sciences. The Institute espouses the view that interdisciplinary conversations among experts in psychology, philosophy, and religion serve to advance our understanding of what constitutes both the mental well-being and the spiritual flourishing of the human person.

The overall mission of IPS is to contribute to the renewal of the Christian intellectual tradition and to the development of a psychology consistent with the teachings of the Catholic Church. IPS remains committed at the same time to fruitful dialogue with voices from outside the Christian tradition. The Institute offers M.S. and Psy.D. degrees in clinical psychology and an M.S. degree in general psychology. Moreover, it initiates research projects through the Scholarly Research Center located in Arlington, Virginia.

The IPS Monograph Series is placed under the patronage of St. Albert the Great, a thirteenth-century man of science and faith, whose life incarnates the human values that the Institute for the Psychological Sciences aims to promote. Those scholars associated with IPS seek to maintain a constructive and critical conversation based on both advanced research about and a high vision of the human person. IPS is committed to integrating what is the best in faith-based traditions and what is judged worthwhile in the several life sciences.

The Institute for the Psychological Sciences Monograph Series

VOLUME 4

HEALING FOR FREEDOM

A Christian Perspective on Personhood and Psychotherapy

Benedict M. Ashley, OP

The Institute for the Psychological Sciences Press
Arlington, Virginia

Distributed by
The Catholic University of America Press
620 Michigan Avenue N.E./240 Leahy Hall
Washington D.C. 20064

The paper used in this publication meets the minimum requirements of American National Standards for Information Science—Permanence of Paper for Printed Library Materials, ANSI Z39.48-1984. ∞

Library of Congress Cataloging-in-Publication Data
Ashley, Benedict M.
Healing for freedom : a Christian perspective on personhood and psychotherapy / Benedict M. Ashley, OP.
pages cm. — (The Institute for the Psychological Sciences monograph series ; v. 4)
Includes bibliographical references and index.
ISBN 978-0-9773-1038-8 (pbk. : alk. paper) 1. Personality—Religious aspects—Christianity. 2. Theological anthropology—Catholic Church. 3. Psychotherapy—Religious aspects—Catholic Church. 4. Catholic Church—Doctrines. I. Title.
BV4597.57.A84 2013
233—dc23 2012050900

To Dr. Gladys Sweeney
of the Institute for the Psychological Sciences
with profound gratitude

CONTENTS

HEALING FOR FREEDOM

one

HUMAN PERSONHOOD

Three Models

The Dilemmas of Psychotherapy

Today the profession of psychotherapy, although still much in demand, is faced with three grave problems. The first is that the increasing use of medical treatments for mental illness (chiefly drugs, but also surgery, electroshock, etc.) seems to weaken the reliance on psychotherapy, although it by no means eliminates it.

The second problem is the great diversity and inconsistency of personality theories and the therapies based on them. Medical diagnoses of physical ills are also often diverse, yet in most cases some "standard" etiology and treatment is generally recognized. For psychological problems, however, the theoretical and therapeutic diversity is baffling. Hence therapists are often resigned to mere eclecticism.

A third and more fundamental problem is that psychotherapists may find themselves split in their professional versus their religious convictions. Nor are they trained to deal with the religious views of their patients in an empathetic way. Instead they are inclined to view the spirituality of their clients as neuroses.

Commendable efforts are being made to achieve a better integration of Christian theology with current psychology, but chiefly by evangelical Protestants who largely overlook the resources of Catholic tradition, which emphasizes the harmony of faith and reason, theology and philosophy. What I propose to do in this chapter is to describe and classify the diversity in personality theory and therapy; then, in the subsequent chapters, I will show how the Christian understanding of the human person can contribute to synthesize these insights and prepare a way for future research on a sounder basis.

The Classification of Personality Theories and Therapies

"Know thyself" summed up Greek wisdom, and we either seek self-understanding or deny the truth about ourselves as too painful to face. The human person is the most complex of all objects of scientific study; as yet there is no universally accepted approach to unraveling its many threads.

Salvatore R. Maddi, in a widely used text,[1] notes that any personality theory must distinguish its description of the *core* of personality from its description of the *periphery*.[2] The core consists of the "overall directionality, purpose, and function of human life" common to all persons. The peripheral characteristics are the various traits that mark different individuals and on the basis of which persons can be grouped into a few or many types. In these terms, Maddi reduces the main current theories of personality to three principal models:

1. The *conflict model* explains personality as the result of a balance between inescapable conflicts. It has two versions:
   a. The *psychosocial version* used by Freud, Henry A. Murray, Erik Erikson (ego psychology), Melanie Klein (object-

1. Maddi, *Personality Theories: A Comparative Analysis*, 6th ed. (Pacific Grove, CA: Brooks/Cole, 1996).

2. Ibid., 14–15.

relations theory), Heinz Kohut (self-psychology), and Eric Berne (transactional analysis); it locates the conflict as between intrinsic drives and external social demands.

b. The *intrapsychic version,* used by Otto Rank, Frederick Perls (Gestalt psychology), and C. G. Jung; it locates the conflict as between different aspects of human nature.

2. The *fulfillment model* explains personality in terms of a striving to fulfill the human potential. It also has two versions:
   a. The *actualization version* of Carl Rogers, Abraham Maslow, Paul T. Costa, Jr., and Robert R. McCrae (five-factor theory); it sees the goal of development as the actualization of one's perceived potential.
   b. The *perfection version* used by Alfred Adler, Robert W. White, Gordon Allport, Erich Fromm, Victor Frankl (existential psychology), and Albert Ellis; it sees the goal of development as the attainment of excellence.
3. The *consistency model* explains personality not in terms of the intrinsic condition of the person but of its tendency to maintain a steady state of reaction to information received from the world. It has two versions:
   a. The *cognitive dissonance version* of George A. Kelly, Seymour Epstein, and David C. McClelland; it holds that persons seek to reduce disparities between their expectations and their experiences.
   b. The *activation version* of Donald W. Fiske and Maddi himself holds that individuals accommodate to moderate levels of self-activation but, through exposure to either excessive or insufficient stimulation, they will seek novelty-activation.

Another author, George Boeree, groups current theories according to three "forces":[3]

3. George Boeree, "PersonalityTheories," last modified 2006, http://www.ship.edu/~cgboeree/perscontents.html

1. *psychoanalytic* theories, which seek explanations of human behavior in the unconscious;
2. *behavioristic* theories, which seek explanations in external behavior in relation to the environment;
3. *humanistic* theories, which seek explanations in conscious experience.

According to Maddi, moderate behavioristic cognitive therapy has empirically proven the most effective of current methods. Although in the United States there are still some 20,000 practicing psychoanalysts, long-term psychoanalytic therapy has not demonstrated its effectiveness. Yet there are elements in it that *are* viable and of practical value. Freud alerted modern thought to the complexity and obscurity of human thought and behavior—even though such truths were not unknown to past ages, as is evident from the words of the Hebrew prophet Jeremiah (17:9): "The heart is deceitful above all things, and desperately sick; who can understand it?"

Christopher F. Monte sums up in a sentence his own discussion of current theories of personality. I believe most psychotherapists today would agree with his statement, which is not very different from that of the prophet Jeremiah that I have already quoted. Monte writes: "No theory, in the present state of the art, and certainly none of the so-called grand theories from psychology's history, can both comprehensively and irrefutably account for the wholeness, the uniqueness, for the universality of human propensities, foibles, drives, abilities and desires."[4]

4. Christopher F. Monte, *Beneath the Mask: An Introduction to Theories of Personality* (Fort Worth, TX: Harcourt, 1999). For a more detailed study, including discussion of the reliability of such evaluations, see Dianne L. Chambless and Thomas H. Ollendick, "Empirically Supported Psychological Interventions: Controversies and Evidence," *Annual Review of Psychology* 52 (February 2001): 685–716. See also L. A. Pervin, D. Cervone, and O. P. John, *Personality: Theory and Research* (9th ed.) (New York: John Wiley & Sons, Inc., 2005).

The Mind-Body Problem

Today psychologists and psychotherapists are generally trained in some reductionist, materialist theory that attributes the "mind" to the brain and its interaction with the rest of the body, independent of spiritual factors; taking the latter into account is ordinarily considered "unscientific." Yet most cultures have believed in the existence of gods, spirits, demons, etc. Even today our bookstores have not only a section of "religious books" but also an often larger section of "occult books" dealing with superhuman "spiritual" forces. These beings may be dismissed as "fantasies," yet they appear on our film screens, on TV and in novels, and as more and more indistinguishable from the realities with which they are mingled. Often such beings are conceived not as "persons" but as impersonal forces, or if personal, not as unambiguously spiritual in the sense of non-material. *Animism*, the belief that spirits inhabit not only animals, but also even trees, springs, mountains, the stars, is widespread. Human spirits are thought to survive the body and ancestor worship is common. Therefore, I will first describe the dualist model of the human person and then provide a history of it, because it is the oldest and most universal, though today the least popular in standard psychology. Without this historical background, complicated as it is, it is not possible to understand the diversity of modern views such as those classified by Maddi.

The Dualist Model of the Human Person

Dualism is the belief that human persons are composed of two natures, one that is material and the other spiritual. Such a construal of the human person, though, is not without its difficulties as to how two diverse natures can constitute a single being. The major question that has been addressed throughout the ages is how the material body and spiritual soul interact in the human person and agency. Many thinkers have chosen only one side of the dyad, taking either materialist or spiritualist positions.

Since our modern scientific tradition finds its origins among the Greeks, we do well to begin our history of dualism with them. The pre-Socratic Greek philosophers provided a mixed but important foundation for the work of Plato and Socrates. Most of these early thinkers struggled to think beyond the spirit-filled mythologies of their day and tried to explain all things in material terms. Thales, the first of them (c. 624–547 BC), was the first to predict solar eclipses, and he argued that "all things are made of water," but he is also reported to have exclaimed, "All things are full of gods!" Parmenides, slightly later (fl. 550 BC), argued that the knowledge of "Being" is possible only because Being never changes, yet he seems to have conceived of that Being as a material sphere. Anaxagoras (500–428 BC), who first explicitly introduced "mind" (*nous*) as the cause of change, called it "the thinnest of things" and thus material. No wonder then, that the noted sophist or rhetorician Protagoras (481–411 BC) declared: "As to the gods, I am unable to say whether they exist or do not exist."

These materialists are to be contrasted with the great Pythagoras (569–475 BC), the first systematic mathematician and mathematical physicist, who headed a cult that believed in the cyclic reincarnation of eternal souls. These souls were doomed forever to be re-embodied after death. It is important to note that souls that had sinned greatly in this life would descend into an ignoble animal body for the next. Pythagoras exemplifies a spiritualist position that did not satisfy later Greek thinkers.

Only with Socrates (469–399 BC) and his great pupil Plato (427–347 BC) was the dualist model given full expression. Plato followed Socrates' dialectical method of answering a problem by progressively eliminating unsatisfactory answers until the true answer ultimately emerged. He saw this method as best exemplified in Pythagorean mathematics, where the elimination of inconsistent and therefore wrong answers to a problem finally led to a consistent and precise answer. He thus discerned that the process of learning is an *ascent* from many imprecise answers to the precise and certain fit. He concluded, therefore, that learning is really a kind of remembering of true ideas innate to the human mind. This notion agreed with Pythagoras's belief in reincarnation, or the descent of an eternal soul into a body; it was also in harmony with the view of Parmenides that truth is impossible for the bodily senses. In Plato's model, then, the human person is an eternal mind equipped with true and certain ideas that has tragically fallen into a material body that causes it to forget these ideas. Later thinkers modified Plato's own model in various ways but retained its essential dualism, which explains human consciousness as independent of the body.

This model today seems entirely "unscientific," but Plato used it to promote the first successful theory in physics, the mathematical astronomy of Eudoxus (408–355 BC), Plato's colleague in the Athenian Academy, which was to become the model of all future centers of scientific research. Unfortunately the Academy descended into skepticism at the time of Carneades (214–129 BC). This despair of reason, which had already been proposed by Pyrrhus (c. 365–270 BC) and was influential into the second or third century of the Christian era, led finally to the confession of Sextus Empiricus (fl. AD 200): "I know nothing, not even that I know nothing." Through the centuries what is called Middle Platonism[5] in Alexandria in Egypt continued until AD 500 to produce important scientists, especially mathematicians.

Meanwhile, across the Mediterranean from this development of thought in Greece, Jewish thought had itself begun, grown, and matured, and then had encountered the thought of the Hellenistic and Roman cultures. The first two chapters of Genesis, standing at the head of the Jewish scriptures, teach that there is a transcendent but personal God who has freely created all things, including the first human person, from "the dust of the earth" and "breathed into his nostrils the breath of life." Thus human persons not only became alive,

5. See Stephen Gersh, *Middle Platonism and Neoplatonism: The Latin Tradition* (Vol. 2) (Notre Dame, IN: University of Notre Dame Press, 1986).

but, unlike other animals, were created in "the image of God." Hence God empowers human persons over all other earthly creatures and tells them to preserve and cultivate the garden of earth.

Then this first human person names all the animals and, finding human personhood different from them, realizes that one who is so lowly an image of God cannot live alone but needs a wife and children to form a community. In this simple, symbolic language, the Jews expressed their understanding of the human person as unified in body and soul, self-consciously intelligent, endowed with feeling, social, full of wonder at the diversity of creation, free and concerned to "name" (understand) environmental creatures so as to control and perfect them. Thus, though the ancient Jews never advanced to scientific research, their understanding of human psychology as it is described in the Bible from so many angles was balanced, deep, and remarkably realistic.

The Old Testament, however, remained vague as to the afterlife, speaking, much as did Greek mythology, only about a shadow existence in the grave. Not until the late Book of Daniel, which was written during the period when the Jews suffered under Persian rule and which was influenced by Zoroastrian dualism, did the Bible speak of the immortality of the soul. In later accounts—found in 2 Maccabees and in the Book of Wisdom (which is perhaps of Alexandrian origin)—of the martyrdom that the Jews suffered at the hands of the Ptolemaic Greeks, the promise of human immortality becomes explicit. By the first century BC the Sadducees believed in a future life but not in the resurrection; the Pharisees of the time, though, did believe in bodily resurrection, as Orthodox Jews still do.

When the Christian Church began to preach the Gospel, it had the problem of inculturating it. How could the Jewish biblical ways of thinking be made meaningful to the highly cultured Hellenistic and Roman civilizations? Philo of Alexandria (20 BC–AD 50), himself a Jew, had already tried to explain the Old Testament in a Platonizing fashion, arguing that Moses was the ultimate source of Greek wisdom. St. Paul gave Christian preachers a better example when he preached to the Athenians (Acts 17:16–32), quoting their poets and alluding to their rituals to explain the Gospel. The Church Fathers painstakingly followed this example.[6]

Gnosticism—a kind of mythologized Platonism—was the first doctrinal danger that the Church faced as it spread the Gospel through a world dominated by a declining Roman empire.[7] The Manicheans—a later Gnostic group so named because of their founder, Mani (AD 210–78)—taught that this world is the creation of an evil or foolish God and that the true God is hidden and only mystically accessible. Hence they recommended that their more perfect believers should release their spiritual souls from their evil bodies by suicide through prolonged fasting.

In competition with these various forms of dualism were the adherents of materialism and skeptism, as I will later recount, who strongly resisted the inculturation of the Gospel. As aids to this inculturation, Aristotle's major works might have presented fewer difficulties, but they were only gradually becoming known.[8] Hence the Church Fathers' obvious choice for terms in which they might dialogue with their pagan culture was (non-Gnostic) Platonism, since it defended both the power of reason to arrive at certain truth and reason's spiritual character. Yet the Church Fathers were careful to reject Plato's belief in rein-

6. For an account of this transition, see Cardinal Jean Daniélou, *The Theology of Jewish Christianity,* trans. and ed. John A. Baker (Chicago: H. Regnery Co., 1964).

7. Historians today no longer accept Edward Gibbon's famous view that Christianity caused this decline, but attribute it to many factors, chiefly military and economic. Christianity may even have delayed its fall. For reviews of current opinions see Hugh Elton, "Late Antiquity in the Mediterranean: The Collapse of the Roman Empire—Military Aspects," ORB Online Encyclopedia, last modified 1996, http://www.nipissingu.ca/department/history/MUHLBERGER/ORB/MILEX.HTM

8. Aristotle's dialogues, now lost, that imitated Plato's style were in circulation, but his works as we now have them were lost until the first century BC. Christopher Shields, "Aristotle," *The Stanford Encyclopedia of Philosophy,* last modified Sept. 25, 2008, http://plato.stanford.edu/entries/aristotle/

carnation, because it contradicted the Church's doctrines of Incarnation and Resurrection. The great biblical scholar Origen (AD 185–254) for a time held for reincarnation, and after his death these views were condemned by Church councils. Plato's dualistic psychology, though, which tended to denigrate the human body by identifying evil with materiality, continued to affect Christian theology.

Among the Eastern Fathers the great Gregory of Nyssa (ca. AD 335–95), influenced by Origen, proposed a whole anthropological theory based on Genesis in which he attributed human sexuality to the Creator's foreknowledge that humanity would fall into sin. He argued that if sin had not occurred human persons, like angels, could multiply by being directly created by God.

The dualist model of the human person took on new life in Neo-Platonism with the Alexandrian pagan Plotinus (AD 205–270), who traveled to Persia and met Indian thinkers, then settled in Rome, where he taught Porphyry (c. AD 232–c. 305), his biographer. It later took on Christian form through the mystical works of Pseudo-Dionysius, an unknown Syrian, who wrote between AD 485 and 518/28. Neo-Platonism, however, did not continue Plato's interest in scientific research but concentrated on systematizing his doctrines to promote the view that the human person must mystically transcend itself.

Before this, in the Western Church, St. Augustine of Hippo (354–430)—so often mistakenly accused of being anti-sex!—after his own conversion from Gnosticism (Manicheaism) first corrected this anti-sex notion and taught that humanity was created to procreate sexually even if it had never sinned. Yet on the basis of his own troubled youth and conversion experiences, he was as aware as Sigmund Freud of the conflictual role of sexuality in human life in its historic condition. His famous *Confessions* is the first autobiography in history that explores human *subjective* insight, on which Cartesianism was to be founded. While in general Augustine, like Gregory of Nyssa, remains a Platonist, his theology is soundly biblical and provides a richly psychological view of human life and its problems.

In the Christian medieval universities from AD 1200 onward, Aristotle's work became basic to the curriculum; yet scholars only gradually became aware how profoundly the Platonic and Aristotelian models of the human person differed. St. Thomas Aquinas (1225–74) was a pupil of St. Albert the Great (c. 1206–80), who wrote the most extensive commentaries on Aristotle's works that were produced in the Middle Ages, adding to it much original scientific material. Yet Albert's reading of Aristotle is, like almost all medieval readings, still touched with Platonism. It was Aquinas's unique achievement to have explicated the profound differences between Aristotle and his master and, on the basis of the Greek's insistence that *all purely human knowledge must be founded empirically on the senses,* developed Aristotle's understanding of the human person in more complete way, as will be shown in some detail in the next chapter.

Aquinas was too critical of Platonism to be as generally favored in his time as was the more traditional Augustinianism of the Franciscans such as St. Bonaventure (1221–74), yet these Franciscan thinkers had also to conform to the Aristotelian standards of logical rigor that more and more dominated the universities as the thirteenth century ended. The Franciscans John Duns Scotus (1265–1308) and William of Ockham (1288–1348), in undertaking their logically rigorous criticism of Aristotelianism, felt it necessary to suppose that human intelligence has the power to know individual things directly without a sensible image, as well as abstractly with a sensible image. This differed radically from Aquinas's view that we know individuals through cooperation between intelligence and sense phantasms. Scotus produced a metaphysics based on a univocal concept of being that was supposed to be valid independent of the sciences based on sense knowledge. Refuting Scotus, Ockham became a nominalist, denying that intellectual abstraction can yield truly universal concepts, affirming rather that it can yield only concepts that signify collections of somewhat similar individuals. Both approaches weakened the power of human reason so much that Scotus was led to doubt the possibility of proving the immortality of the soul by reason, and Ockham the possibility of a certain proof from reason of the existence of God. Thus the way was opened for the later tendency of theologians, including the Reformers, to depend on faith alone to refute a materialist conception of the human person.

From the time of Petrarch (1304–74) humanist laymen of the Renaissance courts, still faithful to Church (but reacting to the clerically dominated universities), shifted attention from the over-refined logicism of nominalism to the study of Greek and Roman belles-lettres. They were entranced more by the literary beauty of Plato's *Dialogues* than by his profound speculations, and they were also taken by the ardent rhetoric and poetry of the Stoics and Epicureans. The Renaissance did, however, see a remarkable advance in mathematics and its application to physics, as a result of the recovery of the works of the many scientists of the initially Aristotelian Alexandrian Museum during its seven-hundred-year (300 BC to AD 400) existence. It is not surprising therefore that at the end of the Renaissance and the beginning of the "scientific revolution" of the 1600s, the Jesuit Francisco Suarez (1548–1617) attempted to reconcile Scotus's Platonism and Aquinas's Aristotelianism. Yet his reconciliation leaned to Platonism, since it made metaphysics independent of natural science, and so yet again a dualist model of the human person was favored.

The scientific revolution was immediately preceded by a period of even more intensely skeptical despair of human reason than nominalism; that period came about through the breakup of Church unity by the Reformation and by the religious wars that followed it. The great mathematician René Descartes (1596–1650), influenced by Suarez's Platonic tendencies going back through Scotus to St. Augustine, sought to find certitude in the "clear and distinct" ideas familiar to him in mathematics, which he thought, as did Plato, come from innate ideas. Yet Descartes gave a remarkable new twist to Platonism by his *Cogito ergo sum*, "I think therefore I am," making self-consciousness the basis of all knowledge, including natural science.

This version of the dualist model can be called *subjective dualism,* and it became basic to "modern" thought and especially the mathematization of modern science, which was so successful in the scientific works of G. W. Leibnitz (1646–1716) and Isaac Newton (1643–1727). It could also, however, end in the pantheism of Benedict Spinoza (1632–77) who identified matter and mind as two faces of a single reality.

Cartesianism's reliance on innate ideas, however, caused the Englishman John Locke (1632–1704) to emphasize the alternative *reductionist* model and to claim that all of our knowledge comes from the senses. His reaction to subjective dualism, however, was only partial, because it retained Descartes' notion that what we first know is not reality but our thoughts about reality. Hence the *empiricist* tradition, which has dominated British-American thought ever since is really *sensationalism* and thus is akin to the Cartesianism of continental philosophy. Moreover, the Scotsman David Hume (1711–76) argued that Locke's psychology reduced the relation of cause to effect to a simple succession of sensations; certitude or even a determinate probability in science therefore becomes impossible.

To escape this revival of skepticism and thus save Newtonian physics, while also providing a system of moral values independent of revelation, Immanuel Kant (1724–1804) devised still another version of the dualist model. He had been educated in the metaphysics of Leibniz and, although he came to criticize its dogmatism, he never escaped from its Cartesian dualism. Kant held, as Locke had done, that science must be based on the evidence of the senses. Yet he argued that scientific "truth" is not the conformity of our minds to reality but only a *consistent* picture that scientists can construct by fitting the data of the senses into categories innate to our intelligences. We are able to do so, he argued, because even in sensing objects we impose the framework of Newton's absolute "space" and "time" on them. The physical reality of the things themselves (*Dingen an sich*), therefore, will always be inaccessible to the human mind. Hence, for Kant and his followers, the existence of a human spiritual self and of God are unknowable to scientific reason but must be assumed for purely practical purposes, in order to support moral, social living. Kantianism thus provided a dualism, distinct from Plato's objective dualism and Descartes's subjective dualism, which we can call *categorical dualism.* In this model of the human person, the intelligence is no longer filled with the innate ideas that for Plato and Descartes gave certitude to truth. Instead, it is provided with a set of mental categories into which the data provide by the senses can be ordered so as to provide the basis of consistent *a priori* reasoning. This model, however, remains dualistic in that the human mind remains unable to reach extra-mental reality, including the human body. Philosophy ever since has struggled to get out of this enclosed, self-constructing mind.

The post-Kantian German Idealists, J. G. Fichte (1762–1814), F. W. J. von Schelling (1775–1854), and G. W. F. Hegel (1770–1831), therefore, each constructed a beautiful monistic "theory of everything" with their own personal minds at the center, as medieval thinkers are so often falsely accused of doing. Continental philosophy ever since has debated Kantianism, as is evident from Kantianism's influence on modern physics, as, for example in the thought of the father of quantum mechanics, Niels Bohr (1885–1962).[9]

This influence is evident, also, in the definition of the "scientific method" commonly taught student physicists today, which is formulated as follows:[10]

1. By observation identify some problem about our understanding of the universe.

9. See Henry Krips, "Measurement in Quantum Theory," *The Stanford Encyclopedia of Philosophy,* last modified August 22, 2007, http://plato.stanford.edu/entries/qt-measurement. Krips shows how Bohr agreed with but also departed from Kant, in whose philosophy so many German physicists of our time are educated. Einstein refused a Kantian anti-realist assumption, but confessed to being a follower of the pantheist Spinoza!

10. See Prof. Jose Wudka, "What Is the 'Scientific Method'?" last modified September 24, 1998, http://physics.ucr.edu/~wudka/Physics7/Notes_www/node6.html

2. Construct a theory to explain what you have observed.
3. On the basis of this hypothesis deductively predict the possible results of some new observations.
4. Test these predictions by experiments or further observations.
5. Modify the theory to fit the observed results better, but without supposing that the results can ever be more than probable.

Just as Kant argued, this method requires scientists to deduce some bit of possible sense data from *a priori* principles, which principles, although suggested by sense observation, are purely mental constructions. Any conclusion drawn from these principles must be verified or falsified by some new observation. Yet all the observed data before and after remain incapable of telling us what the object really is, and thus they have their intelligibility (meaning) only from the logical (usually mathematical) consistency of the mentally constructed theory. We are left, therefore, with a dualistic view of the persons who are scientists, since we describe them as *primarily* theory makers rather than as discoverers of reality. As the holes in this Kantian dualism became evident in the twentieth century, British and American analytical philosophy reduced its own ambitions to a study of the clear use of language in science or in moral debate.

Thus, though pure Platonic, Cartesian, or Kantian dualism of matter and mind finds little explicit support today among psychologists, the very name of their discipline—"the study of the psyche"—betrays the lasting influence of Cartesian-Kantian dualism. This very term "psychology" had a Cartesian origin. It first occurs in 1590 in the writings of a rather pedantic German Protestant philosopher, Rudolph Göeckel (Goclenius). It did not become popular before 1719, when another even more pedantic German Protestant philosopher, Baron Christian von Wolff (1659–1754), a follower of Leibnitz, began publishing his immense textbook *Rational Ideas on the Power of Human Understanding* It was so popular not only in German universities but throughout Europe that it became, as it were, the bible of the Enlightenment. Two volumes of Wolff's textbook were titled *Psychologia empirica* (1732) and *Psychologia rationalis* (1734).[11] Wolff was a thorough rationalist and assumed that what is first known to us is metaphysics, because it deals with innate first principles. This is in marked contrast to the position of Thomas Aquinas, for whom all we can naturally know is based on our senses. Although, like Locke, Wolff gave much more value to sense knowledge than Descartes had done, he accepted Leibnitz's view that *general* metaphysics, or *ontology* (a term invented by the German Protestant Jacob Lorhard, 1561–1609), is concerned not merely with what is actual but first of all with what is "possible." Hence Wolff considered "rational psychology" as a branch of "special" metaphysics that applies "ontology" or general metaphysics to particular fields of knowledge. Thus he distinguished it from "empirical psychology," which is based on sense observation. This insured that the study of mind would be divided into "philosophy of mind" and "scientific psychology" proper, and the terms were preserved by Kant.[12]

11. Some sources attribute it to the Lutheran Reformer Philipp Melanchthon (1497–1560), who Protestantized the German universities, but it is not found in his published works. Others attribute the term to Otto Casmann (1562–1607), but he used it in print four years after Goclenius; see Marko Marulic (pseudonym for K. Krstic), "The Author of the Term 'Psychology,'" *Acta Instituti Psychologici Universitatis Zagrabiensis*, no. 36 (1964): 7–13.

12. "The least object of perception (for example, even pleasure or displeasure), if added to the universal representation of self-consciousness, would at once transform rational psychology into empirical psychology." *The Critique of Pure Reason*, trans. Norman Kemp (New York: Palgrave Macmillan, 1929), Transcendental Logic, Second Division, Transcendental Dialectic, Second Book, Chapter I: The Paralogisms of Pure Reason, p. 330. Kant also says there: "The thinking subject is the object of psychology, the sum-total of all appearances (the world) is the object of cosmology, and the thing which contains the highest condition of the possibility of all that can be thought (the being of all beings) the object of theology" (323). And, "As thinking, I am an object of inner sense, and am called 'soul'. That which is an object of the outer senses is called 'body'. Accordingly the expression 'I', as a thinking being, signifies the object of that psychology which may be entitled the 'rational doctrine of the soul', inasmuch as I am

The Reductionist Model of the Human Person

The materialist view of the human person that is central to the reductionist model was already evident among the pre-Socratics. Their chief question was "What is it made out of?" Consequently they did not query, "How do we know what it is made out of?" The strongest early proponent of this model was Democritus of Abdera (314–271 BC), who reduced all reality, including any extra-terrestrial "gods," to unchanging atoms moving aimlessly in empty space (atomistic materialism).

This model, however, did not receive explicit epistemological formulation until after the decline of the Platonic Academy into skepticism in the third century BC. The Stoics and Epicureans were called "dogmatists" because they were not primarily concerned with scientific research, which seemed to them so much idle speculation. Instead their interest was in promoting more practical and trustworthy ethical values in terms as obvious and motivating as possible; hence sensible and materialistic. The Stoics, led by Zeno of Citium (333–264 BC), argued that the goal of life is consistently carrying out one's moral responsibilities, independent of one's unreliable feelings. To support this view, they pictured the universe as governed by determinist natural laws that control the fundamental natural force of "fire" (energistic materialism) as it acts in a regular cycle of construction and destruction. On the other hand, the Epicureans, or followers of Epicurus of Samos (314–271 BC), argued that happiness is a life of physical pleasure enjoyed quietly with friends and lived free of family cares or of any fear of after-death punishment death for sensual indulgences.

When the military-minded Roman Empire succeeded to the Greek culture, it saw Epicureanism as too "soft" and so favored Stoicism, thereby doing little to advance scientific research except for mil-

---

not here seeking to learn in regard to the soul anything more than can be inferred, independently of all experience (which determines me more specifically and *in concreto*), from this concept 'I,' so far as it is present in all thought" (329).

itary and medical purposes. The Romans did, however, retain much of the rhetorical psychology of the Greek sophists. As the empire became Christian, Platonic dualism came, as we have already indicated, to be favored by the Christian Church and it spread throughout the East and West. After 1200, however, in the Western universities it had to confront the instrumentalist model of Aristotle (see Chapter 2 for an account of this model). During this period of nearly a millenium and a half, the reductionist model, discredited by its materialism, was given little attention.

It is a common historical misconception to think that the scientific revolution of 1600 was a revolt of scientists seeking freedom for their research, against Christian dogmatism. While there were indeed incidents of conflict between the new science and the Church, such as the notorious Galileo Affair, the leading scientists of the scientific revolution, Nicolaus Copernicus (1473–1543), Tycho Brahe (1546–1601), Johannes Kepler (1571–1630), Galileo Galilei (1564–1642), Francis Bacon (1561–1626), René Descartes (1596–1650), and Isaac Newton (1642–1727), were all believers in the God of the Bible and often received ecclesiastical patronage. Moreover, because of their increasingly mathematical methods, these scientists tended to be Platonic in their outlook.

The shift to the reductionist model is first clearly evident in a correspondent of Galileo, a French priest and mathematician, Pierre Gassendi (1592–1655), who remained a good Catholic but who, like the Renaissance humanists, was contemptuous of Aristotle's works because of their lack of rhetorical literary style. Instead Gassendi favored the ancient reductive model, first proposed by the pre-Socratic Democritus (314–271 BC) and promoted by the ancient Epicureans, which reduces all natural things to unchanging atoms moving in empty space. Gassendi was unconvinced by Aristotle's refutation of atomism;[13] he saw no incompatibility between atomism and

13. *Physics* IV, cc. 7–9, 214a seq. Modern physics speaks of "empty space" but then asserts that it is full of gravitons, photons, and neutrinos, as well as "curvature" and

belief in the Christian Creator. Neither did the devout Protestant Christian Robert Boyle (1627–91), "Father of Modern Chemistry," who accepted this Epicureanism in natural science and defended it in theological writings.

After its use in the natural sciences, this reductionist model was extended to the human person by accepting Locke's empiricism, previously discussed, which reduced the distinction between human and animal intelligence to a mere matter of degree and located the former in the human brain. This step, explicitly taken in the eighteenth-century Enlightenment, is the origin of today's secular humanism or naturalism. With its application to the human person, this model has been used to replace the revealed faith of Christianity with a purely rational culture. Secular humanism replaces faith in the help of God with faith in the power of human science to solve human problems. We must think for ourselves! Thus in this respect the reductionists joined the dualist Kant in the advocacy of a secularist individualism. In 1784 Kant wrote:

> Enlightenment is man's emergence from his self-incurred immaturity. Immaturity is the inability to use one's own understanding without the guidance of another. This immaturity is self-incurred if its cause is not lack of understanding, but the lack of resolution and courage to use it without the guidance of another. The motto of enlightenment is therefore: *Sapere aude*! Have courage to use your own understanding![14]

Earlier, in England, Thomas Hobbes (1588–1679) had already taken the step to a frank materialism, arguing that we can know nothing of God by reason except his existence and that He too must be ma-

"quantum fluctuations." Anthony Rizzi, *Physics for Realists* (Baton Rouge, LA: IAP Press, 2008) has named this so-called "vacuum" the "plana"—from Latin for "flat"—and has shown that it is a real substance or substances with properties; see "plana" in his index.

14. *An Answer to the Question: What Is Enlightenment?* (1784) in *Immanuel Kant: Perpetual Peace, and Other Essays on Politics, History, and Morals*, trans. Ted Humphrey (Hackett Publishing Co., 1983), 41.

terial since He created a material world. This materialist trend both in France and England was for a time offset by the influence of Descartes, but when the Cartesian world system was replaced by Newtonianism, French scientists and mathematicians, such as *Julien de La Mettrie (1709–61)* in his *Man the Machine*, adopted materialism in a radical form.[15]

In the nineteenth century this development culminated in the materialist *positivism* of Auguste Comte (1798–1857), who held that science can describe but not causally explain natural phenomena. These materialists, more radically even than Locke, denied any essential distinction between sensation and intellection. Those who did not adopt atheism were deists, admitting God as the Creator, but denying his active intervention in the universe once it was created. While these thinkers made few scientific discoveries, they powerfully influenced the French and American Revolutions. At the same time the heavy mathematization of modern science made it "value free," which stimulated Romanticism to supply a value system. Like the later emotivist ethics of some analytic philosophers, this new value system was based not on human nature but on "feelings" and "preferences": or, as argued by the very influential Jean-Jacques Rousseau (1712–78), on natural inclinations independent of reason.

A major step toward the dominance of the reductionist model occurred in nineteenth-century England when Charles Darwin (1809–82) proposed his theory of the evolution of life and human intelligence by natural selection. Darwinism soon had world-wide acceptance and seemed to finish off any need even for a deistic God or a spiritual soul and to explain the human mind as simply a better adaptation to animal behavior in the face of environmental change.

15. Other scientists and philosophers of this period who were materialists include Comte Buffon (1707–88), Denis Diderot (1713–84), Étienne Condillac (1715–80), Claude-Adrien Helvetius (1715–71), Jean D'Alembert (1717–83), Baron d'Holbach (1723–89) (see his *The System of Nature*), the Marquis de Condorcet (1743–94) and Pierre Laplace (1749–1827).

In Germany especially, Darwinism stimulated materialist views in opposition to the German idealists who had radicalized Kant's views to the point of pantheism, such as Friedrich W. J. von Schelling (1775–1854),[16] and in particular George W. F. Hegel (1770–1831); the latter's system, for political reasons, was sponsored by the Prussian government.[17] Thus the famous evolutionist Ernest H. Haeckel (1834–19) claimed that human consciousness is nothing more than electric currents in the brain. Ultimately materialism took on its most influential social form in the "dialectical or historical materialism" of Karl Marx (1818–83) and Friedrich Engels (1820–95), which, in Marx's own words, "turned Hegel on his head" and was to dominate the political history of the twentieth century.

Another German, Wilhelm Wundt (1832–1920), who is generally considered the father of modern scientific psychology, in his *Theory of Sense Perception* (1858–62) and *Principles of Physiological Psychology* (1873–74) began the use of modern scientific techniques in the study of psychological phenomena. His research in psychology was based on laboratory controlled introspection. He had been a student of the noted physicist Hermann L. F. von Helmholtz (1821–94), who had written a *Handbook of Physiological Optics* that inspired Wundt to study visual perception. Wundt wrote in his *Principles of Physiological Psychology:*

> Psychological inquiries have, up to the most recent times, been undertaken solely in the interest of philosophy; physiology was enabled, by the character of its problems, to advance more quickly towards the application of exact experimental methods. Since, however, the

16. On Schelling, who was particularly concerned with a "philosophy of nature" and its theological implications, see Thomas O'Meara, OP, *Romantic Idealism and Roman Catholicism: Schelling and the Theologians* (Notre Dame, IN: University of Notre Dame Press, 1982) and *Church and Culture: German Catholic Theology from 1860 to 1914* (Notre Dame, IN: University of Notre Dame Press, 1991).

17. Among these materialists were Karl Vogt (1819–95), Jakob Moleschot (1822–95), and Ludwig Büechner (1824–99).

> experimental modification of the processes of life, as practiced by physiology, oftentimes effects a concomitant change, direct or indirect, in the processes of consciousness,—which, as we have seen, form part of vital processes at large,—it is clear that physiology is, in the very nature of the case, qualified to assist psychology on the side of method; thus rendering the same help to psychology that it, itself received from physics. In so far as physiological psychology receives assistance from physiology in the elaboration of experimental methods, it may be termed experimental psychology.[18]

Wundt's use of introspection, however, led to accusations that he had abandoned the materialist position for the dualist, Cartesian "turn to the subject" that initiated modern thought. In fact his introspective method proved scientifically unreliable, since even trained observers of their internal mental processes often disagreed. It was the Russian Ivan Pavlov (1849–1936) who in his experimental study of the behavior of dogs established the laws of classical conditioning and the stimulus-response (S > R) model of explanation. This became the basis of radical behaviorism as it was taken up by the American J. B. Watson (1878–1958) in his 1913 lecture "Psychology as the Behaviorist Views It" at Columbia University in New York in which he rejected all introspection as scientifically unverifiable. B. F. Skinner (1904–90) further radicalized behaviorism by denying that even internal states of the nervous system could be cited as explanatory of behavior.

The Austrian Sigmund Freud (1856–1939), a secularized Jew as committed to scientific reductionism as Watson and Skinner, published in 1900 his *The Interpretation of Dreams* and in 1901 his *The Psychopathology of Everyday Life.* In these works Freud, in sharp contrast to behaviorism and following Wundtian methods of conscious introspection, sought to explain human behavior in terms of instinctive drives hidden in the Id, or unconscious part of the human psyche. These psychic forces manifest themselves only symptomati-

18. Wilhelm Wundt, *Principles of Physiological Psychology*, trans. Edward Bradford Titchner (Sonnenschein, 1904), 2–3.

cally and symbolically, though they can be partially explored through the technique of psychoanalysis. Freud, a physician, had come to this view from his work with Joseph Breuer (1842–1925) on patients diagnosed as "hysterical." He himself says in the first of these books that in his dreams he identified himself with Hannibal. He interpreted this as meaning that Hannibal and Rome symbolize "the opposition between Jewish tenacity and the organizing spirit of the Catholic Church" with which he was fascinated but which for him symbolized the suppression of his hatred of his father.[19]

Although for Freud the core of the human psyche is the unconscious "Id," it is an error, says Maddi,[20] to suppose that Freud considered the Ego to be identical with consciousness, since some contents of the Id emerge, especially in psychoanalysis, although not its totality, and much of the contents of the Ego become hidden by defensive suppression. This is because, according to Maddi, "Even the highest form of [human] functioning, bespeaking exemplary development, is characterized by defensiveness, because the true antisocial nature of the instincts must be hidden from oneself and the world."[21] Thus for Freud, defensiveness—the tendency to ignore, forget, repress the fact of one's inherent selfishness so as to seem, even to oneself, to be a good citizen, "a decent person"—marks all human behavior even at its best. It hides the demands of our three core needs for "life, sexual pleasure, and death" that society restricts.

Behaviorism in its several versions stands in sharp contrast to

19. On Freud and religion see David Bakan, *Sigmund Freud and the Jewish Mystical Tradition* (Boston: Beacon Press, 1975), and Paul Vitz, *Sigmund Freud's Christian Unconscious* (New York: Guilford Press, 1988). Freud's view of the human person was materialist and deeply pessimistic, as is evident in his two famous books *Totem and Taboo* (New York: W. W. Norton, 1913/1950) and *Civilization and Its Discontents* (New York: W. W. Norton, 1930/1962). In the former work he attributed religion and religious ethics to a defensive denial of our hatred of our father as a rival for our mother's sexual favors. In the latter he argued that civilized society can only exist by the painful, and never quite successful, suppression of basic human instincts.

20. Maddi, *Personality Theories,* 38–39, 307–9.

21. Ibid., 39.

Freud and his disciples, yet it too, at least in its radical version, is largely discredited. Now that our knowledge of what goes on in the brain and central nervous system and in the hormonal system is rapidly increasing, Skinner's refusal to include this biological and neurological data seems absurd. Consequently Aaron Beck and others have turned to cognitive therapy (CT), which is based on a study of how the way people think influences their behavior and can be altered by learning experiences.

CT has also been integrated with behavioral conditioning techniques to form cognitive behavior (or behavioral) therapy (CBT). CT and CBT can be tested experientially, not simply by the kind of pure introspection that Wundt unsuccessfully tried to employ but by also observing verbal and non-verbal expression of thought in its relations to other kinds of external behavior and stimulation. This moderation of behaviorism is called the "cognitive revolution" and began in the 1950s, especially with Donald Broadbent's *Perception and Communication*[22] and Ulric Neisser's *Cognitive Psychology*.[23] CT and CBT were considerably influenced by Noam Chomsky's notion of "universal grammar" common to all human languages.

Thus for the treatment of a number of mental disorders these systems have been empirically validated. It should be noted, however, that as radical behavior therapy has given way to cognitive therapies, these therapies fit better into Maddi's fulfillment model than into the behaviorist model of personality. If we grant that humans can learn to control their behavior by the way they think, it becomes evident that central to their personhood is the striving for the realization of their potentialities and even for creative transcendence of their present limitations.

In the twentieth century the philosophical context of these debates in psychology was the ascendancy of materialism in scientific education, which took the German universities and their labora-

22. (New York: Pergamon Press, 1958).
23. (New York: Appleton-Century Crofts, 1967).

tories as its model. Thus religion became simply ignored except in controversies concerning "creationism" and evolution. In British and American analytical philosophy, "analysis" was influenced first briefly by the logical positivism of the Vienna Circle, led by Rudolf Carnap (1891–1970), then in a more lasting way by the "language games" of the Austrian Ludwig Wittgenstein (1889–1951), which devotes itself primarily to clarifying the language of science and of ethics. Only recently has analytic philosophy become interested in the question of the "ontology" or reality of the terms to which scientific language refers, but for most analysts this reality is only material, and "God-language" is treated as meaningless.

The current materialist approach to the human person has undoubtedly gone far to explain much about us that through the ages seemed utterly mysterious. We know today that human structures are determined by the genome and that this genome, present in every cell of the human body, can be understood chemically and physically. The information in the genome makes possible the construction of the human brain and central nervous system and the rest of the body that supplies the brain with its needed energy and the bodily instruments needed to carry out its commands as the person communicates with and interacts with the exterior world.

The human brain itself is known to be an extremely complex set of wire-like cells called neurons that transmit information from one part of the brain to another in a coordinated fashion in a manner somewhat like the calculations of a computer. Materialists, therefore, assume that our human activities, like those of a machine, can be best understood by taking them apart and putting them back together again. This seems to be precisely what science is doing today as it resolves the human person to its genome.

Thus from Freud onward there has been little question in the psychotherapeutic profession that the materialist reductionist model of the person is the only one that has scientific respectability. Any belief in a spiritual reality is interpreted as a defensive projection of physical desires. This position, which is a prominent feature of secular humanism or naturalism,[24] is set forth by one of its leading philosophical exponents, Paul Kurtz, as follows:[25]

> [N]aturalism is committed to a methodological principle within the context of scientific inquiry; i.e., all hypotheses and events are to be explained and tested by reference to natural causes and events. To introduce a supernatural or transcendental cause within science is to depart from naturalistic explanations.

The tenets of a humanistic naturalism have been formulated programmatically by the Center for Naturalism as follows:[26]

> Naturalism as a worldview is based on the premise that knowledge about what exists and about how things work is best achieved through the sciences, not personal revelation or religious tradition. The knowledge we have of ourselves and our place in nature is the achievement of a collective effort to construct a consistent view of the world that permits prediction and control. This effort proceeds by experiment and rational inquiry, and the knowledge gained is always subject to further testing as understanding matures. Wanting something to be true, or having the intense personal conviction that something is true, are never grounds for supposing that it *is* true.

24. For a discussion of secular humanism as a "religion" in the functional sense, see my *Choosing a Worldview and Value System: An Ecumenical Apologetics* (Staten Island, NY: Alba House, 2000), 25–62.

25. "Darwin Re-Crucified: Why Are So Many Afraid of Naturalism?" *Free Inquiry 18.2, 15–17. John F. Post provides another definition:* "[Naturalism holds] the twofold view that (1) everything is composed of natural entities—those studied in the sciences—whose properties determine all the properties of things, persons included,… abstract entities … like possibilities … and mathematical objects … and (2) acceptable methods of justification and explanation are commensurable, in some sense, with those in science"; "Naturalism," in *The Cambridge Dictionary of Philosophy*, ed. Robert Audi (Cambridge: Cambridge University Press, 1995), 517–18, at 517.

26. See www.centerfornaturalism.org, last modified 2006, as well as William Craig and J. P. Moreland, *Naturalism: A Critical Analysis* (Routledge Studies in Twentieth Century Philosophy; New York: Routledge, 2000) for a critical discussion of this movement.

> Scientific empiricism has the necessary consequence of unifying our knowledge of the world, of placing all objects of understanding within a single, overarching causal context. Under naturalism, there is just one, inclusive world in which phenomena arise.

To keep pace with the current popularity of "spirituality," this Center even advocates its own variety, so that today some American "naturalists" who defend strict materialism nevertheless speak of a "naturalist spirituality"!

> Although naturalism may at first seem an unlikely basis for spirituality, a naturalistic vision of ourselves and the world can inspire spiritual experience. Naturalism understands such experience as psychological states constituted by the activity of our brains, but this doesn't lessen the appeal of such experience, or render it less profound. Appreciating the fact of our complete inclusion in nature can generate feelings of connection and meaning that rival those offered by traditional religions.

To the obvious objection that this position is contrary to the convictions of many people whose "spirituality" is based on a conviction that spiritual beings are real, naturalists claim that their views are backed by empirical evidence and are logical, although they do not claim the views to be absolute truth.[27] However, probable truths, if their probability is not zero, must ultimately rest on "absolute" (that is, certain) truths and hence, in fact, naturalism is self-contradictory.

Yet the mind-body problem remains much discussed today even by that present majority of authors who accept materialism or "physicalism," the term that some prefer in view of the fact that modern physics admits the existence of particles that have no inertial mass.[28]

27. See David Papineau, "Naturalism," in *Stanford Enclycopedia of Philosophy*, last modified Feb 22, 2007, http://plato.stanford.edu/archives/spr2009/entries/naturalism/.

28. Ample material on the current state of the question is available in the following: David Chalmers, "Guide to the Philosophy of Mind," accessed June 14, 2005, http://consc.net/guide.html; J. J. C. Smart, "The Identity Theory of Mind," in *Stanford Encyclopedia of Philosophy*, last modified May 18, 2007, http://plato.stanford.edu/entries/mind-identity.

Some hold the "identity theory of mind," which says that mental experiences are nothing other than brain events. Paul and Patricia Churchland proposed "eliminativism,"[29] which holds that while "folk psychology" supposes that we have mental events, just as once people thought that sickness was demon possession, the progress of science will eliminate such beliefs as illusions and it will be known for certain that only brain events really exist. The most common current opinion, however, seems to be what is called "non-reductive physicalism" (actually a version of the reductive model as I have defined it), which claims that, as material substances become more complex, *properties* that are mental "emerge" ("property physicalism").

This emergence is supposed to explain why we all speak about conscious "qualia" such as the feeling of pain or pleasure and images such as dreams, etc. These properties are said to "supervene" on physical states of the brain. Others hold that the same qualium might respond to different physical states; for example, different brain states could be experienced as painful, so that although pain is a sign or "token" of a physical state, it is not unambiguously so. Still others favor "functionalism," which admits that brain states and mental events differ only in their function, that is, that mental events result in certain human behaviors, whereas brain events are neurological changes. Generally the proponents of these varieties of the reductionist model write as if the only alternative to their view is a Cartesian dualism and ignore the instrumentalist model as a third possibility or confuse it with dualism.

29. Paul Churchland, "Eliminative Materialism and the Propositional Attitudes," *Journal of Philosophy* 78.2 (1981): 67–90; and Patricia Churchland, *Neurophilosophy: Toward a Unified Science of the Mind-Brain* (Cambridge: MIT Press, 1986). Daniel Dennett, *Consciousness Explained* (New York: Penguin Books, 1991) is known for holding similar views.

The Instrumentalist Model of the Human Person

The respective advocates of dualist and reductionist models continue to debate and eclectically incorporate attractive aspects of the opposite model into their own theory. Yet from Greek times a third model can provide a profound reconciliation of these two conflicting models free of mere eclecticism, a model that was proposed by admirers of Aristotle and perfected in the work of St. Thomas Aquinas and his followers. I will begin to expound this third, instrumentalist model in the next chapter and apply it modern developments in the rest of this book.

When Pope Leo XIII, in the encyclical *Aeterni Patris* (1879), revived "the solid doctrine of St. Thomas Aquinas" as the basis of Catholic education to offset the anti-Catholic influence of the Enlightenment, it was not known how distorted and confused interpretations of the thought of Aquinas had become by the influence of Christian Wolff as described above. Furthermore a basic split arose between Thomist writers. On the one hand, the University of Louvain Thomistic Center advocated a "Transcendental Thomism" that would reconcile Aquinas and Kant. On the other, there were the more historical views of Etienne Gilson (1884–1975) and Jacques Maritain (1882–1973), who defended the distinction of natural philosophy from metaphysics. These two writers, although much more faithful to Aquinas's empiricism than the Transcendental Thomists, retained Wolff's distinction between natural science and philosophy. Gilson even claimed that Aquinas's commentaries on the works of Aristotle did not express Aquinas's own views.

Since 1950, however, this historical confusion of Aquinas's views has been cleared up, and it is now seen that, for Aristotle and Aquinas, "psychology" as study of human behavior pertains to metaphysics, since the human intelligence is spiritual, and thus *personal* psychology is distinguished from animal psychology (*comparative* psychology), which is the highest part of natural science. As will be shown in the course of this book, for Catholics this view is consistent with the teaching of the Church on the immediate creation of the human soul by God.

Conclusion

The instrumentalist model agrees with the dualist model both in that the human person differs from animals by possessing a spiritual soul that exists after death and in that human intelligence cannot operate in this life except through the instrumentality of the bodily senses and especially the instrumentality of the brain. Against both the other models, the instrumentalist model insists that both (a) the human spiritual powers and their acts and (b) the human bodily powers and their acts are powers and acts of the one spiritual soul of the person, who is a unified substance. This unified substance is constituted from a spiritual soul as its *formal* cause and from a body as its *material* cause. Therefore, the discipline of psychology, which studies the psychic functions of the human person, is an intrinsic part—and indeed the highest part—of natural science; the full study of human spirituality, however, transcends natural science and pertains to metaphysics and (for the Christian) to theology.

two

A MEDIATING FOUNDATION FOR PSYCHOLOGY

The Instrumentalist Model of the Human Person

As was shown in Chapter 1, the instrumentalist model of the human person proposed by Aristotle and significantly developed by St. Thomas Aquinas shares something of both the reductionist model and the dualist model but also differs radically from both. In this book I will spare the reader any scholarly discussion of the relations between Aquinas's thought and Aristotle's; neither will I relate details of the many disputes over the correct reading of their works, matters discussed at some length in my book *The Way Toward Wisdom.*[1] Instead I will write simply of the instrumentalist model developed by their joint effort and refined by later authors.

The instrumentalist model, like the dualist model, holds that the human capacity for abstract thought and the freedom of choice that it makes possible prove that the human person is in one essen-

1. *The Way Toward Wisdom: An Interdisciplinary, Intercultural Introduction to Metaphysics* (Notre Dame, IN: University of Notre Dame Press, 2006).

tial respect spiritual. On the other hand, like the reductionist model, it holds that this spiritual abstract thinking and freedom necessarily depend instrumentally on the concrete information that comes from the bodily senses that rational animals share with subhuman animals. Therefore, animals and human persons have the same kinds of sense and appetitive powers, which (at least in higher animals) depend on a primary, physical organ, the brain; but these common animal powers exist, as does the whole human body, because of a life-giving soul that is not animal but spiritual.

Thus, whereas for the dualist model the human soul and the human body are two different substances, for the instrumentalist model, just as for the reductionist model, they constitute only a single substance. Yet, while for the reductionist model the person is a single *material* substance, in the instrumentalist model, the human soul is non-material (spiritual), though it gives existence to the material body and together with that body constitutes a single substance. This single substance or person is primarily spiritual inasmuch as its spiritual soul survives the death of the body; secondarily it is material, in that it cannot in this life perform its spiritual acts without the instrument of the body. Furthermore, although the spiritual soul survives death, it does not constitute a complete person again until it receives its body back.[2]

This view raises the question whether it is possible that intelligent beings, other than human animals, may exist who are powerful enough to possess a penetrating knowledge of reality without using the instruments of the bodily senses, such as the spirits or angels in whose existence many religions believe. If these exist, human persons must in intelligence rank at the bottom of their hierarchy, since our intelligence is so dependent on an unreliable body that is so subject to disease and chance.[3]

2. See *The Catechism of the Catholic Church*, 2nd ed. (Vatican City: Libreria Editrice Vaticana, 1997), n. 996, on the resurrection of the body.

3. See my essay, "The Existence of Created Free Spirits" in *The Ashley Reader, Redeeming Reason* (Naples, FL; Sapientia Press of Ave Maria University, 2006), 47–60.

Yet our spiritual soul is not imprisoned or entombed in the body, as Platonic dualism holds. It is able to know and communicate with other persons and to control itself and the world freely precisely because it has a body that supplies it with ample information. Hence this body is essential to its spiritual activities, not a hindrance to them, as in the dualist model. In the instrumentalist tradition this view of the human person is expressed by saying that the "form" or "soul" (in modern terms we might say the "organization" of the body) is what makes it a living, acting organism.

Further on I will show how it can be proved with certainty on strictly empirical evidence that in fact the human soul differs from the forms or souls of other animals in that it is essentially non-material, as the instrumentalist model requires. At present I am only trying to make clear that in this model the immaterial human soul actualizes the matter of the human body in much the same way that the material (physical) organization of other organisms actualizes their matter. Hence the human person is constituted by a body-soul unity, in which the spirit-animated body and the embodied spirit are two sides of the same coin.

Note that for a superior spiritual form also to have lesser, material powers implies no contradiction as does the claim of the "property physicalism" version of the reductionist model by its claim that a superior consciousness "emerges" from an inferior material body.[4] What is superior possesses and can give to another something less than its whole perfection, but what is inferior and lacks something superior to itself cannot give that superior thing to another. The notion of "emergence" used by property physicalism is plausible only because of the

4. Materialists do not recognize the contradiction in their claim that a cause can give what it does not have, because they are so used to Neo-Darwinian evolution understood as the emergence of the higher from the lower. This, however, is precisely the problem with Neo-Darwinism as an explanation of the fact of evolution. An adequate theory of evolution must discover a higher cause of evolution; this point will be discussed in Chapter 3.

popularity of the Neo-Darwinian theory of evolution. That theory, if taken not as a *fact* but as an *adequate* explanation of the facts, suffers from the contradiction that will be discussed in Chapter 3.

The term *person* did not come into common use until Christian times and, as we have seen in Chapter 1, various uses of the term have seemed to favor dualism. Only when, in the thirteenth century, Aquinas argued that the immortal souls of the dead before the Resurrection are *not* persons, because they still lack their bodies, was the instrumentalist model adequately proposed. The dead again become persons, as Aquinas believed on the basis of Catholic faith they will, only when in the Resurrection their spiritual souls recover their material bodies and so become once more complete substances. Similarly, current Catholic theology holds that a human person comes into existence only by a direct act of creation of its soul by God. This happens when God completes the process of the fertilization of a human ovum by a human sperm to form a living child so as to give to that appropriate matter the spiritual form that makes it a single substance.[5]

This view does not mean, it should be noted, that God is the cause only of the human soul. As first cause of the universe and its natural laws, God is also the first cause of the parents who procreate the child's body and of the evolutionary process that produced the human species to which the parents belong, as well as of the very act of their sexual intercourse in producing the pregnancy.

The advantage of this view of the human person as a body-soul unity is not only that it mediates between the seemingly irreconcilable dualist and reductionist views. It also retains the scientific advantages of both opposing views, since (a) as does materialist reductionism, it begins *empirically* with the study of the human body, and (b) it posits the existence of a spiritual soul as the unifying principle of that human body only for empirical reasons, namely, the unique character

5. See *The Catechism of the Catholic Church*, nn. 362–68, on the human soul. On the question of when in embryological development the soul is created, see my article in *The Ashley Reader*, "When Does a Human Person Begin?" 329–68.

of human behavior as distinct from that of subhuman animals. The dualist model, by contrast, neglects the fundamental logical and epistemological axiom that in our thinking we must go from what is more certain to what is less certain.

What we are most certain of is the existence of the changing, material, sensible world and our own bodies as part of that world—not that we have a spiritual intelligence by which we know that world. Spiritual reality that transcends the evidence of the senses is less certain to us than what we touch, see, and hear. Hence *if* spiritual reality exists, it must be known by inference from what our senses tell us about ourselves and our bodily activities.

This is an approach directly contrary to the dualism of Descartes, who has so greatly influenced and confused modern thought. Descartes claimed he could doubt the evidence of his senses, yet could not doubt the fact that he was thinking. He said, "I think, therefore I am" (*Cogito ergo sum*); then, on the basis of this supposedly evident and certain truth, he tried to prove that the material world and other persons exist. But this is circular reasoning. I know that I am thinking only because I am thinking about something. If I claim that this "something" is simply my thoughts or myself as a thinking subject, I must then ask myself what I mean by a "thought" or a thinker. A thinker is something that has thoughts, and thoughts are first of all thoughts about what I touch, see, and hear. If I try to think a thought that is not about such bodily, sensible things, or the cause of such bodily things as effects, I come up with a blank.

Moreover, the same difficulty occurs in the supposedly anti-Cartesianism of Locke and the British Empiricists, since, though they rejected Descartes' innate ideas, they accepted that what we directly know are the subjective impressions within our minds, not the real objects that supposedly these ideas represent. Thus empiricism assumes that we know something but does not establish that we know anything but our ideas. The same difficulty arises in Kant's system, since he never explained how he could be sure that sense data are caused by real things, which he had to concede were for him unknowable. Aristotle and Aquinas, for their part, did not deny that persons are thinkers who have thoughts; they did, however, insist that thought as such is one of the most mysterious things that we think about and so it is not the place to begin our search for truth, as Descartes so vainly did.

I become certain that I have an idea of dog only after I have experienced the dog in its reality external to my mind, and I become certain that I have a mind only because I realize I have the power to know such things as dogs. It is only after I have learned something about the real world that I can then call up the memory of a dog, which may be no longer there, and begin to realize the difference between real and merely mental existence. Thus the dualist model violates the fundamental rule that science should move from what is better known to what is less well known.

Those who advocate the reductionist model, on the other hand, although they are methodologically correct in beginning with the empirical observation of human behavior just as they would do in studying animal psychology, in all honesty ought to remain open to the possibility that reality is wider than materiality. Therefore, in this book I will argue for the instrumentalist model of human personhood but will not begin from introspection, as the supporters of the dualist model have usually done. Instead I will proceed from an inductive perspective, as do the psychologists who support the reductionist model, thus going from what is more certain in our experience of the persons we see, hear, and touch to what is less certain, that is, to the hidden causes of these observed effects of human behavior. Whether among these causes, some are non-material, cannot be assumed but must be proved.

Though modern scientific anthropology and psychology certainly have a good claim to have achieved some reliable knowledge, their adoption of a rigidly materialist methodology has led them to accept two fundamental assumptions that need careful criticism.

1. Science should never claim certitude for any of its conclusions, but only probability.
2. Scientific explanations must be only in terms of material causes, because the existence of non-material causes can never be scientifically established.

The first of these assumptions can be accepted if it is understood as a merely *heuristic* or cautionary rule of investigation. Certainly the history of science teaches us that great scientists, such as Copernicus and Galileo, came to conclusions that were in fact true and which they proposed as certain, yet which in fact they had not yet proved. Others, like Newton, thought they had arrived at precise laws that later had to be refined, as Einstein refined Newton's laws of gravitation. Freud and Skinner, from opposite directions, notably advanced psychology, yet their views today are rightly regarded as dubious. Consequently, science must remain open to possible corrections of plausible theories. Karl Popper has even gone so far as to argue that scientific theories can never be verified; they can only be falsified, in order to make room for better ones.[6] Furthermore, postmodernists, as we will see below, argue for "a hermeneutic of suspicion" that raises the question whether a particular theory has gained general acceptance because of hard evidence or merely because it has esthetic, political, or ethical appeal in a given culture at a given time.[7]

Nevertheless, if this first assumption is taken seriously to mean that science *never* achieves certitude, that would altogether eliminate the possibility of genuine scientific knowledge. Is it only probable that

6. See Popper's *The Logic of Scientific Discovery* (London: Hutchinson, 1959) and *Conjectures and Refutations: The Growth of Scientific Knowledge* (London: Routledge, 1963).

7. The term is Paul Ricoeur's: see G. D. Robinson, "Paul Ricoeur and the Hermeneutics of Suspicion: A Brief Overview and Critique," *Premise* II, no. 8 (September 27, 1995): 12. Another example is the notion of "paradigm shift" made popular by Thomas S. Kuhn in his *The Structure of Scientific Revolutions*, 2nd ed. (Chicago : University of Chicago Press, 1970).

our earth moves? No, this scientific conclusion is certain, and not trivially so, since its proof is fundamental to all modern astronomy. Actually to claim that all scientific knowledge is only probable involves a logical contradiction, since statements are *determinately* probable only if they are based on good reasons. If, however, these reasons are themselves merely probable and are also based on other merely probable statements *ad infinitum*, the original statement becomes infinitely improbable! Therefore, probabilism's claim, that science can arrive only at probabilities, is to claim that science is no more probable than irrational assertions that are backed by no evidence at all, and hence to agree that critical scientific knowledge is impossible.

Thus science, to be truly scientific, must be built up on fundamental certitudes that can never be contradicted, and then it must continue in step-by-step advances that establish more certitudes, as in fact it has historically been done. Yet at any given time a great deal of science, probably the greater part of it, remains merely somewhat probable and open to correction. Moreover, even what is established with certitude is always open to refinement and to the exploration of its fuller implications.

Why, then, do so many scientists cling to probabilism? I would suggest that the reluctance to let go of it is largely a product of the unresolved issue of dualism versus reductionism. As I sketched in the history of materialism in Chapter 1, British empiricism grew up in opposition to Descartes' idealism, but it was infected by his subjectivism. Descartes sought certitude in innate ideas, a notion that empiricism rejected and sought to correct by basing science on sense knowledge. Empiricism was nevertheless influenced by Descartes in its supposition that what our senses show us are simply *ideas*. The empiricists supposed that these sensational ideas represented material realities external to our thought, but they never were able to show that this was certainly the case. Hence they eventually accepted David Hume's skepticism—or more accurately his pragmatic probabilism; this was a desperate solution, as we have just seen, and especially for a materialist, since it gave rise to Kant's special kind of idealism described in Chapter 1.

The second of the aforesaid unsupported assumptions often made by modern scientists—that scientific explanations must be only in terms of causes that are material, because the existence of non-material causes can never be scientifically established—is difficult to reconcile with the first assumption. If scientific reasoning can never attain certitude, how can it make scientists certain that material effects are not ultimately traceable to non-material causes? Moreover, if the second assumption is understood as meaning no more than that it is improbable that material effects can have ultimate causes that are immaterial, well, why is this so improbable so as to cause serious doubt? The only evidence they give for their doubt is that once science freed itself from the notion of immaterial causes it made greater progress. Yet historians of science have found it debatable whether religious faith in spiritual realities has hindered scientific advance more than it has promoted it. Many of the founders of modern science were motivated by a desire to glorify God by their understanding of the wonderful orderliness of creation.[8]

The claim that all our knowledge, because it must remain rooted in our sense knowledge, cannot know of the existence of immaterial things through their causal effects on the sensible world, has no empirical justification. To say, as so many do, that the immaterial is entirely outside the scope of science, which deals only with the observable, and then to assert that science is the only type of knowledge—this argumentation arises from simple prejudice. While it is true that the proper object of natural science is the study of material things, it is possible that among material phenomena there are data that can only be explained as the material effects of spiritual causes. If so, then it is not unscientific to give such explanations, since sci-

8. See Alfred North Whitehead, *Science and the Modern World* (New York: Simon & Schuster, 1999; originally 1925).

ence often reasons from what is observed to exist to the existence of the causes of this effect, which causes themselves cannot be observed. No one has ever observed the Big Bang! Thus this second assumption, like the first, must be left open to exploration; it cannot be taken as an indubitable principle necessary for science. For example, as I will show in more detail later, the "Mind-Body Problem" takes very different turns depending on one's assumptions concerning the nature of knowledge and causes.

In order to accept the conception of science implied by the instrumentalist model of the person as methodologically empirical yet open to spiritual reality, however, one has to overcome the deeply rooted prejudice, often implanted in early education, that Aristotle was an enemy of the empirical method and a kind of *a priori* idealist like Plato, Descartes, and Kant. This prejudice was spread long ago by the writings of Francis Bacon (1561–1626), a famous figure in the scientific revolution, who ignorantly alleged that Aristotle was a *deductivist,* interested only in abstract principles, instead of an *inductivist,* concerned with concrete facts of experience. The advance in the history of science in recent years, especially since World War II, has thoroughly discredited such prejudices and made it clear that Aristotle is one of the principal founders of the empirical methodology of modern science, as I argued in Chapter 1.[9]

9. See also the essays in David C. Lindberg and Robert S. Westman, *Reappraisals of the Scientific Revolution* (Cambridge: Cambridge University Press, 1990.) Thus Westman writes in an article "Proof, Poets, and Patronage: Copernicus's Preface to *De revolutionibus,*" 167–205: "It remains one of the great achievements of the history of science discipline, as it grew into a respectable profession in the decades after World War II, that it attacked and gravely undermined the blatant errors and pretenses of this popular Triumphalist historiography" (169f.). He means, by this term, the notion that it was only with Copernicus that genuine science triumphed. As A. C. Crombie shows in his three-volune work *Styles of Scientific Thinking in the European Tradition* (London: Duckworth, 1994), modern science has had its ups and downs, but at all times there has been a recognition that scientific hypotheses must be confirmed by empirical observations.

Post-Modern Anti-Foundationalism

As we attempt to place psychology as the study of human personhood in a critical scientific context, we also need to address the doubts about science being expressed by thinkers who today call themselves "post-modernists."[10] Many post-modernists vigorously attack what they call "foundationalism." Yet what they are really attacking as "foundations" are the *a priori* (prior to sense experience) truths that Descartes and Kant claimed to have established as the basis of the dualist model. Since in this book I accept Aristotelian Thomism, I am also in this sense an "anti-foundationalist," taking the position that natural science in general, and psychology in particular, must be somehow grounded in sense experience. We must consider carefully just what this grounding might be.

Post-modernists do have a serious argument against the claim that science is grounded in sense observation. They point out that Aquinas said, "What is received is conditioned by the state of the receiver" (*Quidquid recipitur ad modum recipientis recipitur*)"; our sense observations are always colored by prior experience, expectations, and intellectual perspectives. Two people of different temperament, background, and interests will experience the same thing or event in quite different ways. The noted semiotician John Deely[11] calls this "the web of signification," meaning that the world-view of each individual is a tissue of real and purely mental signs that require interpretation if the objective and subjective strands in this web are to be distinguished and related.

Philosophers of science today generally accept a view of "scientific method" that recognizes that researchers do not arrive at their theo-

10. See Gary Aylesworth "Postmodernism," *Stanford Encyclopedia of Philosophy, last modified Sep 30, 2005*, http://plato.stanford.edu/entries/postmodernism/.

11. Deely's massive work *Four Ages of Understanding: The First Postmodern Survey of Philosophy from Ancient Times to the Turn of the Twenty-first Century* (Toronto: University of Toronto Press, 2001) discusses this web of objectivity and subjectivity in great detail.

ries by "induction" from observed facts, as Francis Bacon supposed. Instead, after a somewhat random exploration of the data at hand, they create a hypothesis, *deduce* some of its possible consequences (predictions), and then look for facts to support or falsify that hypothesis. If it is falsified, they modify the hypothesis and continue the process. They know that purely deductive reasoning, because it has no other foundation than a hypothesis, by the laws of logic can never lead to a conclusion that is more than probable.

Since our goal, however, is to understand psychology and psychotherapy, we must attempt to establish solid foundations for a scientific empirical approach to the world. Because human persons are known to us first of all as bodies in a visible world of bodies, a science of human personhood, as Aristotle and Aquinas long ago argued, must be built on such solid foundations. We are part of this changing, physical world, which we know empirically through our bodily senses, and consequently we cannot understand ourselves if we do not first see ourselves as physical, chemical, living substances along with other such substances.

One important implication of the fact that every science has a foundational part is that while errors or confusions in that foundation can wreak havoc in the more specific parts of the science, the reverse need not be true. Therefore, it is fallacious to reject, as many do, Aristotle's analysis in his *Physics* of the generic foundations of natural science, merely because he made serious mistakes in the more specific parts of his exposition of natural science. He did indeed make major errors at this more specific level, such as his astronomical hypothesis that the world is eternal and his consequent hypothesis that there are celestial spheres composed of a quintessential form of matter. These mistakes warn us that we need to reexamine his *Physics* critically to see if the mistakes result from still more basic errors in that foundational work.[12] If we discover that these errors originated only

12. See my dissertation, "Aristotle's Sluggish Earth" (River Forest, IL: Albertus Magnus Lyceum, 1958). Previously in *The New Scholasticism* 32 (1958): Part I: "Prob-

at a more specific level, or even if they suggest some refinement of the foundations, such serious errors on Aristotle's part cannot of themselves invalidate his account of the basic principles of natural science, any more than Einstein has invalidated Newton's three laws of motion or his theory of gravitational attraction.

Similarly, when it was learned that Galileo's theory of the tides was erroneous, this did not overthrow the Copernican astronomy that Galileo defended, nor did it refute his own contributions to the more fundamental theory of inertial and gravitational motion. Likewise, Einstein did not prove Newton's Laws erroneous but simply refined them by a firmer grasp of the foundational principles of physics, such as the relative character of the concepts of time and place. Indeed, in this innovation Einstein, as we shall see, revived an ancient Aristotelian position in opposition to Newton's theory of absolute space.

It is also of the utmost importance to note that in natural science one must consider the foundations of a science before beginning to apply artificial techniques of observation. It is often supposed that science has in many cases proved our natural observations, made by our unaided senses, to be false. For example, to our senses the earth does not seem to move; yet science has certainly proved that it rotates on its axis and also orbits the sun. On the other hand, what seems to our senses to be a solid continuous object, such as a static dinner table, has supposedly been shown by science to be a space sparsely populated by molecules, or atoms, or elementary particles in constant motion. On further examination, however, it is evident that such examples do not prove that our senses are in positive error. The "errors" of normal sense knowledge (if they can even be called that) are purely negative; they show us something about the world but are not sensitive enough to show all its details. As we focus the lens of telescope or microscope, the more precise visual resolution provided by these in-

lematics of the *De Caelo*," 1–31; Part II, "Media of Demonstration," 202–34; the biological part was never published.

struments shows us more and more details in what we first saw correctly but only, as it were, in outline. To arrive at finer details than our naked senses are capable of giving us, we need to use instruments and to engage in controlled experiments. This perspective applies to human sciences as well.[13]

Thus ancient Greek and medieval science differ from modern science not so much in their methodology as in the modern invention of observational and measuring tools and in techniques of controlled experimentation. My eyes can provide only an incomplete picture of reality, and the use of instruments may reveal more. Yet if what little I do see could be proved to be in positive error, then no instruments could help me, since if my senses deceive me in reading my instruments, these instruments are of no use. Hence, we cannot use our instruments without first testing them against our ordinary sense experience. The obstinate Aristotelians who would not look through Galileo's telescope had a right to be suspicious of what information this untested instrument might give about distant objects until it had been tested by looking at nearer objects already well known to them through the use of their unaided eyes.

This priority of ordinary experience over artificial observation applies also to observations made by the experimental isolation of objects and the comparison with controls. Experiments have an artificial character and cannot be evaluated without first showing they are consistent with naturally observed facts. Thus we cannot be sure that the behavior of a caged monkey is the same as its behavior in its normal habitat before we have compared its behaviors in both situations. Hence, epistemologically all science depends on basic natural sense experiences; to be valid, conclusions reached through scientific method must be consistent with those basic experiences. The fa-

13. For overviews of modern experimental methods in psychology, see Donald H. Kausler, *Experimental Psychology, Cognition, and Human Aging* (New York: Springer-Verlag, 1991) and *Handbook of Research Methods in Experimental Psychology*, ed. Stephen F. Davis (Malden, MA: Blackwell, 2003).

mous physicist Sir Arthur Eddington once made the famous assertion that all modern scientific knowledge "reduces to pointer-readings on a scale";[14] but without human observers able to read the scale correctly and perhaps check each other's readings, science would be impossible.

Aristotle maintained, against Plato, that among all the sciences, and in spite of the superior clarity and certitude of mathematics, natural science is the first science in the epistemological order. It alone deals directly and immediately with our sensible world in its ceaseless becoming without any other abstraction than the separation of the universal and essential facts from those other facts that are irrelevant to the scientific project. Therefore, there are the four questions any science must ask and answer and keep asking and answering empirically as it moves from general to more and more specific conclusions.

The First Scientific Question: Does the Subject of Inquiry Exist?

What are the certain and solid foundations of scientific inquiry? A thorough answer to this question is beyond the scope of this book devoted to the specialized field of psychology, but it can be presented in summary as follows.[15] Because science must move from what is more certain to what is less certain, it proceeds by asking four fundamental questions in a definite order. Although our sense knowledge, from which all other knowledge is derived, shows us particular facts, the business of science is to derive abstract generalizations ("laws") from these facts. In making these generalizations science must first discover the most general features of its subject and then proceed to study more and more specific features, asking the same basic questions at each level of specificity.

14. *The Nature of the Physical World* (Whitefish, MT: Kessinger Publishing, 2005; original 1928), 259.

15. See my essay "Why First Philosophy Is Last" in *The Ashley Reader*, and more fully in my *The Way Toward Wisdom*.

Science cannot, however, proceed from a genus to its species simply by *deduction*, since the knowledge of the genus tells us nothing about the differences that distinguish its species. Therefore, at each level of specification, science must again return to an empirical investigation of these differences. *Deductive understanding, therefore, always presupposes an inductive, empirical process.*

The first basic question that must be asked at the beginning of a science and afterwards again and again at every level of specification is: "*Does the subject of our investigation exist?*"[16] The notion that arose after Descartes, that it is meaningful to investigate a merely alleged "possibility," is absurd. Just as probability presupposes some certitude, so does possibility. Only in terms of my certitudes about life on our planet can I think meaningfully about the possibility of life on other planets. Even what *appears* possible to me from what I know with certainty, may in fact be impossible, so that my speculations may turn out to be self-contradictory.

The only certain answer to this first scientific question, *Does the subject exist?* must be supplied by our senses, and first of all by the sense of touch, which alone gives us direct contact with the changing world, including our own bodies. (The role of the other senses will be discussed in the next chapter.) Natural science, therefore, is the *science of changeable existents* (*ens mobile*). Note that I say not "of the changing," but "of the changeable" because if things were, as Heraclitus claimed in the late 500s BC, in every respect continually changing, we could not sense them. We sense that one thing changes relative to sensing something else that has a relative stability—as, when I touch a table I feel my hand has changed, but although the table is warmed by that touch it has for a time a stable surface.

We observe not only that our world is made up of changeable things that eventually change but also that there are things that have a rela-

16. Aristotle, *Posterior Analytics*, II, c.1, 89b 23. Also Anthony Rizzi, *The Science before Science: A Guide to Thinking in the 21st Century* (Bloomington, IN: Authorhouse, 2004).

tive stability and identity that permits us to examine them. Hence their changes exhibit a certain uniformity or regularity, regarding which science formulates natural laws. When Newton observed the apple falling—if he did—he must also have recognized that it was the *same* apple that had been on the tree that was for a while in the air, and then lay on the ground, and he noted that this happens to other apples as well.

Aristotle's insistence on sticking to the basic and most certain fact of change explains why he was less enthusiastic than were Pythagoras and Plato about the use, which so predominates today, of mathematical constructs in science (although he recognized their great value).[17] Natural science abstracts only from the concrete particular; mathematics, by contrast, abstracts also from motion and every kind of change. Even when science measures change and time, it does so by imagining time as a "dimension" in which past and future are parts and the present is a point that joins these parts. In reality, however, neither past nor future actually exists (presently), but only the present "now." Moreover, the abstract mathematical representation of physical reality is only approximate; no real, physical circle perfectly fits the mathematical circle. Yet modern scientists have found mathematical constructs so helpful in research that many fall back into Platonism. For example, one of the present leaders of science, Roger Penrose, said in a 2003 interview:[18]

> Usually it's other people who call me a Platonist! I view the mathematical world as having an existence of its own, independent of us. It is timeless. I think, to be a working mathematician, it's difficult to hold any other view. It's not so much that the Platonic world has its own existence, but that the physical world accords with such precision, subtlety, and sophistication with aspects of the Platonic mathematical world. And this does go back to Plato, who was clear in dis-

17. See Sir Thomas Heath, *Mathematics in Aristotle* (Oxford: Clarendon Press, 1949).

18. Quoted in Karl Giberson, "The Man Who Fell to Earth: Interview with Sir Roger Penrose," *Science & Spirit* (March/April, 2003): 34–41.

> tinguishing between notions of precise mathematics and the usually inexact ways in which one applies this mathematics to the physical world. It is the shadow of the pure mathematical world that you see in the physical world. This idea is central to the way we do science. Science is always exploring the way the world works in relation to certain proposed models, and these models are mathematical constructions.

I do not question Penrose's description of the cultural perspective of most modern scientists, but that perspective cannot stand up under critical scrutiny. As the mathematician Kurt Gödel proved, neither the internal consistency nor the completeness of any axiomatic mathematical system can be established without reference to the facts of sense observation.[19] What Penrose's statement really shows is that too often scientists take the foundational assumptions of their science for granted without the careful and critical examination that Aristotle took care to provide.[20]

The Principle of Identity

Granted that science deals properly only with objects that are known by sense observation to exist, its first general principle also becomes directly evident from observation and hence requires no proof. This is the *principle of identity*, "Nothing can exist and not exist in precisely the same way."[21] The truth of this principle is evident from our sensible experience that we cannot touch something that is not real, that is, does not exist.

While it is true that illusory judgments can be made about un-

19. See "Kurt Gödel," *Stanford Encyclopedia of Philosophy*, http://plato.stanford.edu/entries/goedel/#IncThe.

20. See my *The Way Toward Wisdom*, chaps. I–V.

21. This principle is the same as the "Principle of Non-Contradiction" taken in its *real*, not its logical, sense when it refers to purely *mental* relations. The "Principle of Sufficient Reason," which says, "Everything that exists has a sufficient reason for its existence," was proposed by Leibnitz and is often added to the Principle of Non-Contradiction but adds nothing necessary to its function in reasoning.

usual or abnormal sense impressions, these errors can be corrected by more careful observations. An amputee may feel that his lost limb is hurting, but he can correct this impression by touching the stump. In the real, extramental world, the principle of identity is constantly verified. All logical reasoning is based on this principle. If it were not true, any scientific proposition could be both true and false. The tendency of neurotics or psychotics to think inconsistently is clear evidence of their mental disease.

Note, however, that at the level of natural science the principle of identity is still restricted to our experience of changeable beings; it has not yet been extended to apply to non-changeable beings, if, in fact, any such beings exist. Moreover, it is not primarily a logical principle, since its primary reference is not to the truth of propositions with which logic is concerned but to the nature of changeable reality as such. The validity of the laws of logic are established by showing their conformity to the principle of identity, but the validity of that principle in its logical sense is established by reference to its empirical validity, which is defended by natural science. Indeed, the very meaning of any mental relation with which logic is concerned is known only by analogy to real, physical relations. Thus, although logic as an art of reasoning is founded on this principle, it derives its validity from the changeable reality that is the proper subject of natural science. Hence, although in the pedagogical order formal logic is taught before the study of natural science, in the order of knowing, natural science is prior to logic that concerns relations that are purely mental, as well as to all the disciplines that concern reality.

The Second Basic Scientific Question: What Is It?

Once we know that an object exists, if we would like to know it better, a second scientific question presents itself: "*What is the existent subject of our investigation? (Quid sit?)*" The answer to this question must be a *real definition* of the object to be investigated. A *real* definition is distinguished from a *nominal* or merely stipulated definition because it is not simply a matter of word usage but is an empirically grounded description of the object. A real definition should, when this can be empirically ascertained with certainty, state the *essential* nature of the object.

Our essential knowledge of nature is very incomplete and often only generic, but it goes beyond mere phenomena, as phenomenologists also have shown.[22] We know material things through their observed properties, and we often have to be content with this, but the properties of a thing can sufficiently manifest its essence so that we can identify it.

To arrive at the essence, as such, of something more precisely, we need to be certain of its principal and specifying property, to which its other properties are ordered and by which they are unified. Thus we have an essential definition of the human being as a "rational animal" because "reason" is the property that ultimately distinguishes a human person from other animals and is our highest function, which unifies the rest of strictly human behavior.

Note, however, that in such a definition the meaning of both terms, "rational" and "animal," can still be very inadequately known and can be open to much further clarification. Thus, for example, modern science has been able to determine the properties of gold so well that we can distinguish it very precisely from every other element. This is what Aristotle would have called a real, essential definition, although there is still much about gold that we do not now understand and may never learn.

It can be objected that this second question about what a thing is should be the first. How can we know *that* an object exists without first knowing *what* it is that we know? In sense knowledge we observe

22. For a realist interpretation of phenomenology see Robert Sokolowski, *Introduction to Phenomenology* (Cambridge: Cambridge University Press, 2000). Others, including the founder of the school, Edmund Husserl, understood phenomenology to be a kind of idealism.

that a thing exists and what it is simultaneously, but in our intellectual analysis of our experience, the existence or *esse* (to be) is the condition of our being able in our thinking to clarify what it is, that is, to identify it. I pick up a piece of metal, knowing its existence, but only vaguely understanding what sort of metal it is until I have examined it more carefully, perhaps even subjected it to chemical analysis. Only after I have analyzed my observations can I be sure that I can identify it.

It is often denied, especially by nominalists and empiricists but also by Kantians, that we can know the essence of anything, but this denial is commonly based on the mistaken notion that Aristotle thought we know essences exhaustively and clearly (the Cartesian "clear and distinct ideas").[23] To claim that science cannot arrive at an essential knowledge of things,[24] but must remain at the level of the phenomena arises from an exaggerated notion of the clarity and adequacy a concept must have to represent the "essence" of an object. Essential knowing does not require Cartesian "clear and distinct ideas." Even our mathematical concepts, clear and distinct as they seem to be, are capable of degrees of explicitation; an expert mathematician sees more in the prime number 7 than I do! We have some essential knowledge of an independently existing thing if we can identify it by classifying it, as scientists do all the time. Water is essentially H_2O, although that definition omits certain facts we also know about it.

23. Some Thomists cite texts of Aquinas that seem to say that we cannot know the essences of material things. On this point, see my essay "Transition to Historical Mindedness" in *The Ashley Reader*, chap. 2, 13–26.

24. The grave error (in my view) of Jacques Maritain, in his formal distinction between a *dianoetic* philosophy of nature, which penetrates to essential knowledge, and *perionoetic* empiriological science, which he claimed deals only with phenomena, has unfortunately influenced many Thomists. As mentioned earlier in this chapter (note 14 above), Sir Arthur Eddington exemplifies a reductionist approach to scientific knowledge in his *The Nature of the Physical World* (2005), 259.

The Classification of Substances

As we experience it, the world is in a sense "one" but it is also "many." This is evident from the fact that some objects are moving, some standing still; some come into existence; some cease to exist. This independence in existence is only relative, however, since the existence of one seems to have some effect on the existence of others. As noted in Chapter 1, Spinoza thought there is only one substance, whereas Descartes thought that there are only two kinds of substances, mind and matter. On the other hand Locke, beginning empirically as we must do, began with material substances; he then oddly maintained that, although we must assume that material substances exist, we can never know any substance as such but only its *impressions* on us (sensationism). He supposed that, since the term "substance" (Greek *hypostasis*) means "what stands under," it is hidden from us.

We intellectually know things, however, that have existence independently of each other (at least a relative independence) or we could not know anything, since what exists in dependence on the existence of something else can be known only by knowing *that* something else, and so on *ad infinitum*. All that the term "substance" means, therefore, is an independent existent. Substances are not hidden from us. They are precisely what we constantly encounter in our experience, and they are the objects for scientific experiment.

One might ask whether many substances exist or just one substance exists, namely, the universe as a whole, as Spinoza thought. Certainly this does not seem to be the case; the dog I see does not seem to be part of the lawn across which it runs. We can, however, leave this question until later, and simply begin with the fact that at least one changeable being, a substance, exists and this fact provides an answer to our first scientific question.

In natural science (and only in natural science) is the first scientific question about the existence of its generic subject—changeable being—directly evident to an intellectual analysis of our sense experience; therefore, the existence of some substance requires no proof and we can thus proceed immediately to the second question, "What is it?" Since human knowledge proceeds from generalities to specifics, the answer to this question must be a generic definition of any kind of changeable being. This generic concept must be subdivided until we come to the species of changeable substances. Such a logical categorization of a genus into its sub-genera and species is called a "category."

Since natural science studies things that really exist, the first and principal scientific category (classification, taxonomy) of changeable things is that of "substance" (Greek *ousia*), which can be described as any changeable being that has independent existence. I say "described," not defined, because a definition must be in more generic terms than what it defines. "Substance," however, is the most generic of all the terms in its category. It is divided into inanimate and animate things, and modern science has developed remarkable taxonomies of each of these.

Inanimate substances are atoms or molecules, and the atoms are divided into their kinds in the famous *periodic table of the elements*, which orders about 100 species and their isotopes.[25] In turn the molecules are classified into thousands of known varieties of chemicals. Similarly, living things are divided into at least *plants* and *animals*, but today often into what are called the *five kingdoms*.[26] Biologists believe there are probably at least 13 to 14 million species, most of them being insects and microscopic life forms in tropical regions. The human species is located in this category of substances as a living vertebrate animal, a mammal, a primate, and a rational animal or human person.

Although a definition of "substance" is not possible, the concept can be further analyzed phenomenologically by asking, "Just what do

25. See the excellent account of the Periodic Table by Mark Winter, last modified 2011, http://www.webelements.com/

26. See W. P. Armstrong, "The Five Kingdoms of Life," last modified 2008, http://waynesword.palomar.edu/trfeb98.htm.

we experience when we experience some independently existing reality that is changeable?" Our experience shows us that changeable being, since it exists, must be in act. I know it exists because it *actually* touches me. If, however, what touches me were only actual, it could not change; hence, it must also be constituted by the real principle called "potency." This potentiality cannot be directly observed as can its actuality, but can be inferred from the fact of change, that is, its relation to some old actuality that it had but loses as it acquires some new actuality.[27] Thus potency is nothing more than the capacity of a changeable being to be actualized in some new way. In change, a physical reality known by touch is deprived (non-being, negation) of one actuality and receives another actuality.

In the natural science of Aristotle and Aquinas, the potency and act that define changeable being are technically called "matter" and "form" by analogy to our human experience of making something out of pre-existent material, as a potter makes a jug. Thus it is misleading to speak, as is often done, of Aristotle's analysis of the experience of changeables as "the theory of hylomorphism," since he does not propose it as a theory to be demonstrated but simply as an analytic quasi-definition or description of what is phenomenologically manifested by reference to immediate experience.

Modern science, however, uses the term "matter" in a very different sense than do Aristotle and Aquinas, and it seldom even speaks of "potency" or "actuality." Indeed, as the foregoing quotation from Penrose shows, the mathematicization of current science deals with "timeless," static mathematical constructs, which are like Platonic ideas. Nevertheless, scientists still find it necessary in describing any physical object to speak of the material parts of which it is composed (what Aristotelians would call "secondary matter") and they too can-

27. The "relation" mentioned here is not an accidental relation but a "transcendental relation," identical with the very essence of an entity, as it includes an order to some other entity, e.g., as a "shoe" is such only in relation to a "foot"; likewise, matter and form cannot exist except correlatively.

not talk about "matter" without correlating it with some "energy" or "force" by which it changes. They thereby recognize that, as Aristotle insisted, changeable realities cannot be described without considering both their potential and their actual aspects.

Thus a modern physicist would describe the hydrogen atom by reducing it to the elementary particles of which it is composed but would also note that these particles are organized in a structure bonded into whole atoms by nuclear forces. Similarly an Aristotelian physicist would consider this organization and the properties it produces to be the atom's unifying actuality or form by which it exists dynamically in process in some condition of energy or force. Therefore, even for the modern physicist the structure of the atom is not merely the inter-relation of the elementary particles but also the unity that is given it by it principle part, its nucleus, which makes it a stable whole, a dynamic system of forces quite different from a mere loose, static collection of elementary particles.

Note that matter and form in the Aristotelian sense are not themselves substances, since they exist only together and correlatively, never independently. The actuality or form of a changeable being is what gives actual existence to its matter and hence to the whole thing, while the potency or matter limits the existing form. Matter limits form because any substance, by reason of the form that it actually has, exists only as *this* kind of thing and so cannot exist with any of the other forms it might possibly receive by reason of its matter when it changes. Hence the form's actuality is limited, while the matter that limits it is potentially many other things; in fact, the matter can be said to be unlimited in its possibilities.

This simple yet profound concept of prime matter is difficult to grasp because prime matter is known only in correlation to the actuality of some intelligible form. No wonder that in the medieval universities the concept of prime matter was often misunderstood by commentators on Aristotle. Writing in the prevailing Platonic tradition, Duns Scotus, for example, tended to conceive "matter" as the minimal kind of actuality that is possible, and so he held that matter could exist without form.[28] This confusion has carried over into post-Galilean science, and when physicists today think of "matter" and "energy" as the two most basic terms in physics, they generally mean by "matter" not the potency that any particular substances has to be changed but some simplest actual kind of substance out of which more complex substances can be formed; for example, the elementary particles called quarks and leptons out of which atoms and everything else is made. Yet they also recognize that ultimately the elementary particles must be explained as some kind of formation of a cosmic "field" out of which everything emerges and in which every change takes place. Thus modern physics, by reducing matter to a property of a "field," has again approached Aristotle's profound conception of real physical potentiality.[29]

The First Theorem of Natural Science

With this analysis of what we observe changeable substances to be, it then becomes possible to formulate the very first theorem or demonstrated conclusion of natural science.[30]

MAJOR PREMISE: **The actuality of the potential as such** is the generic form of changeable being.

MINOR PREMISE: Change is **the actuality of the potential as such.**

CONCLUSION: Therefore, change is the generic form of changeable being.

28. On this opinion, common to several scholastics of the Franciscan tradition, see Allan B. Wolter, OFM, "The Ockhamist Critique," in *The Concept of Matter*, ed. Ernan McMullin (Notre Dame, IN: University of Notre Dame Press, 1963), 144–66.

29. See the essay of the physicist Charles W. Meisner, "Mass as a Form of Vacuum," in McMullin, *The Concept of Matter*, 609–12.

30. Aristotle, *Physics* III, c.1, 201a10.

In this syllogism the middle term (in boldface) is "the actuality of the potential as such" and, since this is the definition of "change" as it has been phenomenologically described above, this premise is evidently true. For any being, to change is to have its potentiality actualized. This change can be the actualization of prime matter that produces a new substance by substantial change from a previous substance or substances (a molecule of water produced from two atoms of hydrogen and one of oxygen). Or it can be a change in which a substance undergoes merely *accidental* modification, as when H_2O is frozen or evaporates, yet remains H_2O. The major premise of the foregoing syllogism is also evidently true from phenomenological analysis since this analysis shows that all the changeable beings of our sensible experience are composed of actual form and potential matter.

This theorem may seem mere word play or so obvious as to be trivial, but in fact it is fundamental to critical scientific thinking, because it tells us that the whole of natural science must always be a study of change. This does not exclude from natural science the proof of the existence of non-material substances, but by proving the existence of such substances from their material, changing effects, we set the limits of natural science. All of the other properties of the substances it studies will be dynamic properties, because the substances are changeable. Thus whatever we can know about the world of our sensible experience must be known in terms of change as the defining mark of all existent changeable things. In fact modern science really verifies (or falsifies) its assertions by checking them against these observed changes in nature, and not merely by reference to the consistency or inconsistency of these assertions with a theoretical mathematical construct. Therefore, in natural science we will never be dealing with merely static objects, but always with objects that reveal themselves or are revealed through the changes that we observe them undergo.

How absurd then is the often-repeated charge that Aristotle's worldview is static! In fact, his whole enterprise was to save the insight of Heraclitus's *panta rei*, "All is changing," by showing that true scientific and certain knowledge need not be of the unchanging, as Parmenides and Plato thought, but the nature of the changeable world can be explored through sensibly observing its properties and intellectually analyzing how they change and produce change.

The Principle of Causality

Once we have clarified the generic nature of changeable existents in terms of actuality and potentiality, and after the principle of identity is established, a second great principle of science emerges, the *principle of causality*. In current scientific language the term "cause" (as well as its correlative term "effect") has a very limited sense, which can apply only to the *extrinsic* causes of a thing; Aristotle and Aquinas, though, used the term "cause" in a wider sense to include any way in which one reality depends on another for its existence.

Here we are concerned with the *intrinsic* constituents of a changeable substance that are its correlative actuality and potentiality. As we have just seen, the existence of every changeable substance depends on its actuality (matter) and its potentiality (form), but in different yet correlative ways. To wit, the existence of that object is *caused* by and is the *effect* of a *material cause* and a *formal cause,* and these are the *intrinsic causes* of that object. We will see later that every changeable substance also has extrinsic causes.

The Third and Fourth Basic Scientific Questions

All terms in the science of the changeable must be defined in terms of the actualization of potentiality, but we observe that there are not only changes in which an old substance is changed into one or several new substances, but there are more superficial changes in which a substance as a whole retains its identity but is actualized or rendered potential in some particular respect: the ice in my glass melts but is still water. Aristotle called such a relatively superficial change of a substance an "accident" (Greek *symbebekos*, standing with) that is extrinsically caused in the substance by the action of another substance, as for example, when water is heated.

On the other hand, there are aspects of a thing which it always possesses by reason of its essence, and each of these is called a "property" (Greek, *idioi*) or "proper accident"; the property, or "proper accident," can however be distinguished from the essence (a) because the properties are many while the essence is one—for example, H_2O freezes at 0°C, and boils at 100°C and has a refractive index of about 1.33; and (b) because the property of a substance can be latent or manifest in various circumstances although the substance retains its identity—for example, water at various times has different temperatures and phases and refracts light only when light hits it at particular angles. In Latin scholasticism the properties discussed in both (a) and (b) are often called "accidents" and thus change is said to be "substantial" when a substance having an essential identity is produced or destroyed, and "accidental" when the substance remains but one of its accidents changes or a property is manifested or becomes latent.

Both proper accidents and mere accidents are simply aspects of some substance, and their existence *depends* on the substance, which is defined as "that which has relatively *independent* existence." The Cheshire Cat in *Alice in Wonderland* and *Through the Looking Glass* fades away until it leaves only its smile. This jokingly teaches us that a smile, which is an *accident*, cannot exist without the existence of its subject, the Cat; nor can the power to form an expression somewhat like a human smile, which is a *property* of *every* cat.

Since science seeks general laws, it abstracts from the accidental traits of substances in order to discover their identifying properties and then to explain why these properties are necessary to the substance, not merely its accidents. Thus the third scientific question is "*What are the properties of the substance we are investigating*? (*Quale sit?*)" and the fourth scientific question is "*Why does the substance un-*

der investigation have these properties? (Propter quid sit?)." It is important to note that the third and fourth scientific questions are the deductive or explanatory reversal of the first two questions. Once the real definition of a thing's essential nature has been obtained through an analysis of its properties by the method just described and, as a result of that same process, the answer to the third question, "What are its properties?" has become evident, the fourth question, "Why does it have these properties?" presents itself.

Yet at first sight these third and fourth questions, like the first two, seem out of order, since it is through the properties that we come to a real definition of the subject. Science, however, seeks general laws regarding the properties of substances in order that it can give a causal explanation of why these are essential properties and not mere accidents. Consequently we go *a posteriori* to the definition through the properties and then *a priori* in reverse order to explain the properties through the essence of the subject that is their cause. Nor is this process logically circular, because what we observe are many properties, from which we derive an insight as to why they are all related in the essence of the thing. Then from this unified concept we explain the thing's many different properties that we have already observed, and perhaps we predict some other property that we have not before observed and that we can now confirm by observation.

For Aristotle, as I have before emphasized, "deduction" requires us to have first defined both the essence and the properties of the thing through sense observation *before* we attempt to deduce these properties from its essence. Note again that we do not define these properties and essence by an inductive *argument*, as Aristotle is so often misrepresented as trying to do, but by an analysis of the data of observation. This analysis establishes that these properties and the essence are real. In the analysis we first eliminate data that is seen to be merely accidental because the object retains its identity even in specimens in which this feature is absent. This operation manifests the properties of the substance.

For example, we make sure that what is in this glass is water by testing its properties. Second we look for the ordered interrelation of the properties that manifests the unified essence on which they depend. Thus we know it is water because it has all the properties of what we have already identified as other examples of "water."

After we have empirically answered the first, second, and third questions, we can then deduce the observed properties from the observed essence, so as to see the relation of cause and effect between them. In modern scientific method, *unobserved* properties are predicted from a hypothetical model of an object. Then, if these predicted properties can be looked for and observed, the model is verified; if they cannot be found, it is falsified and requires modification. Aristotle would consider that type of deduction logically merely probable and proper to *dialectical* speculation (debate) rather than rigorously scientific proof, because it is deduced from a hypothesis having probability, since it was suggested by the original data, but not known with certitude to be true to reality.

The fourth scientific question, therefore, is, "*How does the essence cause the properties of the substance under investigation?*" Asking this question is the final step of inquiry at each level of specification, for it requires us to make explicit the precise *middle term* or *causal* connection between the properties and the essence. An answer to the fourth question completes our scientific knowledge of the subject at that level of research, but it only prepares the way for more specific study. As we advance in understanding the properties of a thing, our knowledge of the essence becomes more explicit and precisely defined. Since, however, a substance has only one essence—that which places it in the *category of substance*—but it has many kinds of properties, we must next examine in how many generic categories these properties must be classified. This will provide us with a guide for giving a good description of any substance that science observes and investigates.

The Nine Categories of Properties of All Changeable Substances

The category of substance, and the nine categories of properties, are named by univocal terms; each constitutes a classification of physical realities of a certain type: *substance, quantity, quality, relation, action, reception* (often translated "passion" or "being acted on" or "affection"), *place, position, environment,*[31] and *time*. Whether this list is exhaustive is open to question, but even in the light of modern science it is hard to propose any other categories.[32]

All our natural information reduces to *change,* since we cannot sense a thing without it changing our sense organs and being somewhat changed by them. This makes evident that our world is made of relatively independent *substances,* since some appear while others disappear in the process of change. This means that every substance is composed of co-relative actuality (what it is now) and its potentiality or capacity to become something else—otherwise there would be no change. Aquinas calls the actuality of a thing its *formal cause* (or "form," but this does not mean simply its shape); its potentiality he calls its *material cause* or "matter." (In contrast, today, by "matter" is meant a body with actual weight.)

We do not directly sense the unity of a material body but its properties, of which the first is its *quantity* following on its potentiality. Secondly, we sense the various *qualities* correlative to its quantity, of which the first is its limiting shape, and then its colors, etc. Next comes the category of *relation,* since substances are either equal or

31. What I call here "environment" is mentioned in the *Categories* but not in the *Physics*, and the example given by Aristotle is "clothed" or "naked," which is not a property of all material things. What it might be as a property will be discussed in its place.

32. Since the famous seventeenth-century *Disputationes Metaphysicae* of Francesco Suarez, SJ, the treatment of the categories has been assigned by most Neo-Scholastic authors not to natural science but to metaphysics, but this is not Aristotle's or Aquinas's view. Kant derived his own system of categories from the logic of the Leibnitzians, no longer a classification of empirical realities but a set of mental pigeonholes into which empirical data is to be fitted to achieve mental consistency.

unequal in quantity, similar or dissimilar in quality. Relations are not directly sensed but are simply a "between-ness" linking two extremes. Next comes *action* and its correlative *reception,* without which there would be not change. Then come *place, position (orientation),* and *environment.* By *place* is meant the fact that one substance cannot act on another unless it contacts it, since otherwise when a body acts it would change every other body in the world. But a body in place can be rotated, and this is *orientation. Environment* is the wider place in which a substance naturally can exist—for example, a fish cannot live without its environment of water. Finally, of the changes we observe in the world some are more regular than others, as the cycle of the sun is more regular than the weather, and this is *time.*

Some commentators assert that Aristotle's categorical system merely reflects the Greek language and is of little philosophical (scientific) value, but they neglect his discussion of them in his *Physics* where he shows that every changeable thing must have these properties or it could not change. In his work the *Categories,* Aristotle lists, besides the category of substance, nine categories of properties that can also be called accidents. In his *Physics,* he demonstrates (although he does not state this explicitly) that these categories are the necessary properties of any changing thing precisely because it changes. All the univocal words in any human language ultimately refer to one of these broad categories, and from them by analogy we derive words to apply to other things not so directly in our experience. In what follows I will explain each of these categories in more detail.

The Category of Quantity

The simplest form of change, because it is the most superficial, is motion. A changeable substance cannot be in motion without having at least two parts, one that has passed a given limit and another that has not yet passed it. If the substance were not in motion, it would be either wholly behind that limit or wholly beyond it. Hence every changeable thing is a body, that is, it has quantity, which is defined as the property of having "parts outside each other." "Outside" here means that the parts, which coincide at no more than a common boundary—for example, two parts of a line meet only at the common point; two parts of a plane meet only at one line, two parts of a solid, only at one plane. If the parts have common boundaries, then the quantity is continuous; if they have no common boundary, the quantity is discrete.

Discrete quantities are numbers, the units of which do not limit each other and each of which has no parts, though they are parts of some larger quantity—the three units (1, 1, 1) of the number 3 are each indivisible parts of that number 3.[33] The unity and specification of any number is given by the last unit counted (in makes no difference which unit that is). Thus the number 3 is specified by some third and final unit added to the two other units.

The Category of Quality

Again, since the objects of our senses are qualities (color, temperature, hardness, etc.), we could not observe a changeable quantified substance unless it also possessed at least one sensible quality. There are, however, four species of quality, and the existence of those qualities can be verified in various ways. One of these species consists of qualities that are either directly observable in sensation—such as color, sound, taste, smell, pressure, temperature—or that are not immediately evident to the senses but can be known indirectly to exist—such as colors in the infrared or ultraviolet of the spectrum of light or the sound vibrations that some animals can hear and we cannot. A second species of quality is shape or figure, which is sensed by touch

33. Zero, one, the rational numbers (fractions), irrational numbers, imaginary numbers, infinite numbers, and sets, although of great importance in mathematics, do not univocally fit the original definition of a number as "a whole whose parts are discrete" but are only "numbers" by analogy. On this, see the important though controversial book of George Lakoff and Rafael E. Núñez, *Where Mathematics Comes From: How the Embodied Mind Brings Mathematics into Being* (New York: Basic Books, 2000).

or sight as the limit of a quantity, such as the curvature of a line or the cubical or spherical shape of a solid. A third and very important species comprises the powers or functions, whether active or passive, of a body (often called "forces" in modern science) by which it acts on other bodies or is acted upon. For example, electromagnetism in inanimate bodies, or the powers to nourish, grow, and reproduce in living organisms are active powers; the property of metals to be malleable (i.e., pressed into different shapes), or of an animal to be stimulated, are passive powers. Such powers are not directly observable, but the actions or receptions that they make possible are observable. Finally, a fourth species of quality includes conditions (traditionally but misleadingly called "habits") such as the stability or instability of chemical substances or the health or disease of animals; or, in the case of animals and humans, states of openness to learning new behaviors or abilities to act appropriately or inappropriately. These conditions are also not directly observable but can be inferred from observing the actual performance of a substance in various situations. For example, a physician judges health or sickness from "symptoms" of normal or abnormal behaviors or reactions of an organism.

Qualities are correlative with quantities, because quantity is a property that follows on the potentiality (matter) of a substance, whereas quality is a property that follows on its actuality (form). This is so because quantity manifests the fact that a material substance is internally divided into many parts and thus lacks perfect unity. Hence quantity follows from the potentiality of matter, since matter lacks the unification that it can only receive from its form. Conversely, quality manifests form because it expresses the limitation, specification, and power of the substance and its actuality. Certain qualities are the direct object of our senses and therefore are what we know first and best, just as what we directly know of a substance is its actuality. Moreover, we know the extension of the substance into parts or its quantity through its qualities. For example, I know the size of an orange by seeing its colors.

Although quality is first in our *knowledge*, quantity is in *reality* the first of a material substance's properties and the condition of all the rest, just as the potency of one substance in the process of change precedes its actualization by some new substantial form. This real primacy of quantity explains why the science of mathematics is possible, since we can abstract the concept of quantity from all the subsequent kinds of properties and consider it in this abstract, idealized state.[34] Thus the mathematical concept of a circle abstracts from its color but not its figure or shape and from all processes of change. This gives to mathematics clarity, precision, and a type of certitude impossible in natural science, which abstracts only from the accidents of substances. This is why the use of mathematical constructs has proved of such great service as a dialectical instrument of natural science. (Mathematical constructs, though, only approximate the concrete physical realities of the world; therefore, whereas mathematical theories used in science can show *negatively* that certain hypotheses cannot be true of physical reality, they cannot, of themselves, show that *positive* hypotheses are certainly true of physical reality.)

The Category of Relation

Inasmuch as there exist at least two bodies, one acting on the other, it is evident that there must also be a category of *relation* that includes, with respect to quantity, relations of *equality* and *inequality*, and, with respect to quality, relations of *similarity* and *dissimilarity* of qualities. Yet some philosophers—for instance, the nominalist William of Ockham (1288–1348)—have maintained that relations are not real but are merely mental.[35] Certainly there are also some merely

34. When a geometric circle is conceived as an abstract quantity, only the quality of shape as its limit is retained; the substance of which "circularity" is a property is not specified. In conceiving a number, even the quality of shape is left behind, although the *unity* of the parts of the number still reflects the unity of the unspecified substance of which it is a property.

35. For a careful discussion of Ockham's position on relations see Frederick Co-

mental relations—namely, those studied in logic, such as the relation of a predicate of a proposition to its subject, or in language, such as are expressed by terms like "and," "therefore," or "if"—that are analogically derived from real relations. Nevertheless, although it is true that a "relation" existing between two sensible changeable things is not itself an object of the senses, intellectual analysis shows that it is no figment of the mind, since the dissimilarity in size of a tall man and a short woman is certainly real and so is the similarity and dissimilarity of the colors of a male purple finch and its drab-colored mate.

A relation differs from the other categories of properties of changeable things in that a relation is precisely a "between-ness" associating two things rather than modifying them. Thus when we match two red apples and two green apples, the similarity in quality between each pair is real, not a mental projection on our part. Furthermore, since every changeable thing has the property of quantity that consists in having parts, and since these parts also have characteristic qualities, it becomes apparent that the parts can be either homogeneous or heterogeneous, that is, some parts may be equal in quantity to others (I have two eyes, two arms, two legs) or similar (my two eyes are alike, but they are not like my arms, nor are my arms like my legs). If it was not possible to be sure that some real things are really equal in quantity or similar in quality, natural science would be impossible, since measurements of bodies and classification of substances based on similarities and dissimilarities would become impossible and no scientific, universal assertions could be established.

It should be noted that we have been discussing what the Scholastics called "predicamental" relations, which are properties of substances. These relations must be distinguished from "transcendental relations." In our discussion of the categories we have repeatedly seen

pleston, *A History of Philosophy*, vol. III, *Late Medieval and Renaissance Philosophy,* Part I (Westminster, MD: Newman Press, 1946), 68–71.

that causal elements are correlative—that is, that one, by its very definition, implies the other; matter implies form, cause implies effects, a hat implies a head, a shoe a foot, parenthood implies childhood, etc. These relations are called "transcendental" because they add nothing additional to a term but merely state that by its very definition it implies a correlate. To the contrary predicamental relation as a property of a substance add something more to the essence of a substance than the essence itself, since we can think of a human person as a rational animal without thinking of this person as having two legs.

The Two Categories of Action and Reception

As I have shown in discussing the principle of causality, a substance that is actually one thing yet potentially other things cannot change into one of these other things by itself, since that would be to give itself what it does not have. For change to occur, the thing that changes must be a *recipient* and another substance must exist that is the *agent* that has the power to change the first substance. Such a power is a quality that is the property of a substance but whose act is the actualization of another substance, which in turn has a correlative quality of receptivity. Thus we have the category of *action*, which classifies the various powers a substance may have—for example, its mass, by which it weighs down a scale, or its electric charge, by which it attracts or repels another charged object.

Since action and reception are reciprocal, these are also the basis of another species of relation besides the relations of equality/inequality and similarity/dissimilarity already discussed above, namely, the relation of *cause to effect* and *effect to cause.*

It is very important to note that the change of actualization that results from action is not in the agent as such; the agent, in order to give that actualization, must already have it; but the change in actualization is found in the recipient. The recipient, moreover, must have a potentiality for that new actualization. This is expressed in the saying, already quoted, "What is received is conditioned by the state of the receiver." For example, the impression made by a seal pressed on wax will be modified by how cold or hot the wax is.

Some have suggested that only the four categories substance, quantity, quality, and relation are necessary for the work of natural science, but this is not the case. The remaining six categories do indeed imply a relation, but they are not, as such, either real relations or transcendental relations; they form the foundations of real relations other than those between quantities and qualities and between causes and effects. Since change is real and is the effect of a cause, the relation between cause and effect is not the product of our minds but is a fact of nature. The reason that Ockham,[36] and later David Hume (1711–76), could deny the reality of the relation of cause and effect is because this kind of property is only indirectly observed by our senses, as will be explained later.[37]

These twin categories of action and reception are obviously of utmost importance in natural science, since they answer a question that is not answered simply by knowing that some substance exists, namely, the question whether the universe is a single substance, as Parmenides and Spinoza maintained,[38] or many, as Aristotle maintained.

36. On this complicated topic see Marilyn McCord Adams, *William Ockham*, vol. 1, chapter on relations; "The Concept of Relation", in Julius Weinberg, *Abstraction, Relation and Induction: Three Essays in the History of Thought* (Madison: University of Wisconsin Press, 1965); Mark Henninger, *Relations: Medieval Theories* (Oxford: Clarendon Press, 1989).

37. David Hume, *An Enquiry Concerning Human Understanding* (1772): (Indianapolis, IN: Hackett 1993), Chapter I.

38. Benedict De Spinoza, Ethics, Book I, *Ethics:* including *The Improvement of the Understanding*, trans. R. H. M. Elwes (Buffalo, NY: Prometheus, 1989). The continued influence of this idea of the universe on modern science is evident from the statement of Einstein: "I believe in Spinoza's God, who reveals himself in the harmony of all being, not in a God who concerns himself with the fate and actions of men." Arnold Sommerfeld, "To Einstein's 70th Birthday," in Paul Arthur Schilpp, *Albert Einstein Philosopher-Scientist* (Evanston, IL: The Library of Living Philosophers, 1949), 99–105, at 103. Ilse Rosenthal-Schneider, "Presuppositions and Anticipations in Einstein's Physics," ibid., 129–46, shows (144f.) that Einstein believed, while granting it could not be

Given that a changeable being cannot change without action and reception, and also given that the principle of causality shows why nothing can change itself, it follows that our changing world must be made up of at least two bodies that act on each other and are acted upon.

The Four Causes of Every Changeable Substance

To the two intrinsic causes, the formal and material causes we have already established, Aristotle added a third, *extrinsic* type of "cause," *agency* or *efficiency*, which explains change not by something within a body but by the external action upon it of another body, as well as by the body's own way of receiving this action. Such a principle of agency is what we mean today by the term "cause" in natural science and its correlate of receptivity and "effect."

From what has been said it is also evident that efficient causes presuppose material and formal principles, since an efficient cause actualizes (gives a form to) some potentiality (matter) of the body on which it acts. Thus, taken in an *analogical* sense, form and matter, as principles of changeable substance, can also be called "causes," namely, the *formal* and *material causes* of any substance. Yet strictly speaking they are more principles than causes, inasmuch as they do not perform actions. Instead, the actualization or form of a substance is the effect of the action of another substance on some matter, which is not active but wholly receptive.

Aristotle was insistent that a fourth type of causality, *final causality* or teleology (*telos*, goal), is also required for any adequate scientific explanation. Although modern science grew up with the supposition that all observed events are deterministic—so that as the great French mathematician Pierre-Simon Laplace (1749–1827) claimed, if we knew the exact conditions of the universe at any given moment we could exactly predict its entire future—in scientific research this grand as-

proved, that this is the only possible universe and hence God was not free to create any other. This was the meaning of his famous dictum, "God does not play dice."

sumption is really not necessary. There is no reason that science cannot remain open to the possibility of genuinely chance events, free events, and miraculous events.[39] The task of science is simply to account for the *regularities* we observe in nature, without which the world would be a total chaos. Furthermore, to explain a change in terms of its final causality does not presuppose some kind of "purpose" in natural causes, although it raises the question of the ultimate origin of order in nature, as does the very existence of a changing universe.

Why, then, did modern science become so reluctant to speak explicitly of teleology? Ever since Galileo emphasized the power of mathematical constructs in natural science, modern scientists have tended to ignore Aristotle's distinction of the four types of causality and to deny final causality altogether because mathematics abstracts from change.[40] When they must use the concept of causality they usually speak only of "matter" and "energy" (or "force"), that is, the material and efficient causes. Thus today in English the term "cause" is commonly restricted to efficient cause, leaving the other three correlative causes only implied.

Nevertheless, these other three kinds of cause remain indispensable to modern science, although they are cloaked and confused by other terms. Thus the term "information" so widely used today in science, and also such terms as "organization," "system," etc., are equivalent to formal cause. Terms like "function," "vector," "direction," and "regular outcome" take the place of final cause. "Teleology" is denounced as unscientific, either because it is supposed that it implies

39. Chance events are the result of the interference of one efficient cause with the action of another, as when an apple falling straight to the ground by gravity is swerved to one side by the wind. Free events will be discussed in Chapter 5, and miraculous events in Chapter 8.

40. See my article "Final Causality" in *The New Catholic Encyclopedia* (New York: McGraw-Hill, 1967) (1st ed., 5:162–66; 2nd ed., 5:723–27). In mathematical abstraction, beginning with Geometry, not only quantity but the first species of quality—namely figure or shape—remains.

conscious purpose in things that lack intelligence, or because it is supposed to refer to some occult type of efficient cause. Such suppositions are false; a final cause need not be conscious or purposeful, nor is it an occult type of efficient cause, since it is simply the *predetermination* or *direction* of the efficient cause to produce a regular effect. Gravity is an efficient cause that regularly produces the movement of massive bodies *toward* each other; it does not move these bodies apart. Hence gravity is teleological, in that it produces a certain *directed and predictable* change. Scientific *prediction,* which is such a powerful test of a scientific hypothesis, would be impossible without natural laws, and such laws determine the regular outcome of efficient action that is precisely what Aristotle meant by final causality. It should be noted that the term "prediction" is an unhappy one, since science properly concerns present reality, because only the present is strictly real. What is meant is that we know the existence of a cause from its effect and of an effect from its cause, although this relation of efficiency is in fact simultaneous, not sequential.

These four kinds of causation involved in regular change are *correlative.* Material and formal causality are correlative, since to change something is to change what its actuality is to something other. Hence "matter" is the potentiality of some actually existent body to become something else, whereas its "form" is what through change it becomes, while by that very fact it is deprived of its previous form. It can thus be seen that matter and form are not *things* but the two principles of a changeable thing that cannot exist of themselves but only as correlative constitutive causes of an existing body.

Similarly, since efficient causes regularly produce certain predetermined results, the efficient and final causes are also correlative, because the final cause is simply the predictable effect of the efficient cause. Again, the immediate effect or final cause of any efficient cause is the production of a new form in matter that previously had a different form. Thus in regular changes the efficient cause regularly actualizes the material cause with another form, which is the efficient cause's pre-determined result or final cause. Hence the final cause is the *ultimate explanation* of the observed change to which the other three causes are correlative. It is *causa causarum,* "the cause of causes." Amidst the random, chance events in our somewhat chaotic world, there are also law-like, regular events by which that the world exists as an ongoing, relatively stable system through time. Science seeks to discover the laws that govern those regular events and by them to explain what it observes to be factually the case. Chance events are left to history, not to science.

To ignore this correlation of four types of causality, as some modern scientific explanations do, is to ignore our experience that we come to an understanding of the *actual reality* ("form") of the world about us only by observing the results of change; from those observations we infer *what* forces or efficient causes were required to produce this change, in what kind of *matter,* and with *what regular determination of final result.*

Now we can return to the fourth scientific question: "How is the essence of a substance the cause of its properties?" The substance cannot be the efficient cause of its properties, since these are intrinsic to it and are given to the substance along with its essence by the efficient cause that produced the substance. (For example, when the decay of the element uranium produces the element lead, it gives that lead not only its essential nature but its properties.) The properties instead flow (emanate) from the essence as from a *formal* cause, since the essence is the form of the substance. Thus the properties of substance b are caused by the other substance, a, that produced the substance b—for example, the properties of a seed are produced by the plant that bore that seed as its fruit.

In current physics, all scientific explanations ultimately come down to explanations in terms of the four fundamental forces, gravity, electromagnetism, and strong and weak nuclear forces. If, then, we ask, "Why does a body have the power (quality) of gravity (or of electromagnetism, etc.)?" physics can give no other answer than "Gravity is 'natural' to a massive body," which amounts to saying that it is a property *intrinsic to massive matter.*

The Categories of Place, Position, and Environment

For a body to change, it must be in *contact* with another whose efficient causality it receives. Scientists, particularly those working since Newton proposed his great theory of gravitational attraction to explain the solar system, have often debated whether an efficient cause can produce an effect at a distance (*actio in distans* is the Latin phrase). In fact supposed examples of such action at a distance have usually been eliminated from science by the discovery that the action that is to be explained in fact passes through a medium.[41] The problem was raised for Newton because he supposed that gravitational attraction is instantaneous, but today gravity is supposed to travel at the speed of light.

The four fundamental forces of modern physics are attributed to the exchange of "virtual particles" (mesons) between other kinds of particles (hadrons) and by leptons traveling at the speed of light. Moreover, the idea of a vacuum or void extending between material particles has been replaced by the concept of a "field" or "fields" having properties, such as "curvature," which are analogous to qualities. Indeed, the notion of action at a distance taken literally is contradictory. An agent cannot produce its effect except in a specified recipient, since the two (agent and recipient) are correlative, like form and

41. The Nobel Laureate in Physics, Murray Gell-Mann, in his *The Quark and the Jaguar: Adventures in the Simple and the Complex* (New York: W. H. Freeman, 1994), 173, gives this notion of non-locality as an example of what he calls "flapdoodle," which is a misunderstanding of quantum theory. For a Thomistic discussion, see Anthony Rizzi (*The Science before Science*, 234–45), who shows it does not prove that there is "action at a distance" and has developed a better account of the so-called vacuum. On the nature of scientific observation, see also Donald H. Kausler, *Experimental Psychology, Cognition, and Human Aging* (New York: Springer-Verlag, 1991) and *Handbook of Research Methods in Experimental Psychology*, ed. Stephen F. Davis (Malden, MA: Blackwell, 2003).

matter. This specification of the agent to a recipient of its action happens only by the contact (immediate or mediated) of the two bodies. Hence, "action at a distance" would imply that the agent and recipient are simultaneously *in contact* and *not in contact,* and also that a bodily agent can produce unlimited effects. Therefore, for any change to occur, not only must there exist two or more bodies, but these must be in immediate or mediated contact. From this fact follow three categories that are best discussed together, namely, *place, position* (orientation), and *environment.*

That these three properties are distinct is evident from the fact that a body can be rotated and thus change its position while remaining in the same relation of contact with the immediately surrounding bodies, that is, in the same place. Furthermore, it can change this immediate relation to other bodies while remaining in the same environment, that is, in the same general region of bodies. For example, a fish can swim about in the pond that is its environment.

In the *Physics,* Aristotle passed over this category of environment and when naming it in the *Categories* as *echein,* "to have or possess" (traditionally translated in Latin as *habitus),* gives as an example of its categorical uses only "to have on a garment."[42] It is difficult to see how "being clothed" is a category of natural, rather than artificial, reality. Some Thomists have interpreted the term, as I have done, by distinguishing *echein* from *topos* (place), taking *echein* as the location of a body in a region (environment) of surrounding bodies, and taking *topos* (place) as the location of that body by the surrounding and contacting bodies. This is of considerable importance for Aristotle's natural science, since he holds that various types of bodies have specific "natural places" in which they are most stable.

Such natural places apply to all three categories, of place, position, and environment, as I have described them; for example, an oceanic fish is in its natural place when immediately surrounded by water, but

42. *Categories* 15, 15b21.

also when it is not "belly-up," and when this water is a natural body of salt water, not fresh, and when it is not in an aquarium. Modern ecology and environmentalism manifest the importance of this concept.[43]

The Category of Time

Philosophers have spent many pages over abstruse discussions of "time," and the most famous philosopher of last century, Martin Heidegger, maintained that "being" itself is "temporality."[44] In current science there is a strange paradox in thinking about time. On the one hand, some physicists even question the existence of real time, because they confuse time with its mathematical measurement represented as a straight line. In a line, however, all parts exist simultaneously, whereas in time nothing actually exists but the indivisible present "now." On the other hand, the "grand theories" of science today in cosmology and evolutionary theory use the general laws of physics to reconstruct the past history of the universe and conjecture about its future, although these are chance events, unique, once for all, not repeating series of events. The sun has risen many times in history but each time it has shone on an at least slightly different earth.

For Aristotle the universe is a system of bodies undergoing change by acting on each other. Hence it is not strange that we observe that some of these changes—and in the simplest case, motions—are more regular than others. Consequently, the more regular motions regulate or stabilize the less regular motions. For example, the many complex

43. For the many dimensions of this question see, *Earth Matters: The Earth Sciences, Philosophy, and the Claims of Community,* ed. Robert Frodeman; contributing authors, Victor R. Baker et al. (Upper Saddle River, NJ: Prentice Hall, 2000).

44. See the essay of David H. Mason, "Time in Whitehead and Heidegger: Some Comparisons," *Process Studies* 5.2 (Summer 1975): 83–105. Heidegger said that the "being" of "*Dasein*" (the human being) is temporality; since the essence of humanity is, however, to be open to "being," it is not clear that "being" is anything more than this historical reality. Heidegger refused to say anything about any reality transcending history.

changes on our earth are kept in order by the cycles of day and night and of the seasons resulting from the diurnal rotation of the earth and its annual orbital motion. Time is simply this relation between a less regular motion and a more regular motion, and hence for the universe is ultimately its most regular motion.

Currently this most regular cosmic motion is thought to be the rate of the expansion of "space" (Hubble's constant). The radius of the universe, observed from any point within it, is believed to be about 13.7 billion light years, which also represents the universe's age since the Big Bang. The future of the universe may be a Big Crunch in which the cycle begins again, or a Big Rip (Big Crackup) in which all matter, so to speak, burns up, or a Big Chill in which nothing remains but space at zero temperature disturbed only by faint "quantum fluctuations." Thus whether time can be said to have a beginning or an end is a puzzle.[45] If time is infinite, then it must be eternally recycling, as Aristotle supposed, since no particular law-like change can be infinite (since it has a final cause) except by repeating itself.

These ten categories, substances and the nine generic properties common to all material substances, as I have enumerated them, are necessary to describe any natural phenomenon. For example, an atom of hydrogen cannot be well described without saying that it is a natural unity that can exist independently of other atoms. A hydrogen atom is a substance with a certain essential structure, namely, a nucleus with a single proton and one orbital electron, and a meson carrying the electromagnetic force between them, and it is has nine kinds of properties that result from this essential structure.

Hence a hydrogen atom has certain specific kinds and numbers of parts with certain dimensions (quantities). These parts have the capacity to attract or repel other parts or be attracted or repelled by

45. Stephen Hawking, in his *A Brief History of Time* (New York: Bantam Books, 1988), argues that space and time may be limited yet "without boundary"; hence time has no beginning or end. His mathematical model has not yet been given a physical interpretation that could be tested by observation.

them. The atom as a whole has the powers (qualities) to emit and absorb certain types of radiant energy and to enter into molecular combinations with other atoms such as oxygen to form H_2O water. Not only do the parts form a structure, they do so as parts in relation with each other (similar and dissimilar parts with their various causes and effects) and also as a whole. As a whole, the atom is also in relation to other atoms, with which it interacts.

Besides these inner and outer relationships, the atom also has relative qualitative properties, such as result from its capacities to act or to receive actions (action and reception). Such actions and receptions, however, demand that an atom be in contact with other bodies on which it acts or that act on it (place). The orientation (position) and the environment of the atom may also be of considerable scientific interest in understanding its actions and receptions. Thus we can speak of the "natural" place of hydrogen, since it could not exist in the first phases of the Big Bang; neither could it come into existence in interstellar space, but only within some star. In certain kinds of high-energy situations it burns, combining with oxygen to form water. Hence water now exists as a relatively stable entity only within a certain environment in the order of the now-existing universe. One perennial question for scientists studying the planets has been, does H_2O exist on Mars.

Application of Basic Scientific Terms to Study of the Human Person

How do these categories guide us in describing a human person? As we are bodies (*substances*) that come into existence and die, we are material (*potentiality*) but this matter is extremely complex and highly organized and unified (*actuality*). Our bodies have many parts, which in the mature person have a limited range of sizes (*quantity*); these parts, or organs, are structurally differentiated (qualities of the species "shape") in order to be able to perform different functions (qualities of the species "powers"). They do in fact perform the life functions of nutrition, growth, motion, and reproduction that both act on other parts of the human body and on other bodies, and are acted upon, notably in receiving information through the senses (*action* and *reception*). We are able to live, however, only in a suitable *environment* in which we take *places* and *positions* appropriate to our life functions. Our development and mature life take *time*, and a bodily human life has its natural limits. Our psychological science, then, must be built upon these categories, which are complexly correlative. To fail to consider any one of them is to get a lopsided picture of what it is to be a human person.

In addition to these basic terms, natural science also requires certain other terms: (a) The "ante-predicaments" or logical terms necessary to form a classification or category, namely, genus, species, difference and the terms "property" and "accident" already discussed. (b) The "post-predicaments," namely, *opposite, prior, "together with," "motion," "to have,"* or terms that apply analogically to more than one category of being. Of these latter, motion (or, more generally, change) applies to all categories; the other terms are needed to explain the order among the categorical terms (or ante-predicaments). Finally, (c) the terms "one and many," "true and false," and "good and bad," traditionally called the transcendentals or the"transcendental terms" because of their extreme generality, must be used in natural science, although in a more restricted sense (limited to material things) than the one in which they are used by metaphysicians, who extend them to immaterial realities as well.

The universe is made of many complex things that form a unified system. Natural science attempts to discover what they are really like and to formulate what they discover in true propositions, and to winnow out false ones. Finally, the notion of final causality, on which the uniformity and relative stability of the universe and the possibility of finding natural laws is based, entails the notion of what is good and bad (transcendental terms) about the universe, that is, what is constructive of an orderly universe and what is destructive, leading to chaos. Since we human beings are part of this universe and seek to explore and understand it, psychology must be understood in that context.

The Culminating Foundational Theorem of Natural Science

In the foregoing I have so far shown why the foundations of natural science must include the following foundational theorems of natural science:

1. The principle of identity and the principle of causality, which are directly evident from sense observation.
2. The relatively independent existence, evident from sense experience, of changeable substances composed of actuality (form) and potentiality (matter) as their intrinsic formal and material causes.
3. The demonstration of the theorem that "Change is the generic form of changeable being," so that all subsequent theorems must be in terms of change.
4. Why change also requires an efficient cause and why regular, law-like change requires a final cause.
5. Demonstrations of theorems showing that all changeable substances must have a least nine kinds of properties and what these nine kinds of properties must be.

These five must be completed by a sixth, culminating foundational theorem of natural science.

Given the foregoing analytic description of changeable substances, it becomes evident that changes take place not in isolated substances but in interacting *systems* of substances that form a *universe* of which we are a part. Such a system is a causal series of bodies activating other bodies in which any observed effect has to be explained as the result not only of immediate causes but as the result of that whole system of causes. (For example, the life and behavior of an animal ultimately depends on a series of agents through which it derives its energy. This series ends only in the sun, which is the chief source of energy on our planet. If the sun were to cease to shine, our earth would not sustain life.) In current science, there are at least four such causal series ending in the four fundamental forces that are taken simply as "natural."

These fundamental forces (or rather the substances of which they are natural properties) are "prime movers," a notion familiar from mechanics. No machine can operate without an engine or other energy source, and the dream of inventing a "perpetual motion mechanism" that moves itself forever is recognized to be absurd. Such mechanical prime movers are only relatively prime, since the spring of a clock must be wound up, the fuel in an engine must burn, etc.

Therefore the question of the prime mover of the universe as a total system is scientifically unavoidable, although today scientists often do not like to face that question scientifically, because they believe it to be unanswerable or that if it is answered positively, scientific research will somehow be frustrated thereby.

Aristotle, on the basis of such astronomical evidence as was available to him, held that the universe exists in a "steady state" and is an eternal system somewhat like a perpetual motion machine.[46] Today, on the basis of the alternative hypothesis that the universe had a beginning with the Big Bang, the same question presents itself. This Bang is supposed to have been the first in a vast causal chain that has produced our universe and hence is its relative prime mover. "What then caused the Big Bang?" To say either that it "just happened" or "it caused itself" is unscientific, since that type of answer would not be deemed a properly scientific way to answer any other question about our world.

Because this question is general and foundational and is thus presupposed to more specific questions in natural science, Aristotle con-

46. On this see my *Aristotle's Sluggish Earth*, 202–34.

siders it in the last book (VIII) of his foundational treatise for natural science, the *Physics*. Hence that book cannot be, as some have tried to argue, a "metaphysical insertion." The whole structure of the *Physics* provides the terms and premises that book eight uses and culminates in applying them to this great problem.[47]

Therefore, Aristotle, as an honest scientist, asks in *Physics* VIII: how can the system of material substances be in act in its entirety as a system, if no material substance can move itself (that is, if, according to the principle of causality, each material substance is only potentially in act)? Since the material universe—the only one directly observable by us—is an at least apparently stable and well-ordered system, no doubt it contains some material body that is its prime mover, or at least some coordinated set of bodies that are a joint prime mover. Yet this prime mover can only be relatively prime, since it is also a material body that is only potentially acting. While there may indeed be some body that can be said in a sense to be the prime mover of the universe, like a motor in a machine, it is only relatively first, whereas the true prime mover is not itself a changeable body, that is, it is nonmaterial.

In Aristotle's hypothesis, the universal material prime mover was the outer sphere of the universe, which he supposed by its continual and eternal motion keeps the whole universe always moving. Before the Big-Bang hypothesis became current, the similar steady-state hypothesis of Hoyle and Bondi was favored;[48] it held that this material prime mover was the hypothetical, constant "creation" of a small amount of new matter and energy. Today the Big-Bang hypothesis claims this prime mover is the original immensely dense and very small mass of matter (the "singularity") that began to expand at the first moment of the universe's existence.

47. For a modern commentary on the *Physics* that makes this very clear, see Vincent Edward Smith, *The General Science of Nature* (Milwaukee: Bruce, 1958), 366ff.

48. On the history of this theory see Joseph Silk, *The Big Bang* (New York: W. H. Freeman, 2001).

What Aristotle recognized and faced squarely was that regardless of what hypothesis one might accept for this original material, a changeable prime mover could not itself act on anything without being acted upon by some other truly prime, unchangeable, and hence non-material, mover that could act without being acted upon, which is, therefore, in act by its very nature and hence without potentiality. Aristotle's solution, in *Physics* VIII, to this inescapable problem can be formulated in a theorem that, in keeping with the proper methodology of natural science, is not deductive (*a priori*, from cause to effect) but moves from an empirically observed effect to its cause (*a posteriori*).

This argument from effect to cause for the First Cause of the universe and its non-materiality goes as follows.

1. By our senses we observe changeable substances, for example, A, in the process of change and first of all in motion (Z). Thus by critical analysis of this fact we know A exists and we can define it with a real and essential definition by finding a certain unity among its observed categorical properties.
2. Since nothing that is moved can move itself (principle of causality), we know that A's observed motion (Z) must be caused by some other thing B as its efficient cause.
3. The efficient action of B either (a) is essentially identical with the essence of B, in which case it is P, the prime unmoved mover of the motion, or (b) only comes from some mover C, whose action also depends on P.
4. The number of movers that, like C, act to move others only when they are themselves moved cannot be infinite, since, in an infinite series of such moved movers, there is no prime mover P, and so all of the intermediate agents remain only in potency to act and cannot be causes of the observed motion (Z).
5. Therefore P, a prime mover that requires no other mover to act, exists, but it cannot be a material mover, since all material movers act only if they receive their motion (Z) from some other mover.

In this demonstration of the existence of a First Cause of the universe that is immaterial, no term or principle is used that has not already been directly observed by the senses or that is not intellectually directly evident from an analysis of the data of the senses or demonstrated logically from such premises. Thus it pertains to the generic subject of natural science, and is presupposed to all its more specific conclusions, that is, to all of modern science that deals with the four fundamental forces of gravity, electromagnetism, and the weak and strong nuclear forces.

Each of these forces is treated in modern science as a natural property of all or certain kinds of bodies to which all natural phenomena are ultimately reducible (although the problem of the nature of the "dark matter" that is required to account for the major part of the mass of the universe remains unsolved).[49]

A common objection among scientists to speaking of immaterial reality is that this introduces "the God of the gaps," a construct that is used arbitrarily to fill in incomplete scientific explanations. This may be true of the way the design argument is sometimes presented, but it is not relevant to the foregoing argument, which does not fill in any "gap" in physical explanations but is presupposed to the very possibility of any physical explanation. If this immaterial First Cause (the unmoved mover) is omitted in any scientific theory, that theory collapses and nothing remains possible for science except mere phenomenal description of effects without causes—a stance in fact advocated by those who support a positivistic definition of natural science.[50]

Scientists today recognize the four fundamental forces as ultimate

49. See "Dark Energy, Dark Matter," NASA Science Astrophysics, last modified August 19, 2010, http://science.nasa.gov/astrophysics/focus-areas/what-is-dark-energy/.

50. Richard Dawkins, in his violently rhetorical *The God Delusion*; the even more violent publicist Christopher Hitchens, in *God is Not Great: How Religion Poisons Everything;* the philosopher Daniel C. Dennett, in *Breaking the Spell: Religion as a Natural Phenomenon;* and the somewhat calmer physicist Victor J. Stenger, *God: The Failed Hypothesis* all either misstate Aquinas's First Way of proving the existence of the Uncaused Cause or end by saying that the universe "just happened."

to all their explanatory theories. When confronted with the problem of a First Cause, they either have no answer or they rely on a mathematical "Final Theory of Everything,"[51] which is based on some deterministic natural law. A "law" cannot exist by itself, however; it must exist in the material world. They are then forced to show that the existence of this material world is intrinsically necessary. The great physicist Stephen Hawking has now admitted that, since Kurt Gödel proved mathematically that no mathematical system can prove itself to be either consistent or complete, the notion of such a mathematical, necessary final theory is logically contradictory.[52]

As the culminating foundational theorem of natural science shows, however, these forces that pertain to the category of active qualities by which one body efficiently acts on another remain only potentially acting as causes until they themselves are put in act by an immaterial cause. For example, the force of electromagnetic charge—by which the principle particles in an atom (negatively charged electrons and positively charged protons) attract particles of opposite charge and repel those of like charge—is a natural property of electrons and protons; they are therefore, in this respect, material prime movers. Now material prime movers, composed of matter and form, have among their properties some active power in the category of quality. Like a human power to move objects, this active power is only potentially acting, just as are the other material movers it puts into act, since it is in the category of quality, not in that of action. Therefore, just as this material prime mover, a proton or electron having an electromagnetic charge, is needed to explain the phenomena that are its immediate or remote effects, so an immaterial mover is needed to activate this material prime mover if it is to produce these effects. And so we see that modern scientific explanations are incomplete if they stop at some kind

51. See Steven Weinberg, *Dreams of a Final Theory: The Scientist's Search for the Ultimate Laws of Nature* (New York: Vintage, 1994).

52. See Hawking's lecture "Gödel and the End of Physics," last modified March 8, 2002, http://www.hawking.org.uk/index.php/lectures/91.

of bodies whose natural properties are the four fundamental forces.

Furthermore, modern scientists realize that more than one such fundamental force would not produce the universe as a unified system, unless these forces are somehow unified. That is why a principle current task of physics is the development a "Grand Unified Theory" (GUT). At present this takes the form of a hypothesis in which all four forces were originally united in that state of matter and energy that existed at the moment of the Big Bang and only gradually became differentiated. Thus it is supposed that this law of the unification of the forces of matter and energy is a property of material substance.

Since no material thing can change itself, the question remains, "What accounts for this original force being in act?" Natural science cannot escape this question, and, within the limits of its own proper scope and method, it must try to answer it by the foundational principles of natural science itself, as Aristotle tried to do.

The proof of the existence of a first immaterial cause of all material changes given in *Physics* VIII was adopted by St. Thomas Aquinas as the first and "most evident" of his famous "Five Ways" of proving the existence of an immaterial First Cause.[53] The Second Way, from efficient agency, and the Third, from necessity, are variations on this First Way. Once we understand the First Way, it becomes evident that a consideration not simply of the observed motion but of the agents or moved movers that cause the motion leads to the same conclusion, and this is the Second Way. Furthermore, if we consider the efficient causality of these agents, we see that the action of the first immaterial cause is necessary for them to act, since the fact that they are in act is merely contingent, and this is the Third Way. Thus the first three of

53. *ST* I, q. 2, a. 3, c. *Prima autem et manifestum via est, quae sumitur ex parte motus.* "The first and most evident way [to answer the question whether God exists] is from *motion*." See also *I Sent.*, dist. 3; *De Veritate*, q. 5, a. 2; *De Potentia*, q. 3, a. 5; *Comp. Theol.*, c. 3; *In XIII Meta.*, lect. 5, sq. The fullest exposition is in *Summa Contra Gentiles* I, cc. 13–16 and 44.

the Five Ways are based on three effects all related to efficient causality: (1) the effect of motion; (2) the effect of agency of the moved movers; (3) the necessity of the first cause for these contingent agents to act and produce the observed motion.

Of these three ways, the First Way is the most evident because through observing a motion we recognize its agent, and through seeing that this agent cannot act without another agent, we perceive the mere contingency of its action and hence the necessity of a first uncaused cause. The other two of the Five Ways Aquinas uses to prove God's existence, namely those through formal and final causality, follow on this First Way but can here be left to metaphysics.

"Creationism"

Today there is great confusion, especially in the public media, about the way that modern science and "creationism" address evidence for a First Immaterial Cause of the universe. "Creationism" is simplistically placed in opposition to the scientific theory of cosmological and biological evolution. This confusion, for reasons I will soon show, has important consequences for psychological theory. In fact there is no logical opposition between the claim that the existence of the universe depends on a First Immaterial Cause and the claim that the universe evolves, since the First Cause can be the cause of both its existence in a primitive form and its evolution through natural forces to a complex state. This still leaves to science—and indeed demands of science—the task of discovering how these natural forces have produced this evolution.

The confusion has two main sources, which long ago Aquinas cited as the two main objections to his Five Ways:[54] (a) How could a good God produce a universe full of evils; (b) Why is the scientific explanation of the world insufficient?

54. *Summa theologiae* I, q. 2, a. 3, ad 1 and ad 2.

The first of these led Darwin in his study of evolution to become an agnostic and to a 36-year-long battle with depression:[55]

> I cannot persuade myself that a beneficent and omnipotent God would have designedly created the Ichneumonidae [parasitic wasp] with the express intention of their feeding within the living bodies of caterpillars, or the cat should play with mice.... It revolts our understanding to suppose that his [God's] benevolence is not unbounded, for what advantage can there be in the sufferings of millions of lower animals throughout almost endless time?

Aquinas's response to this difficulty points out (a) the distinction between *physical* evil—which is inevitable in a material universe, since the production of one physical thing out of the potentiality of another necessarily destroys the other—and *moral* evil, which God does not cause but permits in those creatures he has given the great gift of free will; (b) that animal pain is physical, not moral, and differs essentially from human pain—a point to be discussed in the next chapter; (c) that because God is infinitely powerful he can and must cause physical evil or permit moral evil only in order to bring about a greater good. We cannot now know by reason what this greater good that is evolving will be, but we should trust God in his transcendent wisdom and love to realize it.

The second difficulty, however, is the one that scientists today have usually raised against creationism, inasmuch as Protestant fundamentalism inhibits the legitimate work of science through its interpretation of the biblical account of creation in Genesis. This is a reasonable complaint, since the "creation science" that fundamentalists

55. Cited in Cornelius G. Hunter, *Darwin's God: Evolution and the Problem of Evil* (Grand Rapids, MI: Baker/Brazos Press, 2001), the first from a letter to Asa Grey (Hunter, 140) and the second from Darwin's autobiography (Hunter, 18). The cause of Darwin's hypochondria has been much disputed, with theories ranging from a tropical infection, or the effect of prescriptions containing arsenic, to psychological problems resulting from a tyrannical father, to the death of his mother. The most persistent view, however, is that it was a depression resulting from his religious struggle rooted in his pessimistic view of evolution.

advocate in opposition to current theories is scientifically very weak. The fundamentalist interpretation of the Bible, however, is also theologically very weak.

The question of whether our world began or not, and whether after it began it developed, is age-old; there have been many mythological accounts concerning this fascinating topic. The first Greek scientists attempted to address the question more scientifically, and the pre-Socratic Anaximander (c. 610 BC–c. 546 BC), who was associated with the first scientist Thales and was perhaps even his teacher, held that all things have developed out of *apeiron* (the boundless). He imagined this as a great ocean out of which non-living substances and then organisms, first of all fish and finally the human species, evolved. The Stoics also supposed that the universe, through its ordering energy of *logos,* went through cycles in which a positive cycle evolved to its present state, only to eventually perish. Aristotle, however, as we have already seen, preferred the hypothesis of an eternal, steady-state universe. Eventually the Church Fathers had to reconcile Genesis chapters 1 and 2 with Aristotle and with Ptolemy's astronomy.

The Church Fathers read the Old Testament in the light of the New. Therefore they based their view of the Genesis creation account on St. Paul's teaching in Romans 1:20: "Ever since the creation of the world, his invisible attributes of eternal power and divinity have been able to be understood and perceived in what he has made," which is supported by the Old Testament not only in Genesis but in passages in Job and Wisdom and elsewhere. Thus for the Bible the point of emphasis is not on when or how creation took place, but that it is totally the work of the One God and is marvelous in its order. For the Church Fathers, such as the apologist Aristides (fl. AD 124?), the main interest is not in the six days of creation but in declaring that God is the Creator of the world from nothing (*ex nihilo*). Origen (AD 185–254), under Platonic influence, read the scriptural accounts of the created world as symbols (analogies) of spiritual realities, and this generally became the patristic approach. St. Basil (AD 329–79), however, in his *Hexameron* (Six Days) attempted to reconcile such symbols with current science, while insisting that the spiritual significance was what was important, since science is always so speculative and uncertain. Yet the fact that it was not easy to reconcile Genesis with the Ptolemaic astronomy and Aristotelian science taught in the Middle Ages had to be faced.

A solution generally accepted in the Latin Church had been provided by St. Augustine (354–430) who, before his conversion, had been a teacher of rhetoric highly expert in hermeneutics and who became the founder of semiotics, so important today. He had declared in his great commentary on Genesis: "We must be on our guard against giving interpretations which are hazardous or opposed to science, and so exposing the word of God to the ridicule of unbelievers."[56] He held for a simultaneous creation of the whole universe but also for its gradual development through the action of the natural forces which were placed in it. Certainly the instantaneous act of the Creator did not produce an organized universe as we see it now. Augustine thought all the elements of the world were created simultaneously but in a confused and *nebulous* mass (*nebulosa species apparet*)[57] in which were the "seed principles" of all the species of things that would eventually emerge. Augustine, however, also insisted that the human spiritual soul could only be created directly by God.

Aquinas went on to clarify this question greatly by pointing out that, of the fourfold sense of Scripture as it is inspired by God, theological reasoning must be based on the literal sense, but that "literal" means the sense intended by the human author, even when this includes symbolic and analogical expressions. Thus the literal sense of the six days of Genesis may be either analogical or univocal. Since Aquinas saw no sufficient reason to think that the human author meant it analogically, Aquinas preferred to take it literally, but was

56. *De Genesi ad Litteram* I, xix, xxi, especially n. 39.

57. Ibid., I, n. 27.

open to Augustine's view that it was analogical, and in fact St. Thomas also admitted that for simple organisms such as worms there could be "spontaneous generation" produced from decaying matter by the sun, though he doubted that more complex animals could be so produced.[58]

Today Catholic Scripture scholars hold that the human author meant the "six days" only symbolically, for two reasons. First, a comparison of the passage with the mythology of those times show that the author intended to refute the errors of the mythology by using its own symbolic style and reversing it; for example, Eve is created from Adam's side as his partner; whereas in the parallel pagan myth, the gods create woman to weaken man so that he cannot rival the gods! In particular, the six days of creation was chosen by the inspired biblical author as a fitting analogy between the work of God and the craftsmanship of a skilled human worker (such as Jesus the Messiah was to be) to show the wonderful order of the universe that so impressed the Jews, but for which they never developed a scientific theory, as did the Greeks.

Second, as we have seen that Basil and Augustine insisted, we should not read Scripture in a sense contrary to the sound findings of scientific reason.[59] Unfortunately just before the "scientific revolution" Luther and Calvin believed that the inspiration of Scriptures

58. *ST* I, q. 71, a. 1, ad 1. On the views of the Church Fathers and further texts of Aquinas on these questions, see the still-useful work of Ernest C. Messenger, *Evolution and Theology: The Problem of Man's Origin* (New York: Macmillan, 1932). On the history of this question see D. B. Fankhauser and J. Stein Carter, "Spontaneous Generation," last modified Nov 2, 2004, http://biology.clc.uc.edu/courses/bio114/spontgen.htm. Also Ian Musgrave, "Lies, Damned Lies, Statistics, and Probability of Abiogenesis Calculations," last modified Dec 21, 1998, http://www.talkorigins.org/faqs/abioprob/abioprob.html .

59. This was the error of the Inquisitors in the Galileo case, who ignored Galileo's invoking of St. Augustine in his defense. On the true position of the Church, see Pius XII's encyclical *Divino Afflante Spiritu*, "On Promoting Biblical Studies," http://www.vatican.va/holy_father/pius_xii/encyclicals/documents/hf_p-xii_enc_30091943_divino-afflante-spiritu_en.html.

was imperiled by the Catholic tradition of the fourfold sense of the Bible. This attitude eventually hardened into present-day Protestant fundamentalism.[60]

To untangle such conflicts between different types of thinking and of truth, it is essential to have a clear, critical "division of the sciences." As we saw in Chapter 1, it is precisely this clarity as to the type of knowledge to which "psychology" belongs that is causing the present confusion about models of human personality.

The Place of Psychology among the Sciences

Where then in the array of sciences should what Glocenius and Wolff called "psychology" fit? As we have seen, Wolff correctly held that psychology is not a single science but pertains to two related sciences. He called "rational psychology" that which dealt with the spiritual aspect of the human person and he assigned this to metaphysics; the other he called "empirical psychology" and thus split "philosophy" from empirical science, with the unfortunate results I have described. I have argued in Chapter 1 that this split arose through Wolff's Cartesian-Liebnitzian idealist dualism, and that therefore, to accept his formulation is to fall to that extreme of the materialist-idealist divide that it is the aim of this present book to overcome.

Better definitions of the two levels of psychology are: (1) *comparative psychology,* whose proper subject is the behavior of animals, including the human animal; since we are bodily beings, comparative psychology is the culminating topic of physical science; (2) *personal*

60. See the article of Peter Harrison, "The Bible and the Emergence of Modern Science," last modified May 24, 2005, http://www.st-edmunds.cam.ac.uk/cis/Harrison/Peter%20Harrison%20-%20lecture.htm.

Harrison, however, thinks that this "freed" modern science from any need to try to reconcile the Bible and science and thus promoted the rapid advance of modern science! He does not seem concerned that it also meant the abandonment, by liberal Protestants, of belief in the inspiration of the Bible and the consequent hardening of fundamentalism and the rise of "creation science" by conservative Protestants.

psychology, whose proper subject comprises the human person, especially the uniquely human aspects of the behavior of human persons, and this is a topic that pertains to metaphysics (Aristotle's "First Philosophy"). Both psychologies, however, contrary to Wolff, are empirical, but comparative or general psychology is part of empirical natural science, whereas personal or special psychology is part of metaphysics while also being empirical, in that it presupposes natural science from whose empirical findings it reasons analogically.

The fact that we are human persons raises the question whether besides the First Cause of the universe there also exist other persons that are part of the system of the universe and whether they are embodied like humans, or "extraterrestrials" living on other planets and perhaps even more evolved than terrestrials, as many scientists suppose, or pure spirits like the angels of the Bible and the Qu'ran or the spirits of Hinduism, Buddhism, etc—topic I will touch on in Chapter 8.

After treating of animal psychology in Chapters 3–5, I will take up personal psychology in Chapter 6, and then its relation to ethics in Chapter 7 and to theology in Chapter 8. In Chapter 9, psychotherapy will be considered as the practical application of both animal and personal psychology to the good life that can bring about the healing of persons wounded precisely at the point where these two types of psychology meet. Thus my aim is to cast some light on the "mind-body problem" so controversial today. As Jaegwon Kim of Brown University writes in his book *Philosophy of Mind:*

> So we find ourselves in a profound dilemma. If we are prepared to embrace reductionism, we can explain mental causation. However, in the process of reducing mentality to physical/biological properties, we may well lose the intrinsic, subjective character of our mentality—arguably, the very thing that makes the mental [to be] mental. In what sense, then, have we saved "mental" causation? But if we reject reductionism, we are not able to see how mental causation should be possible. But saving mentality, while at the same time losing causality

doesn't seem to amount to saving anything worth saving. For what good is the mind if it has no causal powers? Either way, we are in danger of losing mentality. That is the dilemma.[61]

Conclusion

The argument of this book is that the dilemma well stated by Jaegwon Kim arises from a failure to adopt the fundamental principles of science that this chapter has derived from empirical observation and analysis of our basic sense experiences. On the basis of these scientific principles we can now proceed in Chapters 3–9 to give an account of the human person as a body-soul unity. Step-by-step I will try to show how this approach clarifies both comparative and personal psychology and has important practical consequences for psychotherapy.

61. Jaegwon Kim, *Philosophy of Mind* (Boulder, CO: Westview Press, 1996), 236.

three

HUMAN BODIES

Causal Explanations in Psychology

This chapter deals with the human body as a physical organism within our material universe. It is restricted to basic information that may seem elementary to the reader. The fact that a materialist like Sigmund Freud nevertheless explained schizophrenia as the result of family tensions, when today it is known to be due to brain malfunction that requires treatment by drugs, shows the danger of neglecting the physical aspect of psychological illness. On the other hand, today the excessive use of drugs for genuinely psychological problems illustrates the opposite danger. This issue also has important implications for theology as Pope John Paul II has brought to our attention by the term "theology of the body."[1] To steer a middle course it is necessary first to consider the more obvious truth that human persons are bodily organisms.

As explained in Chapter 2, contrary to what students of science are often taught, this requires us to think teleologically in the sense of

1. John Paul II, *Man and Woman He Created Them: A Theology of the Body* (Vatican: Libreria Editrice Vaticana, 2006).

seeking regular processes in material things. We must observe what regular changes produce in our world and in particular in the case of human beings what are the results of their behavior. This is why behaviorist methodology in psychology has proved fruitful. It is only the behavior of human persons that can tell us what we are as human persons, both as to the organization of our material bodies and as to the ultimate outcomes of our way of life.

Religious people, particularly Christians, may at first be uneasy about this critical approach to the human person from its physicality, since for them the truths of faith based on revelation are ultimately more explanatory than what we learn from our senses. Yet authentic faith is not, as is sometimes said, "a leap in the dark." Christians have always held that it is our natural knowledge through sense along with intelligence that leads us to faith, and this faith is not mere credulity, but a firm trust in a God who has made himself known to us by signs of His presence and revelation that are accessible to human reason. While it is true that we need God's grace to submit to this obligation of faith when we meet these signs, yet our reason tells us that we ought to do so, as we ought to learn from any teacher whose trustworthiness has become evident to us. Thus Jesus did not demand faith of anyone without first giving that person signs that should have made it clear that he was to be trusted as a teacher.[2] On the other hand, honest human science must remain open to the possibility that there also exist non-material or spiritual realities that make use of material causes to produce observable effects that surpass merely physical interpretation.

Am I Alone? The Fermi Paradox

After examining the foundations of a scientific study of our dynamic world, we must first locate the human species within the vast

2. This is the subject of my book *Choosing a Worldview and Value System: An Ecumenical Apologetics* (Staten Island, NY: Alba House, 2000).

world system and the amazing diversity of non-living and living substances on our earth. The Catholic Church is often mocked for its obstinate defense in the notorious Galileo affair of Ptolemaic geocentric astronomy in the face of Copernicus's heliocentrism. This is represented as a hopeless effort to keep us humans at the center of the universe and thus magnify our importance. Such mockery overlooks the fact that for the Aristotelianism of the Middle Ages the center of the universe was far from being its noblest place. That superior region was supposed to be the inalterable, perpetually cycling heavenly spheres, while the sublunar central earth was the far inferior *bottom* of the universe subject to corruption and purposeless chance. The paradox of the Incarnation was that God has become man, precisely because man is such a lowly being. The bad angels were thought to have fallen because of their proud refusal to submit to the Word made flesh. As Richard Tarnas has written about the modern view of human significance, as summed up by the greatest of Enlightenment philosophers, Immanuel Kant:[3]

> It could be said that in one sense Kant reversed the Copernican revolution, since he placed man again at the center of his universe by virtue of the human mind's central role in establishing the world order. But man's claim to be the center of his cognitive universe was only the obverse of his recognition that he could no longer assume any direct contact between the human mind and the universe's intrinsic order.

Yet for many, modern science seems to minimize the dignity of humanity still further by placing our tiny earth in a universe so vast that the light now arriving from the farthest objects visible in our telescopes has been traveling for some 13.7 billion light-years. Thus the noted astronomer Carl Sagan two years before his death in 1996 wrote in a very favorably reviewed and popular book *Pale Blue Dot:*[4]

3. *The Passion of the Western Mind: Understanding the Ideas That Have Shaped Our World View* (New York: Ballantine Books, 1991), 348.

4. Sagan, *Pale Blue Dot* (New York: Random House, 1994).

> And if the lights in the sky rise and set around us, isn't it evident that we're at the center of the Universe? These celestial bodies so clearly reveal that we are special. The Universe seems designed for human beings. It's difficult to contemplate these circumstances without experiencing stirrings of pride and reassurance. The entire Universe, made for us! We must really be something. This satisfying demonstration of our importance, buttressed by daily observations of the heavens, made the geocentrist conceit a transcultural truth—taught in the schools, built into the language, part and parcel of great literature and sacred scripture. Dissenters were discouraged, sometimes with torture and death. It is no wonder that for the vast bulk of human history, no one questioned it.[5]
>
> Better by far to embrace the hard truth than a reassuring fable. If we crave some cosmic purpose, then let us find ourselves a worthy goal. On behalf of Earthlife, I urge that, with full knowledge of our limitations, we vastly increase our knowledge of the Solar System and then begin to settle other worlds.[6]

Sagan is also quoted as saying: "For all our feelings of self importance, we are only a kind of biological rust, clinging to the surface of our small planet, and weighing far less than the air that surrounds us."[7] Yet as enthusiastic founder and supporter of the Institute for the Search for Extraterrestrial Intelligence (SETI), which since 1989 has been vainly listening for messages from intelligent life in outer space, Sagan hoped to discover ET's that he believed, without any substantial evidence, must exist throughout the universe. His hope was based only on what is called "The Drake Equation," formulated by his colleague Frank Drake, that on the basis of seven factors estimates the probability of the existence of intelligent life on other planets that is at least as advanced as we are today on our earth. This raises the "Fermi Paradox," as it is called after the great physicist Enrico Fermi (1901–54)

5. Ibid., 15.

6. Ibid, 377.

7. By Peter Warrington in "The Drake Equation and Extraterrestrial Life: A Brief Overview," last modified 1995, http://www.ufoevidence.org/documents/doc277.htm.

"Where are they?" that is, if there are ET's who think like our scientists do, why haven't they already made themselves known to our scientists?

Recently another physicist, Stephen Webb, in a fascinating book *Where Is Everybody,*[8] presented fifty answers that have been proposed to this question by various scientists. He showed that the Drake Equation has done little to answer the question, because the estimates of the magnitudes of the seven factors in that equation differ so widely.[9] Webb's conclusion, which is that of many other scientists, is that "We are alone." He says:

> [T]he expectation that other sentient species *must* be out there itself smacks of arrogance. Or rather, it achieves the tricky feat of being both self-important and self-effacing at the same time. . . . [It] is undeniable that mankind *is* profoundly different from every other species on Earth. We alone have language, a high level of self-consciousness, and a moral sense. We *are* special. But surely our uniqueness could not have arisen by mere chance, by the blind and random groping of evolution, could it? Well, why not?[10]

Webb then goes on to point out that the current Neo-Darwinian theory of evolution holds it to be purely by chance that, once life began on earth, it ever evolved to the level of intelligence in the human species. If we knew the initial conditions when life first originated, we could never predict what life forms would result.

Another factor in this debate over extraterrestrial intelligence is what is called the Anthropic Cosmological Principle.[11] In its strong

8. Webb, *Where Is Everybody?* (New York: Copernicus Books/ Springer-Verlag, 2002).

9. Ibid., 17–22. Another survey of this complicated controversy that provides ample bibliography and comes to very much the same conclusion as does Webb is by John L. Casti, "Extraterrestrials: A Skeptical View," http://home.comcast.net/~gmcdavid/html_dir/fermi.html. See also Peter Ward and Donald Brownlee, *Rare Earth: Why Complex Life Is Uncommon in the Universe* (New York: Springer-Verlag, 2000).

10. Webb, *Where Is Everybody?* 239.

11. This is argued at length in the book of John D. Barrow and Frank J. Tipler, *The Anthropic Cosmological Principle*, with a foreword by John A. Wheeler (New York:

form it is a "Design Argument" for the existence of a Creator God, but in its weak form—accepted by many scientists, including Sagan—it simply asserts that, if the universe were much different than it actually is, life and especially intelligent life, would be impossible.[12] The way Sagan vividly states this is as follows:[13]

> Our universe is *almost* incompatible with life—or at least what we understand as necessary for life. Even if every star in a hundred billion galaxies had an Earthlike planet, without heroic technological measures life could prosper in only about 10^{-37} the volume of the Universe.... Only 10^{-37} of our universe is hospitable to life. Thirty-six zeroes before the one. The rest is cold, radiation-riddled black vacuum.

Thus, in spite of the fact that the universe seems to minimize the importance of human existence, if it were much different than it actually is in its immense size and age and "emptiness," even we, although we are perhaps the lowliest possible type of intelligent life, would not exist! As for those who laugh at the ancients for placing humanity at the center of the universe, we should note that modern science as made three facts clear. First, the earth is placed at the right distance from the sun to get the proper amount of energy that life requires—not too close and not too distant. Second, although our solar system is about halfway out from the center of our galaxy, the center is prob-

---

Oxford University Press, 1986 and 1996) that has been central to this whole debate; see especially, 556–75.

12. "In reviewing the physical laws and the numerical values of fundamental constants, one encounters a remarkable precision in these values such that only small changes in the fundamental constants, such as the strengths of the four forces, Planck's constant, the mass of elementary particles, etc., would yield a universe without galaxies, stars, atoms, or even nuclei, and consequently without the capacity for life ... The constants of nature, such as the strength of the gravitational force, have exactly the values necessary for the existence of stars and planets." Dean L. Overman, *A Case against Accident and Self-Organization*, foreword by Wolfhart Pannenberg (Lanham, MD: Rowman and Littlefield, 1997), 128–34.

13. Sagan, *Pale Blue Dot*, note on page 32.

ably occupied by a black hole into which we would not want to be sucked. Third, the expansion of the universe is causing the galaxies to move apart, so that inevitably we remain at the center of the only region of the universe that can affect us or that we can ever know by the light reaching us at a constant speed equally on every side.

Therefore, we are left with the conclusion that at present science shows a vast and largely chaotic universe that is so constructed that it makes human existence possible on this earth but, as far as we now or may ever know, no place else.

Extraterrestrials and Christian Faith

How does this picture of the universe favored today by science square with Christian faith? Protestant writers today make much of what they call the "Design Argument," referred to above, to prove the existence of a Creator God.[14] As the passage from Carl Sagan quoted just above says, the chances that evolution of life on earth would have produced human, intelligent life are extremely small. From this fact, say these writers, it follows that we are the work of an Intelligent Creator and not simply of deterministic and non-teleological laws of nature. This Design Argument is a modern version of an ancient proof of God's existence most clearly formulated by St. Thomas Aquinas as his Fourth and Fifth Ways through *formal* and *final causality*. Immanuel Kant tried to show that these proofs were reducible to the so-called "ontological argument" of St. Anselm of Canterbury, which involves a logical circularity. Kant's refutation is still accepted by many writers today,[15] but it was based both on his misunderstanding of the medieval arguments and on his idealist assumptions.

14. On this see William A. Dembski, *The Design Revolution: Answering the Toughest Questions about Intelligent Design* (Downers Grove, IL, InterVarsityPress, 2004).

15. Thus Hans Küng in, *Does God Exist: An Answer for Today* (Garden City, NY: Doubleday 1980), after a critique of Kant (536–51), essentially accepts his position by saying that if we are to have a meaningful life we must "trust" that there is a God (568–75).

This Design Argument from formal and final causality that resembles Aquinas's Fourth and Fifth Ways is not, however, according to St. Thomas himself,[16] as evident as his first three ways derived from Aristotle's *Physics* VIII and based on *efficient* causality. I presented the First of these three ways in the last chapter, noting that as stated in the *Physics* and by Aquinas in his *Summa Contra Gentiles* I, cc. 10–14, this First Way is not a metaphysical demonstration but a physical one. This proof, unlike the modern formulations of the Design Argument, does not rest on the details of modern science that may be only probable and are open to debate, but is part of the foundations of natural science that, if denied, opens the validity of the whole scientific endeavor open to the attacks of Hume and the post-moderns.[17]

He shows no awareness of the thorough refutation of Kant's misunderstanding of the Five Ways of Aquinas previously provided by Reginald Garrigou-Lagrange, OP, *God, His Existence and His Nature: A Thomistic Solution of Certain Agnostic Antinomies* (St. Louis, MO/London: B. Herder, 1934–36); Thomas C. O'Brian, *Metaphysics and the Existence of God* (Washington, DC: Thomist Press, 1960); and Cornelio Fabro, *God in Exile: Modern Atheism; A Study of the Internal Dynamic of Modern Atheism, from Its Roots in the Cartesian Cogito to the Present Day* (Westminster, MD: Newman Press, 1968).

16. *ST* I, q. 2, a. 3 c. *Primum autem et manifestior via est quae sumitur ex parte motus.* "But the more evident way [to demonstrate God's existence] is based on the effect of motion. . . ."

17. It is amusing that the noted evolutionary biologist Richard Lewontin, in an otherwise perceptive article, "The Wars over Evolution," *The New York Review of Books* (Oct. 2005), 51–55, refutes the Intelligent Design Argument by writing, "[T]he theory of ID is a transparent subterfuge. The problem is that if the living world is too complex to have arisen without an intelligent designer, then where did the intelligent designer come from? After all, she must have been as complex as the things she designed. If not then we have evolution! Otherwise we must postulate an intelligent designer who designed the intelligent designer who . . . back to the original one who must have been around forever. And who might that be? Like the ancient Hebrews the ID designers fear to pronounce Her name lest they be destroyed, but Her initials are clearly YHWH" (52). Lewontin thinks ID designers are not honest in claiming their argument is science, not theology. What he cites is the proof of the existence of an Unmoved Mover, which is, as I showed in Chapter 3, a presupposition to scientific establishment of any uniform laws. To show that this Unmoved Mover is God, whether He or She, is the task of metaphysics not of theology. Lewontin declares himself an atheist while at the same time proving the contradictoriness of his position!

If the existence of extraterrestrials is ever proved or even if the probability of their existence is considered significant, would this conflict with the Christian doctrine that the terrestrial Jesus of Nazareth is the Incarnate Son of God and the sole Savior? Since it is also a matter of faith that angels are pure spiritual intelligences superior to us terrestrials,[18] it is a revealed truth that ETs in that broad sense do exist. Aquinas hypothesized that more angels exist than all the species of material things and that each angel differs from every other not merely individually but as a distinct species.[19] If this is correct, intelligent substances in the universe may outnumber and are certainly more interesting and dynamic than the material parts of the universe.

If we apply the Fermi Paradox to angels and ask, if they exist and are so superior to us, why do they not communicate with us, we are reassured by biblical accounts of angelic apparitions that in fact they do, and this has been confirmed by many canonized saints and in our times by the children of Fatima.[20] Normally, however, these pure spirits are invisible to us. Aquinas also argues that they cannot act directly on our spiritual intelligences or free wills, but that they can affect our bodies and in particular what the medievals called the *internal* senses.[21] I prefer to call touch, hearing, smell, taste, seeing the *primary* senses and these "internal" senses *secondary* because the objects of at least touch, smell, and taste are perceived with our bodies.

The secondary senses assist us in our thinking, not by putting ideas in our reason, but by affecting the ordering of our thoughts by acting on our imaginations without us being clearly conscious of the source of these images. Thus the evil angels can suggest evil thoughts and the good angels can suggest good thoughts. The pagan sage

18. On this see Paul A. Duffner, OP, "Today's Crisis of Faith," *The Rosary Light & Life* 43, no. 2 (March–April 1990).

19. *ST* I, q. 50, aa. 3–4.

20. On the apparitions at Fatima, Portugal, 1916–17, see "Fatima," last modified 2010, http://www.sacredsites.com/europe/portugal/fatima.htm

21. *ST* I, q. 111.

Socrates claimed that he had a "genius" or spirit that prompted him to do good and warned him against temptation, and many creative thinkers sometimes experience "inspirations."[22] Our human thinking, therefore, may be more dependent on angelic agencies than we suspect.

Revelation tells us nothing about possible extraterrestrials, that is, intelligences other than the human intelligences that are also naturally embodied, but we can speculate on the subject from a Christian perspective, just as materialists do from their perspective. First the omnipotence of God entails the possibility that he has created such beings on suitable planets or elsewhere in the universe.

Second, the assumption of those who seek communication with extraterrestrials is usually that they may be of a different species than we are. If this is the case they may have an entirely different spiritual history than our human history and this raises no contradiction to Christian doctrine.

Third, if the extraterrestrials were of the same species as ours, it would seem according to Catholic doctrine the Jesus, God humanly incarnate, must be their savior also. Aquinas saw no difficulty in admitting that perhaps the Son of God has become incarnate in several individual human persons,[23] so that it would seem that each of these planets might have had its own incarnation of the Son of God, though Aquinas also holds that it would not be fitting for this to take place in a single human community such as that on the earth.[24] If then the churches on such planets would someday communicate, they would all recognize the one Son of God in these different incarnations. Or, God the Son may have become incarnate only on our planet in Jesus of Nazareth. If so, when other planets communicate with us, we will be able to preach the Gospel to them. The Church teaches that the

22. See Brewster Ghiselin, editor and introduction, *The Creative Process* for an anthology of persons reporting such "inspirations" (New York: Mentor Books, 1970).

23. *ST* III, q. 3, a. 7 c.

24. *ST* III, q. 4, a. 5 c.

righteous that lived before Jesus or who today never have the privilege of hearing the Gospel can be saved by Him if they live by such light as they possess. Surely this would also apply to extraterrestrials to whom we are never able to preach the Gospel as it does to pagans on earth who have not been yet evangelized.

Again it seems possible that although our earthly species was created in grace and destined to the beatific vision, since this was a free act of God, He could instead have created our species in "the state of pure nature." Then such creatures would not be destined for the beatific vision but for a purely natural happiness, as now may be the case for unbaptized children.[25] If these humans who were never elevated to the state of grace sinned by turning from their natural end, they would have gone to hell, but no doubt their punishment would be less than is now that of earthlings who reject grace. If someday we contact such merely natural human extraterrestrials we will communicate with them on the rational level, but they will lack the gift of faith and be content with a purely natural idea of God, unable to understand why we hope for anything else, until we open up this possibility to them.

To sum up, there is nothing in Christian doctrine that contradicts the notion of extraterrestrial embodied intelligence. On the other hand it would not surprise or trouble Christians, as it did an atheist like Sagan, that we terrestrials on our tiny planet Earth may be the only *embodied* intelligences in the universe. We are not alone, because the angels are the greater part of the cosmos, and as St. Augustine says, "God is closer to us, than we are to ourselves."[26]

What of the future of the human species? Those who hope to

25. Aquinas supposed that unbaptized children after death are in this state of natural happiness (limbo). The *Catechism of the Catholic Church,* no. 1261, however, indicates that we can reasonably hope for their salvation and most theologians point out that this may be mediated through the parents of the parents and the Church, since the *Catechism* no. 1259 also reaffirms the Church's tradition that catechumens who die before baptism are saved *ex voto.*

26. *Confessions,* 3.6.11.

communicate with extraterrestrials are very concerned that we will destroy our earthly environment by misuse of modern technology before we have been able to invent space travel to some more hospitable planet. The question also arises whether any further evolution of the human intelligence on earth is possible, since the human brain is already so extremely complex. In that case more than one species of embodied intelligences would live on earth side by side, or perhaps our species might be extinguished by the other, or vice versa. Some have speculated that the Neanderthals were of a different species of embodied intelligence but less intelligent than *homo sapiens sapiens* who killed them all.

Current science predicts that no matter what happens to the human species, without divine intervention the earth is doomed by the laws of nature to perish when in perhaps 5 billion years the sun expands into a red supergiant star. Furthermore, it seems that the whole universe will expand until it ends in a Big Crunch, a Big Rip, or a Big Freeze.[27] Certainly the Second Law of Thermodynamics predicts that increasing entropy (decline of energy into purely random motion) will finish it off. Even if a Big Crunch leads to another Big Bang in a perpetual cycle, we can never observe the cycle that preceded or followed the one in which we exist. Thus, although Christian eschatology leaves open just when human history will come to an end in the Last Judgment, the scientific predictions of the future leave ample room for that judgment long before the universe suffers any of these possible conclusions.

The Anthropic Cosmological Principle, even in its weak version, shows us why, even if only on earth embodied intelligent life, or even

27. This is the hypothesis being studied by the Dartmouth physicist Robert Caldwell and his associates; see Robert Roy Britt, "The Big Rip: New Theory Ends Universe by Shredding Everything," last modified Mar 6, 2003, http://www.freerepublic.com/focus/f-news/862439/posts. The Rip would occur when finally the acceleration of expansion for which evidence has recently been found would overcome the force of gravity and tear all matter apart.

biological life, has evolved, the universe must be so spatially and temporally vast for intelligent, embodied life to exist on our earth, even if it does not exist anywhere else.[28] It may seem incredible that a universe with 125 billion galaxies should exist merely to house our tiny earth. Yet this may seem less disproportionate if we note the immense complexity of the human brain. Its cortex has about 10 billion neurons, typically having several dendrites each with about 1,000 to 10,000 synapses that communicate with 1,000–10,000 other neurons, muscle cells, glands, etc.![29]

We Are Bodies among Bodies

To understand our human selves as part of this vast material universe, we need first to ask what we mean by saying it is "material" and second what we mean by calling our environment a "uni-verse," that is a "many that is also one." As we have seen in Chapter 2, in physics today the most basic terms are "matter" and "energy" but the distinction between them is somewhat blurred. Ordinarily, however, the term "matter" refers to a reality that has inertial mass, that is, a certain resistance to being set in motion or otherwise changed by the application of energy.

Oddly, however, physics also admits the existence of particles such as photons that have no mass, yet certainly must be considered to be "material." Furthermore, the distance between the particles in atoms and the so-called "empty spaces" between the stars are filled with "fields" through which energy is transmitted from one point to another, including the still hypothetical "Higgs field" that is supposed to give massive particles their inertial mass. Obviously, therefore, when we speak of the "material" universe the term "matter" has

28. See Barrow and Tipler, *The Anthropic Cosmological Principle*, especially, 556–75.

29. See "The Brain," last modified 2010, http://www.enchantedlearning.com/subjects/anatomy/brain/Neuron.shtml, and "Number of Neurons in a Human Brain," last modified 2002, http://hypertextbook.com/facts/2002/AniciaNdabahaliye2.shtml.

a more inclusive sense than is usually given it by physicists and includes all reality that has a quantitative character.[30]

Hence Descartes, one of the founders of modern science, held that the essence of matter understood in this inclusive sense is *extension* or quantity, that is, the condition by which some whole has parts having only common boundaries (continuous quantity) or which are entirely distinct (discrete quantity). Aristotle, however, had long ago pointed out that although quantity is the most basic *property* of matter, it cannot be its defining note, since the quantity of a material thing changes without that thing losing its identity; for example, when heated iron expands it remains iron. Instead what is most fundamental to our experience of the material world is that it is *ens mobile*, that is, *real* (existing independent of our minds) but *changeable.*

The ancient Greek Democritus thought that the universe is made up of atoms that change only very superficially in their location in space, but modern science has never observed anything that does not change and change profoundly, coming into existence and then being lost in the emergence of other things. In this book, therefore, by "material" I mean not just massive, inertial matter but everything that is a *changeable whole that has quantitative parts.* Hence a vacuum or "empty space" is in fact a material and energetic field even when no massive particles ("matter" as the term is today commonly used) are present in it.[31]

The scientific term "energy," on the other hand, is defined in physics as "the potential or actual capacity to perform work," that is, to cause change in matter. As previously noted, it is thought that it is exhibited in the four fundamental forces naturally inherent in certain material things (1) *gravity* by which all objects that have inertial mass are attracted to each other, the electroweak force that includes both (2) *electromagnetism* (light, electrical charge and magnetism) and

30. For the history of this term see Ernan McMullin, ed., *The Concept of Matter in Modern Philosophy,* rev. ed. (Notre Dame, IN: University of Notre Dame Press, 1978).

31. See Sagan, *Pale Blue Dot,* note on page 32.

(3) the *weak nuclear* force that produces radioactivity, and (4) the *strong nuclear* force that binds the quarks in atomic nuclei into protons and neutrons and holds the entire nucleus together.

Given these concepts of matter (in its inclusive sense) and energy, we can speak of every identifiable material object as a "system,"[32] that is, a unified whole with interacting continuous or/and discrete parts, each of which has continuous parts. For example, our solar system is made up of the sun, planets (and their planets), asteroids, comets and dust that are quite discrete objects, each having its own continuous parts, but interacting with the other discrete parts of the system in their positions and motions by mutual gravitation and electromagnetism. On the other hand, an oyster is a system whose parts are continuous with each other and whose unity consists in the interaction of its organs that permits it to perform life functions of nutrition, growth, and reproduction. Thus a system can have a very loose or very tight unity, depending on the extent to which the parts are dependent on the whole for their stable existence and characteristic actions. Besides natural systems, there are also the artificial systems that we call "machines" and "communities" of living things.

An important principle of systems theory is that in every system there must be a part whose action coordinates and unifies the actions of the parts (a "prime mover," like the motor in a machine) so that the system maintains itself and has some regular behavior. This prime mover's actions cannot be caused by the action of other parts of the system, but it must receive its energy from *outside* the system. Yet at the same time the action of this principal part can be influenced by *cybernetic feedback* from the parts. The greater this cybernetic influence, the freer the system becomes to act on and control its environment rather than be subjected to possibly destructive forces coming from that environment. In any case no system can long survive un-

32. See Bertalanffy, *General Systems Theory Foundations, Development, Applications* (New York: G. Braziller, 1968).

less it is "adapted" to its environment, either by a passive ability to resist destructive actions on it of the environment or the active ability to control and adjust its environment.

In some material systems this coordination and unification of the whole is very loose so that the parts have some activities not subordinated to the control of the principal part or the principal part is little influenced by feedback from the parts. In other systems this coordination, unification, and cybernetic feedback are much greater. Our solar system, or even a star or a planet, are aggregates of heterogeneous bodies that, although they may endure for years, have few properties that pertain to the whole as such, rather than to the individual parts. Thus our earth is made up of oceans, various kinds of rocks, and living things and, although its ecology exhibits a certain unity, it is a very loose one in which the individual bodies of water, rocks, and organisms are easily distinguished from each other as wholes with individual activities. Although some ecologists favor the so-called "Gaia hypothesis" according to which the earth itself must be regarded as a living organism, most biologists would maintain that the unity of the environment and the unity of even the most simple living organism are of very different orders of complexity.[33]

On the contrary, in distinction from such loose aggregates or weak systems, atoms, molecules formed from atoms, and living organisms formed from various kinds of molecules, have their parts so strongly interrelated that when the parts are separated from the whole and observed by themselves they behave very differently than they did as parts of a unified system. These natural units are also quite different than a man-made machine. Even the most intricate artificial system, such as a computer, differs from a living organism first of all in the fact that a computer is a machine whose parts are not naturally related to each other at all but have been combined by human tech-

33. "The Gaia Hypothesis" has been criticized by Richard Dawkins and several others as too teleological.

nology, while a living thing, like an atom or a molecule, is a natural unit whose parts cannot carry on the functions they had within the unit once they are separated from it. Therefore, although some suppose that an animal is simply a set of molecules and a molecule a set of atoms and the atom a set of atomic particles, this is not really the case.

The unity of an atom, a molecule, or a living organism, is not a mere collection of smaller units, nor is it, like a machine, an assembly of parts that can simply be taken apart or put back together. Atomic particles ordinarily exist only within an atom and if expelled by the excitation of the atom to an extreme state of energy can exist apart from an atom only very, very briefly before again being attached to an atom. A quark, one of the two basic types of such particles, has never been observed outside an atom. Thus the "elementary wave-particles" of modern physics that seem to reduce to quarks and leptons, according to one of the founders of quantum physics, Edwin Schrödinger (1887–1961) may not be complete, identifiable substances having independent existence.[34] Furthermore, atoms in the process of binding together to form a molecule are not simply juxtaposed but are modified to become parts of its unified structure. Thus the "reductionism" defended by some scientists, which overlooks this distinction—between systems that are *constituted from* independently existing units, such as a galaxy, our solar system, or an automobile, and those that *are in themselves* independently existing units, such as an atom, a molecule, or an organism—is inadequate to explain the world in which we live. As was shown in Chapter 2, the reductionist model of the human per-

34. On this see Edwin Schrödinger, "What Is an Elementary Particle?" in *Interpreting Bodies: Classical and Quantum Objects in Modern Physics,* ed. Elena Castellani (Princeton, NJ: Princeton University Press, 1998). Schrödinger says, "Now we do observe single particles, we see their tracks in the cloud chamber. . . . Yet we must deny the particle the dignity of being an absolutely identifiable individual" (205). My physicist friend Anthony Rizzi, author of *The Science before Science: A Guide to Thinking in the 21st Century* (Bloomington, IN: Authorhouse, 2004), however, is inclined to believe they are true substances.

son that flows from this view is especially implausible, for the reasons given there.

Evolving Complexity

Both non-living molecules and living organisms, like the atoms from which they are composed, are unified substances. Yet is it sufficient to say that living things are much more chemically complex than non-living things? Does this material complexity result in a different type of observable behavior than is evident in non-living molecules or assemblage of such molecules? Certainly the boundary between non-living and living substances can be difficult to determine, as is evident in viruses that can reproduce only within more complex organisms.[35] The usual way biologists mark out their field of research from that of chemists is to say that living substances (organisms) are *homeostatic* or "self-maintaining" systems in which the output of energy from the system is kept in balance by an equal input of energy. Viruses according to that definition are not living, self-maintaining substances but are fragments produced by living things that infect other living things that accidentally multiply them. As one virologist says,[36]

> Virus particles (*virions*) are produced from the assembly of preformed components, whereas other agents "grow" from an increase in the integrated sum of their components & reproduce by division. [They] themselves do not "grow" or undergo division [and they] lack the genetic information which encodes apparatus necessary for the generation of metabolic energy or for protein synthesis (ribosomes).

Is life, then, an "emergent" property of certain chemical substances, as some writers claim? That assertion again requires us to face the

35. See Nigel Dimmock, *Introduction to Modern Virology* (New York: Wiley-Blackwell, 2007).

36. See A. J. Cann, *Principles of Molecular Virology* (San Diego: Academic Press, 2nd ed., 1997), Introduction, p. 2.

question of the causes of evolution. The fossil record establishes that life has evolved on our earth and that many species of living things that once existed are now millions of years extinct. In an "Address to the Pontifical Academy of Science, Oct. 22, 1996,"[37] Pope John Paul II noted that Pope Pius XII in 1950 in his encyclical *Humani Generis* had spoken of human evolution as a reasonable hypothesis, provided it not be understood to contradict the direct creation by God of the human spiritual soul. John Paul II then went on to say:

> Today, almost half a century after the publication of the Encyclical, new knowledge has led to the recognition of the theory of evolution as more than a hypothesis. It is indeed remarkable that this theory has been progressively accepted by researchers, following a series of discoveries in various fields of knowledge. The convergence, neither sought nor fabricated, of the results of work that was conducted independently is in itself a significant argument in favor of this theory.

Thus the pope acknowledges human evolution as a fact, but then adds that more than one theory of evolution is current and further research is needed to understand that fact.[38] This claim is strongly resented by some evolutionists, but it can hardly be denied that reputable evolutions who all defend Neo-Darwinism, which some prefer to call "The Modern Synthesis," against religious attacks, are also bitterly opposed to each other's versions of that theory. Thus Stephen Jay Gould and Richard Dawkins attacked each other's views in harsh terms.[39]

As we saw in Chapter 2 the Catholic Church was never committed to "creationism" based on a univocal interpretation of the six days

37. Papal Addresses to the Pontifical Academy of Sciences 1917–2002 and to the Pontifical Academy of Social Sciences 1994–2002 (Vatican: Ex Aedibvs Academicis in Civitate Vaticana, 2002).

38. See Laurence Moran, "Evolution Is a Fact and a Theory," last modified Jan 22, 1993, http://www.talkorigins.org/faqs/evolution-fact.html.

39. See Gould's "Darwinian Fundamentalism" and "Evolution: The Pleasures of Pluralism," *New York Review of Books* (June 12 & 26, 1997).

of creation in Genesis 1. Yet the six-day creation of Genesis was generally accepted by Christians until the eighteenth century and on the chronology of the Old Testament was dated to 4004 BC.

In the seventeenth century, Descartes proposed that the earth was produced by a comet hitting the sun and that the earth was much older than the Bible seemed to say. The Swedish biologist Carolus Linnaeus (1707–78) in his *Systema Naturae*, 1725 established a taxonomy of organisms, and the French Comte de Buffon (1707–88) speculated that, because of environmental changes and chance, species do change, but not essentially. He estimated the origin of the earth at about 75,000 years. Erasmus Darwin (1731–1802), grandfather of Charles Darwin (1809–82), extended this to millions of years and proposed the idea of human evolution but without a causal explanation in his *Zoonomia, or, the Laws of Organic Life* (1796). Then Jean Baptiste Chevalier de Lamarck (1744–1829) in 1809 proposed that life emerged from inanimate material and progressed to man by a striving for perfection and the inheritance of acquired characteristics, but his views were strongly rejected by George Cuvier (1760–1832) although even today it is recognized by some evolutionists that this might be a factor influencing survival. Cuvier, however, also accepted catastrophism or violent changes of the earth's surface to explain the fossil record, but this view was rejected by Charles Lyell (1797–1875) and in his *Principles of Geology* (1833) showed that the earth is very old and constantly changing, a position supported by James Hutton (1726–97).

Finally Charles Darwin in *The Origin of Species* (1859) proposed the view that species change through *natural selection* of random variations by a changing environment. He was open, however, to other causal factors. At the same time similar but independent views were formulated by Alfred Russel Wallace (1823–1913)[40] who, in con-

40. See Ross A. Slotten, *The Heretic in Darwin's Court: The Life of Alfred Russel Wallace* (New York: Columbia University Press, 2004). http://www.amazon.com/Heretic-Darwins-Court-Alfred-Wallace/dp/0231130112/ref=sr_1_1?s=books&ie=UTF8&qid=1302724759&sr=1-1 - #

trast with Darwin's agnosticism or atheism, held for a spiritual First Cause of evolution and a spiritual human soul.

It would seem that Darwinism, rather than Wallace's theistic views, has received such universal acceptance because Darwin's agnostic views fit the modern paradigm shift to secularism. Yet its critics pointed out many of its inadequacies and toward the end of the century its favor was declining until it was given remarkable support by the delayed recognition of the discovery of genes and their random mutations by the Catholic priest and Augustinian Abbot Fr. Gregor Mendel (1822–84). Sewell Wright (1889–1988) developed the mathematical theory of "genetic drift," the random fluctuations in the frequency of the appearance of a gene in a small isolated population, which eliminates some genes and then, as the population happens to increase, leads to their domination. This concept was further elaborated by "game theory" by John Maynard Smith (1920–2004) according to which the drift of one set of changes is conditioned by that of others in the situation. Thus genetic drift is a very important and even, as some think, the major, factor in evolution and is not "adaptationist" or "optionalistic." Stephen Jay Gould (1941–2003) and others also proposed what they called "punctuated equilibrium" to explain the fossil record which seems to show relatively short bursts of evolutionary development.[41]

Hence Neo-Darwinism is "neutralist" in that it completely eliminates any implication of finality or evolutionary "progress," but this also means that there is no determined "law of evolution." As one of its main advocates, Ernst Mayr (1904–2005) in his *What Evolution Is,* says:[42]

> Evolution is not deterministic. The evolutionary process consists of a large number of interactions. Different genotypes within a single

41. Wesley E. Elsberry, "Punctuated Equilibria," last modified Feb 4, 1996, http://www.talkorigins.org/faqs/punc-eq.html.

42. (New York: Basic Books, 2001), 121.

population may respond differently to the same change of the environment. These changes, in turn, are unpredictable, particularly when caused by the arrival at a locality of a new predator or competitor. Survival during a mass extinction may be strongly affected by chance.

The theory of the evolution of life on earth has to be thought of in the context of cosmic evolution about which current cosmology supposes the following:

1. Modern quantum theory only predicts the probability of any observable natural event. Hence today some scientists, in order to explain any events that they actually observe, hypothesize that there are many or even an infinity of worlds; we just happen to be in that world where we observe this event that has occurred only here. Yet if these worlds were completely independent of each other, those in one universe could know nothing scientifically of the others. If, on the contrary, they act on each other so that we could know their existence, then the interacting ones must form a single universe. For the reasons I have already given, however, none of these worlds could exist without the One Creator. Hence many world theories explain nothing.
2. Our universe could be eternal and in a cyclical steady state, as Aristotle held. In his hypothesis the celestial bodies cannot alter but naturally move eternally by an intrinsic power from which their motion emanates, as today we suppose gravitational force is a fundamental power of matter always in act. Yet, because the powers of material bodies are always finite, the eternity of their motion requires conservation by the efficient action of spiritual intelligences subordinated to the First Cause. Aristotle did not think, as did the Stoics, that a cyclical evolution and decline occurred, but within an eternal universe this is also a possibility.
3. The universe could be created with material forces that are "programmed" to produce cosmological and biological evolu-

tion in analogy to the genetic development of a plant. Some biologists today speak of "self-organization" or the "emergence" of species or, like Julian Huxley, talk of "panpsychism" (ensoulment of all bodies) in this way. Yet the Creator would have to program this evolution, and created spirits might be the gardeners who cultivate plants to assure their full growth.

4. The universe could be created with material forces that at a low level have intrinsic tendencies to combine, as elementary particles combine to form atoms and atoms to bond into molecules of various species, but are unable to produce life. Evolution of living things would then require the action of spirits to guide chance events to produce a more complex evolution to the level of the human body capable of receiving a spiritual soul directly created by God. Thus Aquinas thought that the sun could produce simple living things (spontaneous generation) but nothing more complex.

At present this last type of evolution best fits the evidence that Big-Bang cosmology and Neo-Darwinism seek to explain. The position that I argued in Chapter 2 that all valid scientific explanation depends on the existence of a First Immaterial Cause does not exclude any of these possibilities. The First Cause, or Creator, although he can when necessary act directly, prefers to work through the natural forces that he has created so as to use the powers he has given them. If, therefore, simple material bodies produce an evolution of species, the Creator is still the First Cause of this evolution. Scientific research, therefore, is entirely free to determine both whether evolution has occurred and, if it has occurred, the manner in which secondary causes have produced it. Thus nothing I have said in Chapter 2 is contradicted by the fact of evolution as regards material bodies, including the human body; nor does it dismiss any theory of how it occurred that is not dogmatically materialist.

Yet the first question to ask about any theory of biological evolution is whether it is a law-like, deterministic process whose outcome, namely, the emergence of life and the ascent from very simple organisms to intelligent embodied persons is scientifically predictable from the initial conditions of the universe and its immediate environment. Ordinarily what we mean by an accepted scientific theory is such a deterministic law that can be verified or falsified observationally. We have seen that among the Church Fathers St. Augustine inclined to this deterministic view, as have prominent modern thinkers like Lamarck, Henri Bergson (1859–1941), or Pierre Teilhard de Chardin, SJ,[43] who argued for a teleological, necessary ascent of species. It seems even today to be the popular understanding of evolution; but, as the evolutionary biologist Richard Lewontin has pointed out,[44] Neo-Darwinism, like Darwin's own views and contrary to those of Wallace, does not suppose any finality in nature, but only endless change, the coming into existence and death of varied organisms.

In the course of evolution there have been at least six major extinctions of many species, such as that of the dinosaurs, which have had various unrelated causes. The fossil record seems to show that terrestrial life began about 3.5 billion years ago, but that in the relatively brief Cambrian period, between 543 and 490 million years ago, all the major forms of life emerged. Yet some species have endured unchanged for millions of years. Thus it seems impractical to observe directly the actual process of evolution in the short time of modern research.

Many claims are made by advocates of Neo-Darwinism that speciation has in fact been observed, for example, in bacteria, fruit-flies, moths, and Darwin's finches in the Galapagos Islands.[45] Such claims

43. Bergson: *Creative Evolution*, authorized translation by Arthur Mitchell (New York: H. Holt and Company, 1911); Chardin: *The Human Phenomenon*, a new edition and translation by Sarah Appleton-Weber (Portland, OR: Sussex Academic Press, 1999).

44. See my comments in note 17 above on Richard Lewontin's article, "The Wars Over Evolution."

45. For examples and bibliography, see Joseph Boxhorn, "Observed Instances of Speciation," and Chris Stassen et al., "Some More Observed Instances of Speciation Events" in "The Talk. Origins Archive: Exploring the Creation. Evolution Controversy," last modified Sep. 1, 1995, at http://www.talkorigins.org/faqs/faq-speciation.html. For a criticism of some of these claims see Jonathan Wells, *Icons of Evolution: Science or Myth?*

are, however, dubious because of the difficulty of distinguishing between variations within a species, such as those produced by breeding of dogs and horses, and a genuine "origin of species." The criterion generally used by biologists to distinguish species is whether or not two populations interbreed and produce fertile offspring.[46] Yet, since in animals the most complex and therefore the most specifying kind of behavior is not reproductive but sensory, the only sure way to define an animal species is by behavior that manifests a special ability to sense and perceive objects. Thus, until animal taxonomy based on this criterion has been well established, attempts to observe actual animal speciation are ineffective.

Today, chemists break down step-by-step the proteins that are the chemical basis of life and thus discover the chemical reactions necessary to synthesis them and then reverse this analysis so as to synthesize the specific protein.[47] These reactions involve only the use of natural forces, but the clue is to find the scenario of the order and manner in which these forces must be applied to produce the protein. The step from one such event to another is not inherent in the process but is determined only by the information in the mind of the chemist. Therefore, it would seem that if such a scenario for ordering and assembling the chemical constituents of a living organism were known, it could be produced in the laboratory. Similarly if the genome of one species could be modified so as to constitute an or-

---

Why Much of What We Teach about Evolution Is Wrong (Washington, DC: Regnery Publishing, 2000), which stimulated a vigorous discussion available on Internet under Wells's name or book title. See also Phillip E. Johnson, *Darwin on Trial* (Washington, DC: Regnery Gateway, 1991) and *Defeating Darwinism by Opening Minds* (Downers Grove, IL: InterVarsity Press, 1997), who on his website has joined the fray. Prominent defenders of Neo-Darwinism against such critics are Daniel C. Dennett, *Darwin's Dangerous Idea: Evolution and the Meanings of Life* (New York: Simon and Schuster, reprint 1966) and Richard Dawkins, *The Blind Watchmaker* (New York: Norton, 1986).

46. See Marc Ereshefsky, "Species," in *Stanford Encyclopedia of Philosophy* (Stanford, CA: Stanford University, 2010).

47. E. J. Corey and Xue-min Cheng, *The Logic of Chemical Synthesis* (New York: John Wiley, 1989).

ganism of a different species we could reproduce the history of events that we now reconstruct as "evolution." Chemists have in fact discovered how to produce thousands of complex organic compounds from lifeless chemical elements.

Yet to assert that life has "emerged" from lifeless chemical processes it is necessary to propose at least hypothetically a *proportionate efficient cause* for the greater complexity and unification that enables living things to nourish, grow, and reproduce. These activities are not properties of the chemical compounds that supply the proportionate material cause of the organism, but of the dynamically united system of compounds. Therefore, the proportionate cause necessary to produce the system of the living organism must be supplied with the information necessary to guide this complicated process, each step of which has no necessary causal connection with the previous step, but must be determined by such information.

Michael J. Behe, in *Darwin's Black Box: The Biochemical Challenge to Evolution,*[48] heated up the controversy over natural selection by his theory of "irreducible complexity" in living things. He claims that no evolutionist has yet even *proposed* a testable, detailed hypothesis of the chemical synthesis required to explain how the genome of one species could be step-by-step changed into that of another species in such a way as to avoid frustrating the process by a fatal mutation.[49] Therefore, he thinks that evolution should be considered the effect of "Intelligent Design" but proposes no designation of this Intelligent Designer. In Chapter 2, I presented the much more fundamental argument for a non-material Unmoved Mover from the very fact of motion on which all natural science depends.

However these controversies about the causes of evolution will

48. (New York: Free Press, 1996). His many articles answering his critics are listed on www.arn.org/authors/behe/html, last modified 2009.

49. *Darwin's Black Box,* 173–86. An attempt to answer this has been given by John Catalano, "Publish or Perish," last modified Jan 25, 2004, http://www.talkorigins.org/faqs/behe/publish.html. Many pro and cons of Behe's argument are to be found on the Web by browsing on "Michael Behe."

eventually be resolved, they make clear that Neo-Darwinism provides only an historical reconstruction of a series of unique past events not a law of nature by which either the origin of life or its direction of development can be predicted. Only "the fittest survive," but why did the environmental changes on our earth proceed in such a complex and systematic way as to produce our human bodies?

These difficulties are why Neo-Darwinism has given rise to many modifications, supplements, or alternative theories, yet none have gained the general acceptance of biologists. Thus Stephen Jay Gould and Nils Eldridge proposed a theory of "punctuated equilibrium" that modified Neo-Darwinism so as to explain such spurts of evolution as seems to have taken place in the Cambrian.[50] Similarly James P. Brock, *The Evolution of Adaptive Systems,* while acknowledging natural selection, modifies it by "structuralism" or "adaptive equilibrium." Thus he argues that evolution proceeds both in a linear and a radiating manner in which more than one species develops directly from an original species.[51]

Others have gone further and sought other ways to mitigate the chanciness of evolution by natural selection, yet without introducing teleology. Thus Daniel R. Brooks and E. O. Wiley argue that, although organisms by their homeostasis seem to decrease the randomness (entropy) required by the Second Law of Thermodynamics, at the same time they increase the entropy of the environment. Due to this interaction life is necessarily *directional,* tending to increasing complexity (Dollo's Law, proposed in 1890 by Louis Dollo).[52]

Lynn Margulis also thinks that the random accumulation of mutations (genetic drift) is an inadequate cause for evolution.[53] Instead of

50. Stephen Jay Gould, *The Structure of Evolutionary Theory* (Cambridge, MA: Belknap Press, 2002).

51. James P. Brock, *The Evolution of Adaptive Systems* (San Diego: Academic Press, 2000).

52. Daniel R. Brooks and E. O. Wiley, *Evolution as Entropy*, 2nd ed. (Chicago: University of Chicago Press, 1986).

53. *Symbiosis in Cell Evolution,* 2nd ed. (New York: W. H. Freeman, 1993).

the competition for survival of natural selection she and others emphasize the impact of cooperation between organisms and of *symbiogenesis*, that is, the incorporation of the genes of one organism in another. Still others, such as Stuart A. Kauffman,[54] refine Neo-Darwinism with the concept of "self-organization," defined as a process by which a system, especially an open system, increases its internal organization automatically without guidance or management from an internal source and often exhibits emergent properties. Unquestionably, living systems once constituted are self-organizing. Non-living systems such as atoms and molecules, planetary systems, and galaxies also tend to states of stability. Nevertheless, the very concept of "system" must be understood in a way consistent with the Principle of Causality that, as shown in Chapter 2, states that "nothing can change itself." Thus, living organisms are "self-organizing" only in the limited sense that they can develop and function as a system because they are guided by information provided by their genes and nutrition provided by their environment. Whether the genome of a species includes the information needed to constitute a new species remains unproved.[55] We must therefore conclude with the words of a prominent advocate of self-organization, Francisco J. Varela, who says:[56]

54. *The Origins of Order: Self-Organization and Selection in Evolution* (New York: Oxford University Press, 1993).

55. Kauffman, in a recent interview with members of the International Society for Complexity, Information, and Design in which he was asked whether the "design argument" is sound, frankly replied, "I doubt it, although who really knows. I search for laws of self-organization, like the emergence of collectively autocatalytic sets and metabolisms as phase transitions in critically complex systems, as an alternative. But it is still just theory," last modified Nov 15, 2002, http://www.iscid.org/stuartkauffman-chat.php.

56. Humberto R. Maturana and Francisco J. Varela, *The Tree of Knowledge: The Biological Roots of Human Understanding*, trans. Robert Paolucci (Boston, MA: Shambhala, 1992, rev. ed.), 115. On the variety of theories of evolution see also *Evolutionary Theory: Paths into the Future*, ed. Jeffrey W. Pollard (New York: Wiley, 1984), and Lance Grande and Olivier Rieppel, *Interpreting the Hierarchy of Nature: From Systematic Patterns to Evolutionary Process Theories* (San Diego, CA: Academic Press, 1994).

In fact, we have no unified picture of how the evolution of living beings occurs in all its aspects. Though there are many schools of thought that seriously question understanding of evolution by natural selection; this view has prevailed in biology for more than sixty years. Whatever new ideas have been bruited about in terms of evolutive mechanism, however, those ideas cannot discount the phenomenon of evolution.

Kinds of Living Organisms

The period during which the earth was being formed and before life on earth began is called Hadean Time and lasted from 4.5 billion years ago to about 3.8 billion years ago. During this time the sun was being formed from dust clouds by the force of gravity until it reached a temperature and interior pressure that initiated nuclear fusion and, as other particles collected to form the planets and the earth, began to shine as we now see it. This period was completed by the cooling of the molten earth and the production of the materials necessary for life.

During Archaean time, 3.8 to 2.4 billion years ago, as the crust of the earth was forming, the earth's atmosphere was still too toxic for most kinds of life, but at about 3.5 billion years ago life began with one-celled organisms that lacked a cellular nucleus but could obtain energy from carbonic molecules that then carpeted with slime the shallow coastal waters. At about 2.7 billion years ago the first nucleated one-cell creatures appeared. Then in the Proterozoic Era 2.5 billion to 544 million years ago, due to the activity of certain one-celled organisms the oxygen in the atmosphere increased and other one-celled organisms that were able to live in extreme environments became abundant. Then, probably from these latter cells, other one-celled organisms that had nuclei developed sexual reproduction that provides the recombinations of genes that favors evolution that eventually produced nucleated multi-celled organisms.

In the late Proterozoic (Vendian Time, 650 to 540 million years ago) the first fossils of a worm-like animal appear. Yet only with the first era of the Paleozoic Epoch (543 to 248 million years ago) did a great explosion of life forms evident in fossil remains begin in the Cambrian Era. The Cambrian lasted only from about 543 to 490 million years ago, but its fossils represent most of the major groups of animals now extant, including vertebrates.

As we survey this advance of life from one-celled to multicelled living substances we must ask, "What kind of a natural unit is a living organism?" To answer this question the empirical method used by Aristotle and Aquinas still has value. They tried to determine the *functions* (acts) of organisms by the *problematic objects* they are competent to deal with and from these functions infer that the organism has *powers* or capabilities it possesses in order to deal with these problematic objects. What we observe are not these powers, but the functions in relation to their objects. For example, we can infer that a bee is able (power) to fly toward (function) those flowers that have nectar (problematic objects) and not to those, which lack it. The bee's power is not directly observable but is inferable from its observed behavior. As behaviorists say, the powers of an organism are a "black box" into which we cannot look but we can infer its contents from what goes in and out of the box.

Why do I say *problematic* object? An organism, in order to live ("survival of the fittest"), must satisfy various needs and avoid dangers, and each of these involves objects that present life problems to be solved. All living things have at least three kinds of needs and hence problems that they must solve by appropriate functions. (1) They need to develop themselves from a simpler to a more mature form. (2) They must get the matter and energy from nutrition (solids, liquids, and gases) needed to maintain themselves and perform the first two kinds of activity as well as get rid of waste. (3) They need to preserve the species by reproduction. Thus what characterizes a living thing is self-development, maintenance (*homeostasis*), and reproduction, and unless the organism has the powers to perform these problem-solving functions, it and its species will perish. In fact, in the millions of years of terrestrial life, perhaps 90 percent of all species that once existed have now perished. Darwin's theory of evolution rests on the principle that it is this struggle to survive environmental changes and competition with other animals that has formed the living world. This theory in many ways corresponds to Adam Smith's (1723–90) economic theory of free market competition. It must be added, however, that besides competition in the ecological system, *symbiosis* or cooperation is also an important factor. For example, many plants reproduce and survive only because they are pollinated by bees that live off their nectar.

It might be argued that non-living atoms and molecules are also in a sense, as we have said, self-organizing, but this similarity is only analogical. Atoms and molecules organize themselves simply by adding new parts and connecting them to what they already have. Yet they cannot do this unless some efficient cause at least brings them into contact with each other and usually supplies them with additional energy. Thus hydrogen and oxygen, even when mixed, do not unite unless ignited by a spark of energy. Even the simplest living thing transforms and develops the matter and energy it draws into itself into a vastly more complex and intricately unified system than any molecule. One has only to compare the formation of crystals of sugar at the bottom of a glass of water into which they are dissolved to a plant growing out of a seed and producing new seeds to see how immensely non-living self-organization differs from living self-organization.

The scientific force of this analogy between non-living atoms and molecules on the one hand and living organisms on the other, however, lies in the fact that in both cases we must infer the powers of a thing from its functions in relation to their problematic objects. Atoms and molecules survive change by appropriate adjustments just as do organisms, but in different ways. Non-living things survive by the restoration of the balance of their inherent forces; living things survive not just by returning to equilibrium but by complex functions of development and reproduction by which they dominate their environment, obtaining from it what they need and attacking their enemies.

Until recently living substances were classified in two "kingdoms" of animals and plants. Then taxonomists came to prefer five kingdoms in two divisions: (1) bacteria (prokaryotes, lacking a cell nucleus) and all others (eukaryotes with nucleated cells), which are divided into (2) the mainly single-celled protists and the many-celled (3) fungi, (4) plants, and (5) animals. In this classification the protist kingdom is a very loose collection of very different species. More recently taxonomy has become *cladistic*, that is, based on clades or groups having a common evolutionary origin. This yields three "domains," two of which are relatively very simple: prokaryotes (cells without nuclei) divided into (1) bacteria and (2) archaea, and (3) the nucleated, many-celled eukaryotes that probably divided from the archaea after the archaea had split from the bacteria. The cell wall of archaea and the cilia by which some of them can move about are, however, chemically very different than those of bacteria, so they are often able to live under extreme conditions of temperature or salinity of their environment and many produce methane.

Although the bacteria and archaea lack nuclei, they do have a central DNA genome, but this is not surrounded by a nuclear membrane as in eukaryotes. Thus the substantial unity of each member of these two domains is provided by this DNA that contains a vast fund of information to guide their functioning. The information contained in the DNA of these two prokaryote domains is relatively low compared with that of the nucleated eukaryotes, but is far superior to that in the structure of non-living molecules and atoms. Under the guidance of this genome other parts, called ribosomes, produce the proteins needed to perform life functions, taking in food from the environment and reproducing the species.

Notable among the prokaryotes are the cyanobacteria or aquatic blue-green algae that possess the remarkable power of photosynthesis by which they gather energy from sunlight. Their remains have survived as the oldest known fossils and have produced much of the oil deposits on which so much modern technology depends, and provide nitrogen fertilizers in our soil. Most importantly they oxygenated the earth's atmosphere making life on earth as we know it today possible. Furthermore at an early date some cyanobacteria became incorporated (symbiosis) in eukaryote cells as their chloroplasts and thus produced the green plants on which most of animal life depends and today contribute about 50 percent of the earth's atmospheric oxygen.

Reproduction at this prokaryote level is asexual and by cell division (mitosis), but some prokaryotes take in DNA from other organisms or viruses. It is believed that in turn some of the organelles found in the cells of higher organisms were first taken up from these simpler organisms. The archaea, because they do not depend on oxygen, are able to live in extreme environments: in the ice at the earth's poles, around deep-ocean vents, in hot-springs, deep in the earth, throughout our cities and in the human body. Although some biologists hold that there are millions of species of prokaryotes, it is questionable what constitutes a "species" for prokaryotes, since the definition of species used for sexually reproducing organisms is their mutual infertility, and prokaryotes not only do not reproduce sexually but often interchange genetic material from one "species" to another.

Taxonomists also differ as to whether the bacteria or the archaea are the earliest form of life, since the more evolved eukaryotes seem to have evolved not from the bacteria, but from the archaea. Once life appeared on earth about 3.5 billion years ago these prokaryotes for 2 billion years ruled the planet alone; they still constitute some 90 percent of living material on the earth. Thus these one-celled creatures in billions cover the entire globe, in the seas, over every object on the land, deep in the earth, and even high in the atmosphere with a layer of living matter that is the necessary basis of more complex forms of life.

The eukaryotes, as already mentioned, are many-celled organisms with cells that have their DNA enclosed in a nucleus and are divided into the protists, plantae, fungi, and animalia. The protists are a loose grouping of more than 80 types of organisms, some of which are one-celled and others multi-celled, such as algae, slime-molds, diatoms, etc., whose relationships still remain controversial, The plantae get their energy by photosynthesis and, according to a recent theory, appeared on land with the fungi just before the Cambrian explosion, but have left fossil evidence dating from only about some 475 million years ago. Some 270,000 now existing species of green plants have been so far identified. They divide into those that reproduce by spores, such as mosses, which lack a vascular structure, and ferns, which, like all higher plants, are vascular, and those that reproduce by seeds. Seed plants divide into those that enclose their seeds in cones, such as the evergreen trees, and those that enclose them in ovaries and produce flowers. Finally flowering plants divide into those whose seeds have two leaves, such as grasses and lilies, and those whose seeds have more than two leaves, such as roses or sunflowers.

While this cladistic division into three domains is important for evolutionary theory, it remains true that if we define living things most fundamentally by whether they have or do not have *cognitive* capacity then, as Aristotle did, we can count as "plants," all life forms, whether perokaryotes or ukaryotes, that lack the sense organs that characterize "animals." This, however, raises a question about powers of *locomotion* that Aristotle considered to depend on powers of sensation. His reason was that an organism needs to move in order to react to food, a mate, its straying offspring, members of its hunting pack, or to dangers when these objects are located at a distance. Yet it can do this only if it has organs by which it senses these distant objects and also instincts based on these sensations. We now know, however, that "plants," in the broad sense just mentioned, can also have locomotive powers to respond to stimuli, such as the movements of some cells by hair-like cilia or flagella, by the flowing movements of amoebae, or by the turning of a sun-flower to the light, or the snapping shut of venus-fly trap at the touch of an insect. These motions, however, are not clearly responses to distant object as distant but only to contact. That even this response to contact is not that of the sense of touch we will show in the next chapter.

At least 72,000 of identified species of fungi exist today. They live off dead organic material and one type, the lichens, live by combining with certain bacteria. Most vascular plants also could not live without the fungi that live in their roots and supply them with some necessary nutrients. Fungi are divided into chytrids (thread-like organisms with flagella that are mainly marine), bread molds, yeasts, and club fungi by way they produce their spores, but they all have an alternation of an asexual and a sexual phase. Although they appeared about the same time as the land plants, they seem genetically closer to the animalia. What most strikingly marks off the animalia from the plantae and the fungi, as we have already said is the possession of sense organs, but they are also distinguished by the fact that the animalia depend on other living things for all their energy, except the oxygen these breathe and this is used to digest such nourishment from non-animals.

Since we human persons also are animals this means that our lives depend on energy derived from a living environment that has deep roots going back to the bacteria and archaea, which derive at least some their energy directly from non-living matter and from plantae that derive their energy from sunlight.

Fossils have been found that date from the Vendian epoch more than 550 million years ago that show the existence of Ediacaran animals that were multicellular and rather complex, soft-bodied organisms that, however, bear little resemblance to any animals we now know. After that period in what is called the "Cambrian explosion" seemingly quite suddenly (it actually took some 30 million years, though that is brief compared with the history of the planet) representatives of most all the modern phyla of animals appear in the fossil record. Some paleontologists, however, think many of these phyla had originated much earlier. If there was such an "explosion" of species possible causes are (a) an extinction at the end of the Vendian that opened the way to new species; (b) the increasing oxygen in the atmosphere; (c) the origin in the Vendian of the homeobox or HOX genes that make possible new and important gene relationships. In succeeding geological periods many species were lost but the Cambrian phyla developed extensively.

There exist today some 1,324,000 Animalia species (1,272,000 invertebrates, about 2 percent still exist and have been described, but it is estimated that at least 14 million exist, most being microscopic forms of life or insects in tropical regions. Yet only about 1 percent of all animalia are bigger than bumblebees. Today, under the conditions of modern technology, the decline of biodiversity has become dangerous to the human species, the same species that is probably the chief cause of that decline.[57]

The animalia (metazoa) are also multicellular. Like the fungi and unlike plants, they have to derive their nutrition from materials produced by plants, and are unlike both plants and fungi in that their cells are enclosed by membranes but not by walls. Throughout their life cycle these cells contain both sets of chromosomes, except for sex cells that have only one set. Most of them clearly manifest the power of sensation by which they can move about in their environment to obtain food or mate or avoid dangers, but there are borderline cases. One-celled amoebas move about and seem to respond to distant influences. Even plants exhibit "tropisms" that are responses to the environment as when the sunflower moves to face the light or the venus flytrap closes on an insect. On the other hand, sponges (porifera) that seem very loose collections of cells have enough genetically in common with animals to be classed as the most primitive type of the animalia.

In contrast to these simplest animals, also called parazoa, that do not have true tissues, the "true" animals (eumetazoa) are divided into organisms with radial symmetry such as the hydras and jellyfish, and

57. See the United Nations publication: UNEP-WCMC *Global Biodiversity: Earth's Living Resources in the 21st Century* (Cambridge: World Conservation Press, 2000).

those with bilateral symmetry. The latter divide into the flat worms and the nematode worms that lack a true body cavity against those animals that have such a cavity that develops into their digestive tract. These are either protosomes, in which the opening of this pocket of cells in the adult becomes the mouth, or deuterosomes, in which this pocket in the adult becomes the anus.

Protosomes, whose cells divided spirally, include first the annelida or segmented worms such as earthworms and leeches. Second are the arthropoda (over a million species): crayfish, lobsters, barnacles, crabs, shrimp, and at least a million species of insects, perhaps only 10 percent of the real number of such "bugs" that live in many habitats. Arthropods are also segmented but have jointed appendages annelida lack. Third, are the mollusca (some 70,000 species, including snails slugs, bivalves, squids, and octopi), which are not segmented.

The deuterosomes include the echinodermata, which are not segmented, and the chordates, which are. Thus segmentation either developed separately or, more likely, was lost by the mollusca and echinodermata, the latter of which have radial symmetry only in the adult. The sea squirts and amphioxus have only a semblance of a central nervous system, while the true vertebrata (450,000 species) have a backbone of many segments, a clearly developed head and a skull, and a closed circulation of the blood. These are divided into fish (300,000 species); reptiles (7,000 species), such as lizards, snakes, turtles, crocodiles; birds (10,000 species), amphibians (6,000 species) such as frogs, toad, salamanders: and mammals (5,000 species).

Early in the Cambrian, as soon as plants in the form of mosses had invaded the land, animals, probably at first arthropods, followed. About 300 million years ago the reptiles with whom originated the large amniotic egg that contains an ample supply of nutrition for survival on land originated. Meanwhile the seas were swarming with fish. From the reptiles, close relatives to the dinosaurs, arose the birds winged for flight and also, but less closely related to dinosaurs, the mammals.

The first mammalian appeared about 130 million years ago but began to flourish only after the mass extinction of the dinosaurs in the Cenozoic epoch. They are characterized by the breastfeeding of their young, have hair, and three inner-ear bones; they are divided into monotremes—such as the duck-billed platypus and the spiny anteater (which lay eggs), marsupials (such as opossums), which bear their young so undeveloped that they must live in a maternal pouch, shrew-like insectivores, the Tasmanian wolf, bandicoots, marsupial moles, kangaroos, wallabies, wombats, koalas, and the more evolved placental mammals, whose young are born in a relatively mature condition.

These placental mammals include the following arranged in their genetic relationship according to some taxonomists: (1) sloths, armadillos, pangolins; (2) rabbits, hares, pikas; (3) rodents such as mice, rats, squirrels, gophers, porcupines, and beavers; (4) elephant shrews; (5) primates such as monkeys, lemurs, gorillas, chimps, humans; (6) tree shrews; (7) bats (1000 species!), flying lemurs; (8) insectivores such as shrews (other than the marsupial shrews), moles, hedgehogs; (9) carnivores such as dogs, cats, bears, raccoons, weasels, hyenas, and the sea dwelling seals and walruses; (10) even-toed ungulates (antelope, such as deer, camels, pigs, cows, sheep, goats, hippos, camels); (11) cetaceans who are also aquatic (whales, dolphins, porpoises); (12) aardvarks; (13) odd-toed ungulates such as horses, tapirs, rhinoceroses); (14) rodent-like hyraxes; (15) aquatic manatees, dugongs, and sea cows; (16) elephants. This places us human persons cladistically with the *primates* that are most closely elated to the elephant shrews and rodents on one side and the tree shrews and bats on the other! Thus among the mammals we are the middle between the sloths and the elephants.

The oldest primates probably developed from shrew-like nocturnal insectivores that lived in tropical forests and were somewhat like modern lemurs or tarsiers. They had stereoscopic vision and hands suited for grasping with nails rather than claws, and rather large brains. These features enabled them to seek fruits and insects at night. The earliest fossils date from some 55 million years ago and some believe they originated 65 million years ago after the dinosaurs were extinct, though others think they originated still earlier. The prosimians, from whom descend the modern lemurs, lorises and tarsiers were very diverse, but most species became extinct when the monkeys appear—the old-world monkeys about 34 million years ago, the new world species 30 million years ago. The apes appear at about 7 million years ago and soon divided into the line leading to the modern gorilla and that leading to the chimpanzee, bonobos, and humans. African forests were shrinking and grasslands developing where bipedalism was advantageous. It is thought that since our human line is omnivorous this may indicate that it descends from animals living in grasslands boarding lakes and they probably ate protein and fat-rich insects, while another line now extinct living in mixed grass and woodland was vegetarian.

The hominid line separated from the monkey line and at 6 million separated from the ape and *australopithecus* line, and then at about 2.5 million separated from the *homo robustus* line, descending through the *homo heidelbergensis* line at about 1.5 million years with an off-shoot in the Neanderthals who lived from about 200,000 to 30,000 years ago, arriving at *homo sapiens sapiens* not earlier than 200,000 (some say 130,000) years ago with clear evidence of the modern human brain and human intelligence evident in the art-work of Cro-Magnon man of 35,000 years ago. Present genetic and perhaps linguistic evidence shows that the origin of such true humans took place in Southwestern Africa.

Much wonder has been expressed over that fact our nearest hominid relative the chimpanzee shares about 98.7 percent of our genetic code. How could a 1.3 percent difference explain that we are intelligent persons and they are supposedly not? This small difference, however, corresponds to some 240,000 code changes. Even though many such code changes may have no appreciable phenotypic significance, this is a huge difference. Researchers have studied more than 12,000 genes from the brain and liver tissues of human, chimpanzee, and orangutan specimens. They found that since the time of the split between our species and the chimpanzees, the proteins manufactured by the human brain have increased fivefold over their increase in chimpanzee brains, although the change in the liver of the species has been much the same. Thus what was significant about human evolution was the complexification not of the total genome but of the genes relating to a particular organ, the remarkable human brain.

When our human species still had only a few thousand members, perhaps only 7,000 generations ago, it spread into the Middle East about 150,000 years ago, and thence into Asia 73,000 years ago and into Europe 51,000 years ago. It was, however, so needy and so adventurous that it soon began to occupy the whole globe, and according to other studies reached Australia and the Pacific Islands in several waves beginning about 40,000 to 33,000 years ago (although to Japan perhaps only 30,000 to 10,000 years ago and to Hawaii perhaps not until AD 300 and to the Americas (according to the DNA study) perhaps 30,000 years ago.[58] Racial differences among members of *Homo sapiens* amount only to 1 percent of the 80,000 genes and 3 billion bases in the human genome. At first humankind was still so widely scattered that each tribe, probably originally of a few thousand at most, quickly became isolated and lived on a simple economy of hunting and food gathering.

What kind of body, then, has this vast evolutionary process formed for the human species? It is a body that is able to perform those actions which distinguish that species from other living organisms and especially from its nearest evolutionary relatives, the great apes. Of these the chimpanzee is today closest to us genetically, differing from us, according to the latest studies, only about 5 percent, although it is the interactions of genes, not their sheer number that is most important for

58. DNA studies reported in Science Times of *The New York Times* (May 2, 2000), D1.

the phenotype. We differ radically from the chimpanzee most evidently in our ability to speak a true language, that is, one that consists not merely of signals but includes word such as "and" and "therefore" that signify syntactical or abstract logical relations.

We need such a language because we are social animals in a unique way based on a family unit in which the male not only impregnates the female, drives off other males who might mate with the female or destroy his offspring, but remains as a constant companion of the female and a trainer of his offspring, as well as a food-gatherer for the whole family. Moreover these families gather in larger units in which there is transmitted a *culture* that is not merely instinctive but, like human languages, is freely invented in diverse ways by different groups of humans and includes invented technologies by which humans gain a remarkable and increasing control over their environment. These larger units also invent diverse forms of government by which the community is united in common action to which different members make special contributions by playing different roles.

The Organ Systems of the Human Body

The human ability for this unique type of behavior is clearly dependent on the fact that we have larger and more complex brains than other animals, even than the chimpanzee which, when taught by humans, can closely imitate many human activities but does not, like humans, invent these activities. In the next chapter this remarkable primary organ of the human body will be described more fully.

Does this mean, as some have argued, that only when the brain develops in the fetus that a human being comes into existence? Modern biology answers this question by showing that the brain is constructed by the human organism guided by information that it already possesses when it exists as a single fertilized cell (the zygote) produced by the fertilization of a human ovum from the maternal parent and the sperm from the paternal parent each bearing half the chromosomes needed by the new organism sexually reproduced. At that time, although the organism has no brain, its nucleus contains all the information needed to construct a brain and the organism has the capacity to build the brain and all the rest of the baby who is to be in the body of its mother, nourished by her, for some nine months. Half this genetic information is derived from the male parent and half from the female parent.

As the zygote divides into many cells, each containing a replica of the original nucleus, certain of these cells become dominant, while others that form the amniotic membranes that protect the growing embryo and the placenta through which it draws nourishment from its mother are produced under the guidance of the genome in the dominant group of cells. This group of cells then quite quickly structures itself into a bilaterally symmetrical fetus of the vertebrate type and soon the "neural streak" that will become the central nervous system appears and finally the beginning of the brain. Thus there is a continuity of a primary organ from the nucleus of the zygote to the brain of the fetus.

Hence those who claim that during the time that twinning can sometimes abnormally take place in the human species the embryo is a mere collection of independent cells (and hence only after implantation or when the neural streak occurs can we say that this human organism is a human person) cannot explain the known facts. If the cells that are totipotential as long as twinning is possible are independent of each other, why do they not each develop into a fetus? Much the better explanation of twinning is to apply what we now know of cloning and say that from conception one human person existed, not as a collection of independent cells, but as a normally developing single organism constituted from interacting cells, just as in an adult human person. Then, either by some genetic defect or developmental accident, one or a small set of these cells became detached from the original person and developed as its genetically identical clone or twin. Thus, present embryology leads to a more than merely probable conclusion that the human person originates at conception, that is, the fertilization of the ovum, as the one-celled zygote that is programmed genetically to construct the mature adult person in a continuous life span.

Thus the bodily life of the human person begins with the zygote and continues until brain death, always under the guidance of a unique genome. It can be added that even identical twins are not strictly "identical" since, besides the genes in the original zygote, there are mitochondria in its cytoplasm that are now known to have some, though perhaps minor, hereditary effects. In the first cell division of the zygote the two new cells receive different parts of this cytoplasm and hence different mitochondrial factors, so that if twinning takes place then, or at some point in the embryo's early development, the multiple offspring have somewhat different inheritance. Thus every human person is unique not only in having different bodily matter but in their actual bodily composition.

In the evolution of various species of animalia that I have listed, a nervous system first appears in invertebrate animals. Sponges have no nerves. Jellyfish have a nerve net, starfish a nerve ring with a peripheral nerve network, flat and roundworms have a nerve cord, mollusks have intercommunicating neurons called "ganglia" and among them octopuses have quite complex nervous systems. In flatworms, which have a bilateral symmetry, a long nerve cord with a bigger ganglion at the head appears. In arthropods, including insects, a true brain appears.

All vertebrates have a brain enclosed in a skull and the human skull notably exceeds in size that of other primates, and the complexity of the human brain far exceeds our present knowledge. Thus it consists of an immense network of more than 10^9 neurons that receive information from the external senses and process and store it. Each neuron has from 10,000 to 100,000 fibers connecting it with other neurons. Thus the total connections within the brain number about 10^{15}, vastly more than any computer that humans might build.[59]

59. Dean L. Overman, *A Case against Accident and Self-Organization*, foreword by Wolfhart Pannenberg (Lanham, MD: Rowman and Littlefield, 1997), 66.

If the brain is the principal organ of the human body, of what use to it are its other differentiated parts? Since the brain is an information processing center it needs an input of data and this is supplied by the external sense organs; touch, taste, smell, sight, and hearing. Only when it has such data transmitted from the external senses does the brain (a) integrate the data received from the different senses into a unified image of objects, e.g., a dog as it is seen as of a certain shape and color, heard as something that barks, with certain kind of odor, and felt as warm and fuzzy (b) store these images in a form that can be recalled and remembered in its temporal sequence, for example, the dog I saw two days ago (c) in recalling these images separate them from their temporal sequence, modify them, and combine them in various ways as we do in dreaming or fantasizing (d) evaluate them as pleasant or painful, useful or harmful. Medieval writers distinguished these four secondary sense processes as the work respectively of the "common sense," memory, imagination, and in animals instinct and in humans "the cogitative sense" or animal or particular intelligence and taking them together called them the "internal senses", but as before mentioned I prefer to call them the secondary senses, since they deal with information given by the primary senses.

Touch also informs the brain about the state of the other parts of the body and stimulates these to perform their various functions. Our brain, however, constitutes only about 2 percent of our total weight. In order to carry on living functions the brain needs an input of energy and it receives this from the blood that circulates through it, especially because that blood supplies it with oxygen (which it has received from the lungs) that releases energy. So dependent is the brain for a constant supply of this energy that if deprived of it for five or six minutes it is seriously injured and very quickly dies. Brain function is possible, therefore, only if we also have a *circulatory* system (heart and its network of blood vessels) with its blood and a *respiratory* system (the lungs and the trachea and nasal passages leading to them). The respiratory system supplies the blood with the oxygen necessary to burn nutritional substances and thus supply the brain and the body with the energy it requires for its vital activities.

Besides the circulatory system for the blood there is also the *lymphatic* system (vessels, nodes and nodules, spleen, and thymus gland) that circulate lymph through the heart but in a different network of vessel. This *lymph* is a fluid that seeps from the blood into the tissues and is returned to the blood. There is no pump for this system but muscular pressures and the expansion and contraction of the lungs move the lymph, while, as it collects, valves prevent it from flowing back in the tissues and empty it into the blood much the way that the venous blood itself returns to the heart. What is especially significant in this system is that it maintains the *immunity* of the body from foreign substances by producing cells that identity these substances and isolate them and, if possible, destroy them. The liver also supports this defensive activity.

This nutritional material that is burned as the fuel of the body is supplied by the *digestive system* (mouth, teeth, tongue, throat, esophagus, stomach, small intestine, liver, gall bladder, and pancreas) and the wastes produced are disposed through the excretory system as solid wastes in the large intestine and as liquid wastes in the kidneys, bladder and urinary tract.

The *endocrine system* consists of many types of glands producing *hormones* that stimulate or depress various bodily functions and thus complement the nervous system in regulating the body. For this reason it will be discussed in more detail in the next chapter.

The *reproductive system* in the female includes the ovaries to produce the female gametes or ova (eggs) and the uterus connected to the ovaries by the Fallopian tubes to nourish and protect the human child as it develops. The uterus opens through the cervix into the vagina. In sexual intercourse the semen containing the sperm of the male is injected into the vagina through the male penis and this semen is produced in the testes and associated prostate gland. Females also have a prostate (Skene's gland) with similar functions. The male gametes are motile cells that seek out an ovum and, penetrating it, stimulate it to development and contribute to it the genetic component required for its fertilization. The fertilized ovum thus becomes a new human organism and at once begins to develop itself to form a one-celled state (zygote) of the complex multicellular human body through a remarkable series of transformations that takes some nine months. (The main structure is attained in about a month, and the remaining 8 months are devoted to detailed structuring and growth in size.)

The *skeletal* and *muscular systems* not only enable to the body to maintain its other structures and assist the other bodily systems, but also enable the human person to move about in the environment and modify it. The *integumentary* system (skin, nails, hair) protects the whole body and is the organ of the sense of touch, although this sense also makes us aware of internal changes in the body. These three systems are chiefly responsible for the external appearance of the body by which human beings need to communicate with each other. We do so by speech that uses our lungs, our throat, and our mouth, tongue and teeth that pertain to several of these organ systems as special functions. But we also do so by our facial expressions and the gestures of head, limbs, hands, feet, and torso. One has only to watch a mime, an actor, or a dancer (or an Italian!) to see how forceful and subtle such non-verbal language can be. Indeed it would seem that it is the original language out of which speech and other vocal sounds emerged and took on conventional meanings as can these gestures, for example, in the sign language of the deaf and mute.

The Beauty of the Human Body

Artists have always considered the beauty of the human body in its external visual appearance to be the most perfect kind of beauty. Other animals and plants have beautiful shapes and even more brilliant colors than the human body. Landscapes, skies, clouds and the radiance of sun, moon, and stars, of fire and snow, of mountains, oceans, and rivers, all have their special beauty. But the human body with its expressive face and gestures, notably in the rhythms of dance or sports, has the superior beauty in that it directly expresses the human mind and feelings that will be discussed later. These have an intimate meaning to us that make other natural beauties somehow distant. Since beauty consists precisely in an order that is well grasped by the knower, we are instinctively sensitive to human bodily beauty that fits our own capacity for knowledge so perfectly. We are made to see the beauty of other human beings and they somehow are made to be seen by us.

This attractive, socializing, empathetic beauty of the human body is seen first of all in the beauty of children. Because their bodies are still immature, they lack the full shape and qualities of the adult human body, and there is always an element of the comic in the incongruity between their obvious humanness and yet immaturity. Babies are "cute." As children grow they sometimes advance in beauty as they mature and have something special because of the fresh, clean emergence of the human form that often deteriorates in adults. Yet they also at times exhibit the awkward gawkiness of something still in process, as often in adolescence. Full beauty is attained only in maturity and, alas, does not last very long as the body ages and finally dies. "Where are the snows of yesteryear?"[60]

In full healthy maturity, however, the human body can have overwhelming beauty that can express many human qualities. The first of these is that which signals the female and the male readiness and capability for the sexual intercourse required for the preservation of the species. Charles Darwin, the discoverer of biological evolution, put great stress on the importance of such erotic attraction for the "survival of the fittest." He showed how in animals it is often the male who has the most vivid display of beauty.

60. The "Ballade des dames du temps jadis" ("Ballad of the Ladies of Times Past") is a poem by François Villon.

In the human race, however, it is the female who has the curves, the softness and clarity of skin, and the facial coloring and expressiveness and the beautiful hair that is attractive to the male and indicate her fertility.

The male body, on the other hand, by its greater height and muscularity, beard, and other body hair expresses power rather than beauty and the power of impregnation of the female, as well as the power to protect her and her children, especially during her pregnancy. Yet both male and female bodies, each in its own mode, have the beauty of symmetry, subtle coloration, and flexibility in motion that have always delighted artists as well as attracted the opposite sex. Thus human physical beauty is not only erotic and sexual but also expressive of qualities of character and vitality. We are all impressed by the appearances of others even when not erotically attracted to them and in all cultures accentuation of this impressive beauty is sought by dress or cosmetic enhancement.

Some will point out that standards of physical beauty differ from culture to culture and are a matter of style. Moreover, individual tastes differ, and *de gustibus non est disputandum.* This fact, however, merely points to the definition of the beautiful, that it is a certain conformity between the known object and the cognitive powers of the knower. Consequently we find beautiful what we have become accustomed to or what fits us because of our individual temperament and experience. Yet, this subjectivity itself implies a relative objectivity.

As St. Thomas Aquinas says,[61] an object can be perceived as beautiful only because it objectively possesses a certain completeness and proportion of its parts that "shines out," is especially clear to the perceiver. Consequently, underlying differences of style and individual taste, are aspects of physical reality that appeal universally to human knowing because of the nature of human cognition. Thus in a mod-

61. For a profound commentary on this, see Jordan Aumann, OP, *De Pulchritudine: Inquisitio Philosophico-Theologica* (Valencia: University of Salamanca, 1951).

ern museum that exhibits art works from all cultures and periods, much may at first not appear beautiful to some visitors, but as they become acquainted with these works and put off their customary expectations, they find beauty in the art of every time and culture, even in what at first appeared to them ugly and meaningless.

After this consideration of the wonderful physical system that is the human body, in the next chapter we will begin to consider the *psychological* level of *homo sapiens*, not forgetting, however, that we are primate members of the chordates, which are animalia, composed of molecules and atoms and ultimately of matter and energy. What is our future? As we saw at the beginning of this chapter, enthusiasts for space travel hope that we will eventually be independent of our earth and move out into space, but even they know that the survival of our species is entirely problematic. Not only may we make the earth uninhabitable by destroying its ecology, but the universe itself may be running down.

The Future of Our Universe

Material systems, whether strongly unified like natural units or weakly unified like a solar system, do not always remain the same. They originate, evolve, or are extinguished in the course of time and we know of nothing material, not even the whole universe that is changeless. If ours was a "steady-state" universe, as Plato and Aristotle long ago supposed and in recent years Hoyle and Bondi hypothesized, then its changes would have to be *cyclical*, repeating over and over in what the philosopher Nietzsche called "The Myth of the Eternal Return."[62] Today most scientists believe it much more probable that our universe began less than 14 billion years ago with the Big Bang in which all the matter of which it now consists was condensed

62. On this model of the universe accepted in many cultures, see Mircea Eliade, *The Myth of the Eternal Return: or, Cosmos and History*, trans. Willard R. Trask (Princeton, NJ: Princeton University Press, 1954; 2nd ed. 1974).

in a "singularity" or point. This singularity then began to expand, first by an extremely rapid inflation, then more slowly, but now increasingly, and will continue to expand forever.

According to the Second Law of Thermodynamics or Entropy (increasing disorder or random behavior) accepted by science today, any material system inevitably runs down unless it receives a new-input of energy from without since, whenever a material agent acts, some of the energy it expends is wasted as heat, that is, the random motion of matter that can never again be used to perform constructive ordered work. This is why physicists laugh at crackpots who claim to have invented a perpetual motion machine. Thus our universe as it expands is becoming ever less dynamic since its parts are distancing themselves from each other and becoming always less capable of changing other parts. Finally it will reach a condition where matter is so thinned out that almost nothing will be happening! Therefore, our universe, like that of each human being, and of the human race as a whole, is a "being-toward death."

While, as already noted, some cosmologists conjecture that at a certain time the universe will begin to contract in a Big Crunch and return to its original state, it appears that we have no way of proving such a cycle of Bang and Crunch, since the Crunch would eliminate all traces of the previous cycle. Moreover it seems that the law of entropy would demand that each cycle would be less dynamic than the previous ones, so that ultimately all change would die down except occasional weak and random "quantum fluctuations" in a featureless material field of minimal energy. Others guess that it might end in a Big Rip or a Big Chill.[63]

It also seems probable that the universe is not infinite in size (as

63. Others have proposed an "ekpyrotic" universe produced by two universes colliding with each other and other speculate about an infinity of possible universes, but readers must understand that science progresses by "brain-storming" theories, most of which are eventually eliminated by the facts of observation. These are only dialectics, not to be mistaken for established truth, but serving a legitimate purpose in research.

some Renaissance thinkers hypothesized) but finite. If it were infinite and one part could influence another, it would seem that the night sky would be infinitely bright (this is called Olbers Paradox), but Aristotle already made a similar argument;[64] or, the force of gravity would be infinite in every direction, and obviously this is not the case. Present cosmologies suppose that the universe is finite in size, although soon after the Big Bang it underwent a sudden violent expansion.

Whether in fact the universe has always existed or exists only for a finite time seems to be, as St. Thomas Aquinas long ago argued, a question that human reason cannot answer, because our knowledge of the universe is limited to its conditions and developments within a finite time-frame. This should be understood, however, in the sense that, whereas we certainly know that changeable objects can last for a finite time, we do not know whether it is even possible for a finite body to exist for an infinite time, though we also do not know the contrary. Thus the hypothesis that the universe had a beginning is more probable than that it did not, and present scientific data agrees better with that supposition than with the one Aristotle chose. It should be observed, therefore, that the Greek notion of the world, far from glorifying humanity as some say by placing man at the center of the universe, actually emphasized his inferiority to the gods or spirits that moved the heavens. While our earth was thought to be at the center, that was the most ignoble part of the universe and man, whose home it was, was the least intelligent of intelligent beings and the slave of the gods.

The Bible's view, by contrast, although it believes in angelic creatures superior to man, sees human beings occupying a special role in the history of the world. The Second Person of the Trinity, or God the Son, did not become an angel but a human being, Jesus of Nazareth, and through his human life and death brought humanity salvation and will bring ultimate glorification to the whole universe. The

64. *Physics* III, c. 204b26, "Elements have contrariety with each other … if one were infinite the others by now would have ceased to be."

striking difference between the Greek conception of the universe and the Jewish conception found in the Hebrew Scriptures is that for the Greek philosophers the universe was eternal and hence *cyclical.* For the Platonists this was taken literally so that every event would be exactly repeated an infinite number of times. Aristotle saw a difficulty in this notion since, if it were true, how would one cycle be distinguishable from another? He remedied this by distinguishing between numerical difference and specific identity, so that each cycle would be numerically and thus materially different from every other, yet specifically and thus formally the same. The Stoics, like Hindu thinkers in their myths of Shiva the Destroyer and Krishna the Creator, dramatized these cosmic cycles by imagining them as periods ending in the burning up of the world and its recreation.

In contrast to this cyclical view that is *ahistorical,* since it reduces history to mere repetition, the Bible emphasizes history as a series of unique events having an unrepeatable beginning and an absolute conclusion in timeless eternity. Although one of its books, *Qoheleth,* has the weary refrain, "Vanity of vanities! All is vanity and there is nothing new under the sun!" this only acknowledges the very human world-weariness that gave rise to the pagan "Myth of the Eternal Return"; it is strongly offset by the more profound revelation of Genesis, "In the beginning" and of the Apocalypse, "I am the Alpha and the Omega, the Beginning and the End" (Rev 21:6). Our present scientific picture, since it begins with a Big Bang and ends not cyclically with a Big Crunch followed by another Big Bang, fits the Biblical view much more easily than did the efforts of St. Thomas Aquinas to reconcile Aristotle and the Bible.

For Aristotle, only the region within the sphere of the moon is subject to qualitative changes and thus to chance events and therefore to history in the proper sense. In order to have an eternal universe endlessly cycling, he argued that most of the universe was made up of heavenly spheres in which the sun, moon, planets, and stars were embedded and which was made up of a different kind of matter than sublunar and terrestrial matter. This matter from which the celestial spheres was composed was a solid, transparent, and in part luminous material, subject only to rotational change and hence moving without friction. Since no physical force has the infinite power necessary to keep these heavens rotating through infinite time, Aristotle concluded that each independent set of spheres must be moved by an intelligent, but bodiless spirit, like a Christian angel. Aristotle based this theory (no more implausible than some modern cosmologies) empirically on the claim of Babylonian astronomers, who in 10,000 years of observation had never seen any significant change in the planets or stars, and theoretically on his choice of the hypothesis that the world is eternal.

No wonder then, that the philosopher Martin Heidegger defined an authentic human life as one in which we face the fact of death and that all history is the death of the past and an unknowable future. Hence to be honestly intelligent, Heidegger argued, is to live in anxiety and dread in the midst of historical change beyond our control. Does this not seem a dilemma for psychotherapy, which can only quiet human anxieties by helping people face reality realistically, since that means ceasing to deny one's inevitable anxiety about inevitable death! Later on in this book we will ask whether any answer to this dilemma is possible. The answer given by the noted physicist Freeman J. Dyson when asked about the future of conscious life offers not much comfort.[65] He said, "The most plausible answer, is that conscious life will take the form of interstellar dust clouds.... An ever-expanding network of charged dust particles, communicating by electromagnetic forces, has all the complexity necessary for thinking an infinite number of novel thoughts." When questioned further as to how such a cloud thinned out in a space of billions of light years could think consciously, he answered, "Well, how do you imagine a couple of kilo-

65. See Jim Holt, "Alvy Singer's Terrible Fear," last modified March 4, 2004, http://www.slate.com/articles/news_and_politics/slates_10th_anniversary/features/2006/how_will_the_universe_end/alvy_singers_terrible_fear.html

grams of protoplasm in someone's skull being conscious? We have no idea how that works either."

Dyson did not like to admit that if nothing but matter exists, conscious life will simply be extinguished. If, in fact, the material universe is running down to nothing or almost nothing, "Why" (as Heidegger also asked) "is there anything at all?" It would seem that after the Big Bang matter would have expanded uniformly without any structure in a featureless homogeneity that would amount to a kind of completely full nothingness. Science has still not satisfactorily explained why as matter expanded definite structures developed within and produced identifiable objects. The Second Law of Thermodynamics, however, is compatible with developments like the turbulence we see in a river as it descends to the ocean. While on the whole the matter is moving in a single definite direction, at various points back-currents develop in which, in a relatively small area, the water eddies backward and for a moment reverses it direction, that is, a decreasing entropy or *negentropy*. Moreover, not only does the Second Law permit regions of negentropy in the universe, but it does not predict the *rate* of the increase of entropy, so that it permits fairly stable, enduring objects to appear and endure for a considerable period. Thus if the original matter of the universe developed certain random irregularities in its changes, the force of gravity would produce aggregates of massive matter such as the stars and eventually some black holes of matter so dense that they would not emit radiation as long as they endured. These stars would then collect in perhaps 10^{11} billion galaxies, of which a typical galaxy might contain 10^{11} times the mass of the sun, perhaps around some great black holes at their cores, and these galaxies would collect into super-galaxies. In our galaxy, around the star we call the sun orbits our small earth in a loosely coordinated system around that much more massive body. This system has existed for some 4.5 billion years, but the earth and other matter that orbits the sun will, as their velocity is slowed down by interaction with other matter, eventually fall into it and the sun itself will explode and its matter cool into dust.

It may seem absurd for a psychotherapist to perceive a suffering client against this grandiose background; but a client's perception of themselves and their ultimate fate is colored by where they see their lives in this historical context. For example, a devout Catholic client might perceive him or herself in the light of the full revelation of the nature of the Triune God and of God's providence in Jesus Christ and in the time of the Church that awaits Christ's second coming. Buddhists must see themselves in a very different context and secular humanists in another. In our multicultural state of affairs, Christian clients must suffer conflicts between their faith-perspective and the secular humanism that dominates our public media, as the recent excitement over the novel *The Da Vinci Code* has highlighted. While it may seem impractical for therapists to try to view a client in this broad context, suffering clients have to confront the whole historical universe every day and night and in their dreams!

Conclusion

In this chapter I attempted to place the human being, whose psychology we seek to study, in the context of the universe and its history of which human persons are physically a minute part, yet in their complexity among its most remarkable parts, as that universe is now understood by natural science. We have arisen in the universe through an evolution whose direction, it would seem, has been determined by sheer chance and we depend on a relatively simple solar system but also on an extremely elaborate terrestrial environment in which there are millions of other species of organisms in a gradually shifting ecological balance. Yet our uniquely complex brain has made it possible for us to discover this much about the universe and our planet, and gain a degree of control over its forces. Whether and how long, however, we can maintain ourselves is unknown. It depends on, among other things, such as a possible collision of our earth with an asteroid, on whether we can understand our human psychology well enough to preserve our freedom from enslavement by the psychoses, neuroses, and addictive vices that threaten us with self-destruction through ill-conceived modes of psychotherapy.

The therapist must not neglect the genetic, physiological, and neurological aspects that play a role in mental illness and that may have pharmaceutical or surgical remedies, yet must not simply refer clients to physicians without providing sound diagnosis of properly psychological malfunctioning which may be linked to these physical causes or be independent of them.

four

SENSING AND FEELING

The Information-Gathering Sense Powers and Their Organs

Organisms at the plant level of evolution are able to make limited responses to their environment, and their movements are said to be *nastic* if the direction of this response is independent of the direction of the stimulus, or to have *tropisms* if the organism responds by a directional growth or curvature to a greater stimulus from one side or the other. One type of tropism is a *phototropism*, such as the turning of a sunflower in the direction of the sun; similarly, the leaves of the telegraph plant jerk in the sunlight. Another type is *gravitropism*, seen positively when a root tip grows downward, or negatively when the growth of the plant curves or bends in response to an object that touches it, as a vine clings to a trellis. *Hydrotropism* is a growth response toward water. Some plants—such as the Venus flytrap, which quickly snaps shut on insects, and the sundews, pitcher plants, and the rootless bladderworts—are carnivorous, seizing and digesting insects for food.

Note that some of these movements are simply the result of the effects of the environment stimulating plant growth. Other movements, such as that of the Venus flytrap, seem to involve a chemical exchange that resembles a nervous current. Yet none of these movements give evidence of the transmission of an image (*species impressa*) that characterizes animal life, and the plants are without a nervous system or muscles. Thus those biologists who call them "sensitive plants" are only using an analogy to animal sensation; the plants approach the borderline between plant and animal but do not pass it.

Descartes thought that animals are automatons that have no consciousness. Most current scientists would consider this absurd, yet many make no essential distinction between plants and animals or between animal psychology and human psychology. In fact, some can see no essential difference between human psychology and a man-made computer. They suppose that when we have improved our computers they will be truly able to think—even to think better than we can. It is necessary, however, to recognize some very essential differences between a computer and an animal and a human animal, although all three have in common the processing of "information."

Animals are distinguished from plants in that they have sense organs and obviously react to information they receive through these organs. The fact that, if these organs are inhibited or injured, animals can no longer make their normal responses shows that they have *awareness,* that is, "consciousness," of objects external to themselves. More complex animals also give evidence in their behavior that they feel pain and pleasure in their own bodies and are aware of their bodily movements. This raises the difficult question of what we mean by "consciousness."

First of all, "consciousness" is not necessarily "self-consciousness." The fact that an animal is aware of its little ones and runs to protect them as they stray does not of itself indicate that the animal knows itself as an organism that has conscious awareness of objects. Animal sensation, as far as their behavior gives evidence, never goes beyond singular things precisely in their singular sensible characteristics. An animal's world is made up of pressures and temperatures of external objects felt by touch and by smells and tastes in mouth and nose, colors and shapes seen by the eyes, and sounds heard by the ears. Part of this sensed world is the animal's own body, which is known to it principally by touch, as one part of the body contacts another, or as it reacts to contact from without. As noted in the previous chapter, these are sometimes called "external senses," but more accurately "primary senses," since the animal also has "secondary" senses such as memory and imagination, which process the information from its primary senses.

Some animals are aware of objects or distinctions between objects that our human senses do not detect. For example, dogs have an acute sense of smell by which they get information that escapes us. On the other hand, they may not sense things that other animals can sense; for example, not all animals have two-dimensional vision, and some are colorblind. The human face, as compared to the snouts of most mammals, has evolved, it seems, to reduce our noses and the sense of smell in favor of our eyes, which are placed for binocular vision, since we have survived by dependence more on vision than on smell. Yet as close as chimpanzees approach human behavior there is nothing in their behavior that cannot be explained by awareness of individual objects, not of their own process of knowing these objects; their conscious awareness is not self-consciousness.

Computers and robots can be built that are somehow "aware" of their surroundings and internal states. Are computers "conscious?" To answer this we must first note the basic fact that computers are not alive; they do not construct themselves but are constructed, programmed, monitored, and repaired by human beings. No doubt we humans can construct better computers than we have thus far, computers that will more and more approximate human behaviors that require awareness of objects.

Contrary to common opinion, Aristotle and Aquinas do not state that consciousness or *cognition* in animals differs from other material processes because it requires the admission of some non-material (spiritual) factor that animates an animal's body. Instead they point out that most material changes consist in the production of a new form (formal cause) in matter (material cause) so that a new thing results; sensation, on the other hand, consists in the modification of *one form by another form*, that is, the modification of the form of the sense organ by an alien form so that the act of the sense organ is made similar to (assimilated to) the object. Sense cognition, though, can be said analogously to be "spiritual" in that, as a kind of change, it transcends the limitations of material matter-form composition,[1] and vision can be said to be more "spiritual" than the other senses.[2]

Thus when I touch an object, not only is my hand changed by a new shape (a new form in the matter of my hand, so that my hand is changed), but in addition the power (form) of my hand to manipulate objects is modified by information about the shape of the object, so that it is guided in its act of manipulation by the shape of the object. This modification of our activities in relation to objects by information received from those objects is *awareness* or sense cognition of those objects. In making robotic machines, we imitate this modification of the machines' behavior by cybernetic or feedback devices, but we do so by programming the machine—it does not ultimately program itself; but living awareness or cognition is precisely this power of an organism to do this for itself. Even if we try to copy this ability, by programming the robot to program itself, the ability will always be limited by the program we impose on it; the living organism, by contrast, is independent of any human programming.

The Five Primary Senses

In primary sense cognition, the information received through the sense or senses is always simply that of *singular*, concrete things. Later

1. *Sentencia Libri De Anima* I, lect. 10, l. 159.
2. Ibid., III, lect. 6, l. 668.

we will see how humans have not only this type of cognition but also a cognition of abstractions, which opens up much wider possibilities of knowledge to them than the possibilities shared with animals at the level of sense cognition. In the terminology used by St. Thomas Aquinas, the information or form of the object as it modifies the form of the sense organ and thus enables it to make the act of actually sensing the object is called the *species impressa,* that is, the impressed or received form or likeness of the object—for example, the visual image in the retina of the eye. In primary sensation, however, there is no *species expressa* or production of an image, since, for example, when the eyes are modified by the *species impressa* they are immediately conformed to the visual object. When I see you, I am not seeing an image of you in my imagination, but I see you simply as an existing visual object. On the other hand, when I *imagine* you, I call up an image of you even if you are not present or no longer exist. This is a very important point, since if we sensed only images we would never know the real world. At some point in our knowledge we must make contact with reality, and we do so in our external sensations, where we know real objects, not just representations of them. If we deny this, we will be forced to contradict ourselves whenever we avoid an obstacle to our movement or reach out for a chocolate offered us.

This primacy of information is especially true of the sense of touch,[3] which is the most basic of all the senses and is possessed by all animals. The organ for touch is not only the external skin (the integumentary system) but also interior nerve endings in the body and the viscera. Its proper object is diversified into the sensations of pressure, of temperature (the bombardment of molecules), and of pain and pleasure according as the body is in a normal or abnormal condition. Such sensations are prior to other sensations, since we can close our eyes in a silent odorless room and yet experience the contact of

3. *The Psychology of Touch,* ed. Morton A. Heller and William Schiff (Hillsdale, NJ: L. Erlbaum, 1991).

our body with other bodies. Thus touch forms the context of movement in space and time for all other sensations.

The object of smell is odors, and of taste, flavors; since these tell us about our food they are probably common to a degree to all animals. Since taste involves contact with the object and odor only with some effluvia of the object, these senses tell us little about distant objects and thus have an affinity with touch. While they are important in facilitating our eating, they seem to be of much less importance and acuity in humans than in many other animals.

The object of vision is color. Some persons are color-blind, by which we mean that they can distinguish only a few colors, but even normal persons perceive and distinguish only a limited range and number of colors—some eight pure colors (red. orange, yellow, green, blue, violet, and black and white). Other colors appear to us as blends of these. (Some other animals, by contrast, can see infrared and ultraviolet colors we cannot perceive.) Vision, however, gives us much more detailed information than the other senses and extends to vast distances—to the very stars. Moreover, by the aid of our two eyes we have three-dimensional vision, seeing things in perspective and depth.

Finally, hearing has as its object sound, or vibrations in the air. Although our hearing does not extend to such distances as our seeing, hearing does give us signals of distant events and the directions in which they lie. Moreover, because humans are social animals, we need hearing not just to get signals of warning or attraction as do other animals, but for speech. Thus, through speech we can get information that lies outside our vision and in the past.

Besides our perception of these different bits of information special to each sense—which are all *qualities* of things—we perceive through these qualities certain aspects of things that are accessible through more than one sense, and these are called the *common sensibles: motion,* and the quantitative properties of things, *number* and *size.* These common sensibles enable us to perceive the changing character of the material world and its fundamental categorical property of quantity.

The special organs of the primary senses are rather evident; terminating in various branches of the nervous system, they are said to be *peripheral.* Today it is generally supposed that acts of primary sensation are in the brain, but, as we said above in explaining the *species impressa,* Aristotle and Aquinas held that these acts are in the special organs. This must be the case, because it is in the organ that the contact between the existing object and the perceiving subject occurs, and without this contact we could not know reality. The fact that, for example, the severing of the auditory nerves from their connection with the inner ear and the occipital lobe at the back of the brain, or a destruction of this area, causes deafness does not disprove this, since an organ acts as an instrument of a whole organism; when separated from the whole organism, the organ is unable to act. Currently there is extensive research on the structure and function of all these primary sense organs.[4]

Touch is found in the skin or surface of the whole body, which in humans, as distinguished from other primates, is relatively hairless, an adaptation that increases the human skin's sensitivity. Touch is, however, also found within the body (*somatosensory* system), especially in the muscles, and some want to distinguish this as a sixth special sense of equilibrium or balance and to add a seventh sense of temperature. Therefore touch is now considered a "general" rather than a special sense, because it is distributed through the body and does not depend, as do the special senses, on special organs with special receptor cells. By touch we get information not only about the shape and hardness or softness of extra-body objects but also about the condition of the body, including its injuries, and we thereby feel pain or at least discomfort.

4. For a comprehensive, up-to-date view see Aage R. Moller, *Sensory Systems: Anatomy, Physiology and Pathophysiology,* first edition (San Diego: Academic Press, 2002).

Touch is the most basic sense.[5] The famous case of Helen Keller, blind and deaf from childhood and for some years mute, who even so became a well-known writer and lecturer, beautifully illustrates how fundamental the sense of touch is.[6] Because it is basic, touch is the "sense of existence"; and this has been recently confirmed by "sensory-deprivation" experiments that show that persons floating in water of body-temperature in silence and the dark soon begin to hallucinate, because they no longer can distinguish between sleep and waking.[7]

The Secondary, Processing Senses and Their Organ, the Brain

The information gathered by the special organs of touch, taste, smell, vision, and hearing needs to be processed by secondary senses; in addition to the *species impressa* they receive from the primary senses, the secondary senses themselves also produce a *species expressa,* or an image ("phantasm") that substitutes for direct contact with some existing object.[8] Animals must have such images to guide their responses to their environment or to the pleasurable or painful states of their bodies. As the organs of the five primary senses are at the periphery of the body so as to contact the outer world, the processing of the information received from these organs is the work of the most complex organ that guides the functioning of the whole human or-

5. Aquinas, *Sentencia De anima* II, lect. 3.

6. See Dorothy Herrmann, *Helen Keller: A Life* (New York: Knopf, 1998).

7. Debates about the senses date back to Galileo, who in his *The Assayer* opened the way to the idealistic sensationism of Locke (which is still followed by many scientists) by arguing that most qualities of things are merely subjective impressions; hence we can rely only a mathematical natural science. Galileo gave as an example that one might feel an itching sensation when touched by a feather, and thus fail to distinguish the light touch of the feather on the skin from the itch or the resultant condition of the skin. In fact, both sensations provide information that is objective, but one has as its object the feather external to the body, and the other the state of one's skin internal to the body (as the contraction of a muscle is internal to the body).

8. Aquinas, *ST* I, q. 84.

ganism, namely, the human brain, protected by a protective and enclosing skull of bone and cartilage.

The brain itself, however, is a soft mass of cells, amply supplied with blood by a special network of arteries and veins.[9] The most significant cells of the brain are the branching neurons that transmit chemical and electric signals. When these signals reach the tips (synapses) of the branches (dendrites), the cells release molecules (neurotransmitters) that in various ways communicate with and otherwise affect adjoining cells through their own dendrites. The brain generates only 10 to 12 watts of electricity—about as much as a flashlight—and about 90 percent of the brain's cells are *glia*, cells that merely support the active neurons, yet the brain is the most marvelous of systems.

The brain, as prime mover, directs the three parts of the total nervous system. The first part or *central* nervous system is made up of the spinal chord, at the top of which is the brain. The second or *autonomic* system combines two subsystems that balance each other: the *sympathetic* subsystem system, which activates the heart's action and capacity, the blood vessels, kidneys, and digestive organs, and the *parasympathetic* subsystem, which relaxes them. The third or *peripheral* nervous system extends from the spinal chord and consists in the sensory and motor nerves. It is also the site of reflex movements, such as automatically raising one's hands if it touches something too hot.

Even in some very primitive animals, a threefold division of the brain appears: the *hindbrain* or *brain stem,* the *midbrain,* and the *forebrain.* It is the forebrain that has undergone the greatest expansion and complexification, so that in humans it covers the other parts. The hindbrain is so named because it connects the forebrain to the spinal chord and thus regulates the rest of the body through the central and peripheral nervous systems and receives messages from the primary sense organs. It consists first in the *medulla oblongata,* which contains

9. See John Nolte, *The Human Brain: An Introduction to Its Functional Anatomy,* 5th edition (St. Louis: C. V. Mosby, 2002).

a small area (the "olive") that helps us detect the direction from which we hear sounds. In the lower part of the medulla the *pyramidal motor nerves* coming down from the forebrain cross over to the opposite side of the spinal cord. Behind the medulla is the *cerebellum,* which is thought to coordinate habitual routine movements, timing, balance, and posture so as to free our attention to meet new situations.

The medulla is joined to the midbrain by the *pons,*which transmits messages between the body and higher centers; with the medulla oblongata, the pons is important in regulating breathing, heartbeat, contraction of blood vessels, and other reflexes such as sneezing, coughing, and vomiting. The midbrain is important for reflexes in the visual and auditory systems, and especially for voluntary movements of the body; if it is seriously injured, the victim is rendered comatose.

The forebrain is still more complex: first, it contains the two *thalami,* which are the gateways to the higher centers of the brain; they process the sensory signals going to these centers. The thalami have important influence on sleep and waking, and when seriously injured can induce permanent coma. Second, surrounding the thalami are groups of cells called the *basal ganglia,* which integrate movements; these cells are affected in Parkinson's disease. Under the thalami are the two *hypothalami,* whose main function is to monitor and adjust physiological processes such as blood pressure, temperature, hunger and thirst, sexual arousal, and the sleep-waking cycle, etc. Yet they also link the nervous system to the endocrine system in order to regulate its release of hormones, especially from the pituitary gland, which is about the size of a pea and projects from the hypothalamus. These organs can be considered part of the *limbic system,* which also includes the *amgydala* (involved in fear and aggressive emotions) and other groups of cells regulating heart beat, blood pressure, and attention, notably the *hippocampus* (involved in forming long-term memories and learning) as well as the *nucleus accumbens* (involved in physical pleasures and addictions to them). The *olfactory bulb,* related to the primary sense of smell, is also part of this system.

The outer and major part of the forebrain is the *cerebrum*, which today is thought by psychologists to be the main organ of touch, perception, imagination, and interpretation of sensory impulses; by physicalists it is thought to be the main organ of intelligence, judgment, planning, and decision-making. The cerebrum surrounds the previously mentioned structures, its surface portion, the *cortex*, being remarkably folded so as to fit into a limited skull—if spread out, it would fill an area of about 2½ square feet. It includes about 10 billion neurons with 50 trillion synapses. It is made up of six thin layers of neurons ("grey matter") whose cells have branching projections (*dendrites*) that connect with other cells (*synapses*). Under these is much "white matter"; it transmits nervous impulses from one part to another of the "grey matter" and to the lower parts of the brain and spinal chord. The folds of the cortex have ridges or *gyri* and valleys or *sulci*. There are also four ventricles or cavities in the brain continuous with spinal chord's central canal and filled with a special fluid.

The outer part of the cerebrum or *cortex* is divided into lobes as follows: *occipital* (from Latin, back of head), and *frontal* (front of brain) separated from the parietal by the *central sulcus* at top of brain, and from the temporal by the *lateral sulcus*. The *parietal* (from Latin for "wall") area is at the top of head toward the back and has two parts: the front area integrates sensory input, especially from vision, while the back area constructs a spatial coordinate system. Trauma to the left parietal lobe can cause difficulty in writing, mathematics, and language, while damage to the left parietal lobe leads to difficulty with dressing and washing the body, in making things or drawing. The right parietal-temporal lobe is concerned with non-verbal memory.

The *occipital* (from Latin, back of head) lobes are visual centers. Injuries to them can result in defects of vision or total blindness and also visual illusions or hallucinations. The *temporal* lobes (from the Latin for temple) or sides of the head are under the occipital and parietal areas and beside the ears. They relate to auditory sensation and perception, but injuries to them can also cause disorders of visual perception, difficulties in the organization and categorization of verbal material and language comprehension, and impaired long-term memory. Left-side lesions result in decreased recall of verbal and visual content (for example, recall of faces) and of speech. Right-side lesions result in decreased musical abilities. Right-side lesions can also affect recognition of visual content (e.g., recall of faces). Seizures of the temporal lobe can have dramatic effects on an individual's personality.

The *somatosensory* area includes the portions of the sulcus that divide the parietal from the frontal part of the brain; closest to the temples, it can be mapped with areas related to the mouth and face, and, at the top of the head, with areas related to the legs and feet. Between such areas in the lobes are association centers connecting motor and sensory areas and probably storing memories.

The brain has two hemispheres linked by an arch of white matter, the *corpus callosum,* which, if absent or severed, causes lack of awareness in one hemisphere of events in the other. There is, however, a lesser link, the *anterior commissure*, between the two *olfactory bulbs* and the *amygdala.* The left hemisphere relates to the right side of the body and the right hemisphere to the left side of the body. The left is somehow related to learning language, mathematical calculation, and music. The right is more involved in spatial orientation, face recognition, body image, and the appreciation of the fine arts. In the human eye the right side of each retina goes to the left hemisphere and the left of each retina to the right hemisphere. Speech mainly is a function of the left hemisphere, but the right shares in this function and can learn to substitute for the left. Two areas are especially important: when *Broca*'s area, at the bottom of the left frontal lobe, is destroyed the patient becomes unable to speak, while if *Wernicke*'s area (near it but in the temporal lobe near the auditory cortex) is injured the victim cannot understand the speech of others. The angular gyrus, just above and behind Wernicke's area, is involved in reading and writing.

There are many connections between the limbic system, which is related to emotional life, and the cortex. The whole brain is protected by three layers of membrane and floats in cerebrospinal fluid. The functional differences between the two hemispheres of the cerebrum and its possible connection with mental differences between male and female persons are very controversial questions. In males the left hemisphere seems dominant, while in females the two hemispheres are more alike.

There is evidence that on the average men do better in spatial and mathematical reasoning and women in verbal skills, but this is only a matter of averages. It is also probable that emotionally men tend to be more aggressive and women more empathetic and that this can be explained as an evolutionary adaptation to their roles in the family.[10]

Research on the brain began with behavioral observation and surgical interventions that showed a connection between abnormal behavior and brain trauma; it can now be carried out with a number of devices, notably electroencephalography (EEG), which measures electric current in the brain, and brain scans such as axial computerized tomography (CAT), magnetic resonance imaging (MRI), magnetoencephalography (MEG) and positron emission tomography (PET), each of which has special advantages.

Today our acquaintance with remarkable computers that are also information-processing machines furnishes us with a useful analogue for our brains. At birth the human brain seems to be much less pre-programmed with detailed instincts than the brains of most animals;[11] it is thus ready constantly to acquire more information. Yet human infants certainly do have instincts to cling to their mother and suck her breasts. Face perception, disgust reactions, social behavior

10. See Doreen Kimura, "Sex Differences in the Brain," *Scientific American*, May 13, 2002.

11. Pioneers in the study of insect behavior, which is especially important for research on instinct, were Eugène Marais (1872–1936), and Konrad Lorenz (1903–89), who is widely credited as being the father of ethology, the study of animal behavior, because of his early work on imprinting.

("altruism"), and language acquisition seem to have instinctual foundations, because they are common to the whole human species. Yet the analogy of our brain to a computer should not be exaggerated. A computer is programmed to operate according to a logic that is called a "formal system." We saw in Chapter 2 that the mathematician Kurt Gödel proved that no formal system can prove its own consistency, nor can it provide a solution for every problem that can be raised in terms of that system. The human brain, however, that invented the computer and programmed it, can always invent new programs or new computers that can solve the problems insoluble by previous computers or their programs. In other words, the human brain has a power of invention that can always go ahead of any computer and do it one better.

Gerald Edelman, a physicalist and a Nobel laureate in physiology and medicine, has vigorously argued against the computer-brain analogy and proposed as an alternative what he calls "neural Darwinism."[12] The total number of synaptic connections peaks when the child is between six and eight months of age and then begins to decline; at ten years old, the number has diminished by half, as the most-used synapses have been strengthened and the less-used ones have been destroyed. The process seems to be analogous to Darwin's "survival of the fittest." Hence the brain, according to Edelman, is not a pre-programmed system like a computer but is a selectional system in which pattern recognition (categorization) leads to novel outcomes so that, as he says:

> The number of possible connections these cells can make exceeds the number of particles in the universe. . . . The thalamus is located in the center of the brain and is about the size of your thumb. It relays signals from all senses but smell to the cortex of the brain which, through manifold loops and pathways, "speaks back" to the thala-

12. *Remembered Present: A Biological Theory of Consciousness* (New York: Basic Books, 1990).

> mus. Competition for advantage in the environment enhances the spread and strength of certain synapses, or neural connections, according to the "value" previously decided by evolutionary survival. The amount of variance in this neural circuitry is very large. Certain circuits get selected over others because they fit better with whatever is being presented by the environment. In response to an enormously complex constellation of signals, the system is self-organizing according to Darwin's population principle. It is the activity of this vast web of networks that entails consciousness by means of what we call "reentrant interactions" that help to organize "reality" into patterns. The thalamocortical networks were selected during evolution because they provided humans with the ability to make higher order discriminations and adapt in a superior way to their environment. Such higher order discriminations confer the ability to imagine the future, to explicitly recall the past and to be conscious of being conscious....There is a constant interplay between what is remembered and envisioned—an image—and what is actually happening in the senses. We now know that this interplay is enabled by reentrant interactions between the thalamus and cortex. The brain can speak to itself and the conscious brain can use its discriminations to plan the future, narrate the past and develop a social self.[13]

Edelman distinguishes between a lower consciousness of sense objects and a higher consciousness by which we reflect on our thinking. His view is closer to Aquinas's view than the computer analogy, but it resembles theories such as those of Stuart Kauffman,[14] who seeks to support Darwinism by the notion of "self-organization," which attributes to physical systems—especially living systems—a power to increase the inherent order of such systems. In Kauffman's biological theory, the order is increased through catalytic processes. Like Neo-

13. Gerard Edelman, "Neural Darwinism," *New Perspectives Quarterly*, 21.3 (2004): 62–64, last modified May 12, 2004, http://www.digitalnpq.org/global_services/nobel%20laureates/05-12-04.html.

14. Stuart Kauffman, *At Home in the Universe: The Search for the Laws of Self-Organization and Complexity* (New York: Oxford University Press, 1996).

Darwinism, such a theory does not assign a cause that is proportionate to the effect it seeks to explain (although it is more plausible than computer-program explanations).

No doubt our brains, because they are physical, have finite limits to what they can do. Hence the question remains open whether the brain itself, marvelous instrument that it is and one that is necessary to human thinking, can be the ultimate explanation of human thought; but we will have to take up that question later. What is important here is that the brain is clearly the primary organ of the body that unites the body's operations. This is why today we recognize that when the brain dies, and only then, does the human person die, that is, cease to have bodily existence as a whole organism.

The Four Secondary or Processing Senses

In current terminology, two secondary senses are distinguished, *imagination* (the production of images) and *memory* (the recording of images supplied by the *imagination).* Aristotle and St. Thomas Aquinas, however, added to these two secondary senses two others: the synthetic sense (*common sense*) and the *estimative sense* or *particular reason.* The value of this fourfold distinction becomes evident if we observe what animals do with the information they receive. An animal may react to a single sensation (it might flee the nipping of its body), but more often it exhibits a response to another thing—food, water, its mate, its offspring, or an enemy animal. There is every reason to suppose that the animal perceives another animal not just as a color or sound but as a whole that is seen, heard, smelled, and perhaps touched or tasted; that is, it does seem that at least the higher subhuman animals have the ability to synthesize the data received from different senses so as to form an integrated image of something that possesses all these different kinds of qualities. This ability to synthesize different kinds of sensory images to form an integrated image is often called the *common sense*, but as we will see later, this must not be confused with what we mean when we say that someone "lacks common sense." Hence I will call it the *synthetic sense.*

What is the organ or brain-center in which the synthetic sense (the "common sense") is located? A clue is furnished by research on the sensory condition called *synesthesia* due to which, for example, when a certain sound is heard the person seems to see a color or vice versa; the condition is noted especially in children.[15] Some locate this secondary sense in the cortex, but it is more likely located in the limbic region in the hippocampus, but with connections to cortical centers in the left brain.

In the *memory,* integrated images formed by the synthetic sense as well as images received from particular senses are stored (as *implicit* memory) and may later be recalled to consciousness (as *explicit* memory). For Aquinas, memory is a secondary sense whose objects are images of particular things seen at a given time and in particular circumstances.[16] I remember the dog that barked at me as I passed my neighbor's house this morning on my way to work. Today, however, psychologists use the term somewhat more generally and vaguely and distinguish between *procedural* memory, which records routine actions or habits that can be unconscious, and *declarative* memory, which can be implicit but becomes explicit when recalled to consciousness; this latter is more like what Aristotle and Aquinas meant by "memory." A better distinction, that has been verified in modern research, is between the powers of *short-term* and *long-term* memory.[17] If we were to retain all the data of our experience we would be overwhelmed. In fact we are able to "keep in mind" much of that data only for the short period during which we are using it to react cor-

15. See Patricia L. Duffy, *Blue Cats and Chartreuse Kittens: How Synesthetes Color Their Worlds* (New York: Owl Books/Henry Holt, reprint ed., 2002).

16. *ST* I, q.78, a. 4.

17. See Humberto Gutierrez and Christopher Ormsby. "A Brief Introduction to the Brain: Memory," Instituto de Fisiologia Celular, Mexico City, UNAM, accessed June 15, 2011, www.ifc.unam.mx/Brain/index.htm.

rectly to a particular situation. Long-term memory, however, may last a lifetime. It retains only a portion of what our short-term memory has retained briefly; it allows most of our experiences to fade away.

It is often said that "an elephant never forgets." Whether this is true, certainly some animals do retain what they have learned for a long time, as in the well-authenticated cases of dogs and other animals that have returned to their homes from great distances. Certainly among human individuals, the power of memory greatly differs; to a degree it can be trained. It also tends to weaken in old age, and it can be lost by various accidents (*amnesia*). Without memory, animals could not learn and we could not have a past.

What is the organic site of human memory? Procedural or implicit memory can be in many parts of the brain, since in all of them nerve synapses form and may persist for long periods. As already noted this retention of behavioral patterns is located in the lower brain, especially in the cerebellum and in the forebrain in the amygdala and is long term. The real question is about declarative memory, which is consciously recalled either spontaneously through association or deliberately. According to Freud, part of our "mind" is unconscious yet active and influential on our conscious mind. Certainly in our dreams and in daydreams all sorts of memories emerge that have been long forgotten.

The special site of memory is probably in the hippocampus in the inner fold of the temporal lobes, since damage to these areas produces various types of *amnesia* (which, however, can have other causes).[18] Yet we all have had the experience of not being able to remember the name of someone whom we know quite well. It may still be somewhere in our memory but for the moment is inaccessible until the right association brings it to mind. As one declarative memory becomes linked by association with another, the hippocampus seems no

18. See "Memory, the Brain, and Amnesia," accessed June 15, 2011, http://www.psychology.mcmaster.ca/3vv3/chapter9.htm.

longer to be required for recall, but the recall is produced by the prefrontal lobes of the cortex and in the parahippocampal cortex at the base of the brain.

Memory is a remarkable power, but the power of imagination (in the stricter sense of the term) is even more wonderful.[19] When we recall an image recorded in memory we can also *abstract* from the spatial and temporal context in which we formerly observed it. I can imagine a "giraffe" without thinking of the zoo where I saw it or the day or year I saw it. Moreover, I can change this image by further abstraction, as when I imagine a little giraffe, although the only one I have ever seen is a big one, or a blue giraffe, though none exists. Finally I can combine one image with another and imagine a giraffe with horns like a deer. "Fantasy" or "imagination" is indeed a marvelous power of constructing a world I have never actually experienced. If we analyze the contents of our imagination, we will see that our wildest fantasies are constructed from actual memories taken apart and recombined.

Furthermore, no matter how reconstructed these fantasies are, they retain the *concrete* character of what we have sensed. For example, if I try to imagine "three things," no matter how "abstract" I make them, leaving out what those "things" are, their color, shape, and size, etc., they always remain at least vaguely as "pictures" (or some kind of representation from one of the other senses). For example, if I try to imagine a "noise," it will be somehow more or less loud, harsh, or musical. Thus the kind of "abstraction" that the imagination can perform is never able to leave out all the concreteness of the various sense experiences from which it was derived. As we will see later, this is quite different from the kind of abstraction that we make, for example, in mathematics, when we think of "three." That "three" has no hardness or softness, or warmth or cold, no odor or taste, no color or sound, no location in time or place. It is just three identical units added together and nothing else.

19. See Paul Harris, *The Work of the Imagination* (Oxford: Blackwell, 2000).

Current psychology presents three types of theories about imagination, none of which has universal acceptance: pictorial or quasi-pictorial theories, descriptive or propositional theories, and perceptual activity theories.[20] All agree on the semantic notion that our imagining involves *intentionality* and *consciousness*; that is, something in our brain stands for, "intends" (is a sign of), objects in the extra-mental world and thus makes us conscious of them. I imagine my dog running about in the yard and then go to look for him. The *pictorial* theory supposes that this is to be explained by supposing that in my brain I have a picture or a quasi-picture or representation of my dog running about in the yard.

The *descriptive* or *propositional* theory claims that what is in the brain is a language (mentalese), such as would be in a computer, that has little relation to the thing signified. Some analytical philosophers take this view in order to explain how we can often communicate to someone who does not know our spoken language. This theory, however, overlooks the fact that in such situations we can simply point to objects.

The third view attempts to mediate between the other two. According to *perceptual activity* theories, perception is a process in which we step-by-step categorize information (that is, group similar items and distinguish them from other such groups) in view of some purpose, but without ever producing a final picture or description. This third theory accounts for the fact that when we recall something we have seen, we are usually unable to answer questions about all its details, but only certain salient features. For example, I remember how at a football game, a certain player in a red uniform passed the goal line, but I cannot recall whether he had the ball under his right arm or his left. This experience, however, does not contradict the Thomistic notion of an image in the sense of a *species expressa*, since

20. See the articles of Nigel J. T. Thomas, modified last June 11, 2011, http://www.imagery-imagination.com/.

as I have defined this notion it can have various degrees of precision.

What is the part of the brain that imagines? There is evidence that the right side of the brain seems more active than the left in fantasizing; the left, for its part, is more active in language ability. Injuries to the prefrontal cortex and other evidence make it clear that the area in front of motor centers must be the site for imagination, creativity, attention, and planning. This is in accordance with evolutionary theory, since this part of the human brain is comparatively the most developed. The misguided practice of surgical prefrontal lobotomy, common in the middle of the twentieth century, resulted in patients who acted like robots. This part of the brain has elaborate connections with the sensory centers that supply it with information.

Besides the common sense (synthetic sense), memory, and imagination, the behavior of animals evidences a fourth and very important kind of sense data processing, called by Aquinas the *vis aestimativa* (estimative power) in animals and the *vis cogitativa* (thinking power) in humans.[21] (*Vis cogitativa* is translated by some as "discursive sense," but I prefer "evaluative sense.") Animals are not only aware of their environment, but they *evaluate* it, reacting to some objects positively, to others negatively. Much of this evaluating behavior is not learned.

I once visited Carlsbad Cavern in New Mexico and saw countless thousands of bats clinging to the roof of one of the caves. The guide told us that little bats are born on the ceiling of the cave and for some time cling to their mothers, but eventually the mother bat shoves them away and from the immense height of the cave they fall in the darkness. A few hit the bottom and die, but most little bats drop into the air and somehow discover that they know how to fly about, never touching the bottom, and they eagerly begin to pursue the flying insects on which they must thenceforward live on their own. We must infer that they have an innate knowledge of what they must do to fly

21. For a collection of Aquinas's texts, see George P. Klubertanz, SJ, *The Discursive Power: Sources and Doctrine of the vis cogitativa according to St. Thomas Aquinas* (St. Louis, MO: Modern Schoolman, 1952).

and survive, since they have never before experienced this life problem and yet they solve it. We call this innate knowledge "instinct," and more generally it is the *estimative sense* or "animal intelligence." What I have related of in the case of bats, the migration of birds, the nest-building of birds, the making of honeycombs by bees (this list could go on and on)—these are wonderful instances of instincts.[22]

Much of animal behavior has this evaluative character, which tends to distinguish what is desirable from what is undesirable and to give some appropriate response to each stimulus. This evaluation adds other additional information that was not sensed but is first of all innate or unlearned to the data of the primary sense organs, after the sense data has been processed by memory, common sense, and imagination. Because this sense evaluates or estimates the object as desirable or dangerous it guides the animals' responses to its environment. The wonderful adaptation of animals to the problems of their environment has always awed human beings, since dumb animals often seem more competent in solving the problems of their environment than humans do. This amazement is expressed not only in the earliest art of humanity—cave paintings of animals—but also in the mythology of peoples living close to nature and of the ancient Egyptians, which ascribes to animals a mysterious wisdom that surpasses human wisdom and seems to show that animals are our superiors. Certainly we can learn much from animals.

In addition to having well-developed instincts, animals also learn from experience; they can often be trained by human beings to do new tricks, and this ability to learn increases with the complexity of animals, so that a chimpanzee can learn much more than an oyster. Nevertheless, an analysis of animal learning will show that its learning is always a refinement of some innate type of behavior. Animal trainers know that they can teach an animal tricks by conditioning

22. On how such insect behavior exhibits "self-organization" and "stigmergy" (social behavior) see David Gordon, "Collective Intelligence in Social Insects," accessed June 15, 2011, http://ai-depot.com/Essay/SocialInsects.html.

their reactions through little rewards and punishments, but only if they take advantage of the animal's basic instincts. If a horse did not like sugar and dislike the blow of a whip, it could not be trained to do what the rider wants, nor could it learn to carry the rider unless it already knew how to trot and run or stand still. Yet anyone who has a pet dog knows how wonderfully the animal can learn to live with its master and "relate" to its master, in some ways like a human child. Indeed, the evaluative sense is most like human intelligence, though as we shall explore in the next chapter, it differs from it in significant ways.

What is the physical site of the evaluative sense? In the next section this will become clearer after the nature of the *affective* as distinguished from the cognitive work of the brain has been discussed. Without using the term "evaluative sense," however, neuropsychologists emphasize that the pre-frontal lobes, besides their cognitive functions, are intimately linked with the emotional functions of the limbic system. Since evaluation results from the association of an image with an affective drive, persons with trauma of these areas often exhibit defective practical judgment and behavior. Also important for practical judgment, however, are the linkages to memory centers that explain the operant conditioning of behavior.[23]

The Affective Sense Drives

The fact that primary sense cognition is ultimately processed by *instincts,* which show the animal that an object is desirable or should be avoided or attacked, leads us to infer another and different set of powers in animals that are not cognitive but appetitive or *affective.* They are *drives,* which, when stimulated by the presentation of objects to sense cognition, move the animal to particular kinds of activity—for example, the drive to eat or to approach a mate, or to run

23. See Arnold H. Modell, *Imagination and the Meaningful Brain* (Cambridge: MIT Press/Bradford, 2003).

from an enemy. In modern psychology these are often considered under the title of "affectivity," "emotion," or "feelings" but such terms can lead to confusing them with the cognitive powers. In fact our animal drives are not, as such, forms of cognition and hence are not in themselves conscious. For example, our need for food and water produces drives within our bodies even when we are not aware of being hungry or thirsty. When such an inclination, instinct, or drive is stimulated it causes changes in the body and these changes are registered in consciousness as pleasant or painful (or at least uncomfortable) primary sensations; it is these sensations (not the instincts themselves) that we call "feelings," "emotions" or "affections." For an animal to react to them in a practical way is, then, the work of instinct, either as innate or as it is modified by learning. Descartes questioned whether animals have feelings at all, but we know that they do, not only because *we* too have feelings, but because we see animals react to objects that they evaluate positively or negatively. A cat purrs quietly, relaxing its body to gentle stroking, whereas it arches its back, draw back its lips to show its teeth, and hisses at a dog; the actions in the former case clearly indicate pleasure, and in the latter case, defensive anger.

Although it is easy to list the basic drives of animals as they correspond to the life functions we have enumerated, it is not so easy to classify the bodily changes and their sensations that result in "feelings." We know in our own experience how complex states of feeling can be and how they often seem to be in conflict with each other. Aquinas, however, gave a very simple and useful classification, of which modern psychologists are too often unaware.[24] It was derived from Aristotle's *Rhetoric,* or art of persuasion. This fascinating work was based empirically on the experiences of Greek political orators, who were trying to move their audiences to favor or disfavor some proposed course of action. Its content resembles what is taught in courses on advertising, about what sells and what does not.

24. *Summa Theologiae* I, qq. 80–81 and I-II, qq. 22–48.

- Drives
  - Simple Pain-Pleasure Drives
    - Possessed (SATISFIED): JOY
    - Sought (DESIRED): YEARNING
    - Sensed (PLEASANT): ATTRACTION
    - Sensed (UNPLEASANT): DISLIKE
    - Avoided (REPELLED): FEAR
    - Endured (PAINED): SUFFERING
  - Complex Emergency Drives
    - Aggression
      - ATTACK
      - HOPE
    - ANGER
    - Endurance
      - PATIENCE
      - DESPAIR

FIGURE 4-1. Drives and Emotions

According to Aquinas, the drives that we become conscious of as bodily emotions can be classified broadly as is shown in figure 4-1, "Drives and Emotions." It should be noted that the names for such emotions are varied and are often not very precise.

To illustrate the classification, consider your feelings as you sit down to dinner and see what is on the table. You see the dish you like as pleasant and *attractive,* and you reach for it with a feeling of *yearning* or desire, and as you eat it you feel *satisfied.* On the other hand, it may be that you do not favor the dish; you feel that it is unpleasant, and, as you try, out of politeness or necessity, to eat it, you feel *fear* or anxiety that you will end up *dissatisfied* with the meal. Such feelings are simple, in that they imply the pleasurable or the painful object and motions toward or away from it. If you desire the food and someone pulls it away before you can get it, you grow *angry.*

Sigmund Freud originally tried to explain all human emotions in terms of the pleasurable and the painful; he called the drive toward the pleasurable the *libido* (Latin for "desire"). Furthermore, he thought that this drive was typified by the infant's pleasure in touch, since that involves the whole body, and he argued that the libido develops into erotic or sexual desire. Such a theory is called "pansexualism." It is indeed probably correct as regards the pleasure of touch, since touch is the most basic sense; but it seems to exaggerate the sexual aspects of touch, since, for survival, an organism has the more basic needs for food, comfort, and security. It can be granted Freud, however, that sexual pleasure seems the most intense sense pleasure that animals experience, and it seems that without it they would neglect to take the trouble of reproducing their species. This judgment seems also born out by the great difficulty human beings experience in controlling their sexual desires in order to contribute to their total welfare.

Freud eventually came to recognize a second principle or drive that is necessary to explain human behavior; he unfortunately called it "the death wish," because he found it manifested in suicide and other self-destructive forms of behavior. It is hard to infer, however, that self-destructive behavior results from a special innate drive rather than from a morbid distortion of some other drive, since it seems to contradict the evolutionary doctrine of the "survival of the fittest." Later psychoanalysts have developed a "two-drive theory" in which, in addition to the pain-pleasure drive, animals have an "aggressive drive." The morbid behaviors, which Freud explained by a "death wish," are then explained as neurotic states in which aggression that is naturally directed against external enemies is turned upon the aggressor's own self.[25]

The empirical basis for inferring this drive is found in observations that show that human and non-human animals often desire some object that is *arduous*, that is, some pleasurable object that is

25. See Karl Menninger, *Man against Himself*, reprinted (New York: Harcourt, 1985).

hard to get or some painful object that is hard to escape. Such drives, therefore, are complex in that the difficulty involved is painful, yet the object the animal seeks is pleasurable, or at least, if it is painful, escape from it gives pleasurable relief. Thus *hope* is the drive that arouses the animal's aggressive powers when it sees it must overcome some obstacle to its pleasure or that it may be able to overcome some enemy that threatens pain. *Aggression* taken specifically is the animal's instinct to attack its enemies or to make a great effort that often involves risk and pain in order to obtain pleasure, as when male animals fight each other for a mate or a female animal risks serious wounds in defending her offspring against an enemy. The fierce energy displayed by animals in such dangerous situations show that there is a certain pleasure even in the risky and painful fight. Sometimes painful situations cannot be avoided and then endurance is necessary and can result either in *patience* when the animal suffers but keeps going on its way in spite of the suffering, as when a weary animal keeps on going until it reaches home; or it can end in *despair* and grief. *Anger* is the drive that is aroused when the animal feels itself caught in a hopeless situation, yet is too desperate to immediately despair, but instead prepares to use all its powers to destroy an enemy it cannot avoid.

Even in non-human animals there can be a conflict and confusion of emotions; one sees this conflict exhibited in the behavior of a dog confronted by a stranger holding out a bone. Fear is felt at the approach of a stranger, then desire for the bone, and so a kind of confusion of behavior reflects this struggle of feelings. It is often noted today that rape is more an act of violence than of sexual love, yet it is sexual sadism also. We are only too well acquainted with such emotional confusion and conflict in our human lives and the sometime contradictory actions that result.

One of the big points of Freudian psychology that has good clinical backing is that this conflict of feelings can result in two levels of feeling, one clearly expressed and another concealed from self and others. This situation can exist even at the subhuman level: we observe a certain amount of deviousness and shrewd dissimulation in predatory animals. Many a zookeeper has suddenly found himself attacked by an animal that he supposed was just being its usual friendly self. Hence Freud developed the notion of the *id* (Latin for "it" in contrast to *ego* or "I") or unconscious mind that seemed contradictory; how can mind be unconscious? The confusion can be clarified by considering what is meant in ordinary experience by "attention" and "intention" even at the animal level of consciousness. A pet dog lies passively for a whole hour but lifts up its ears and becomes *attentive* when its master enters the room with a bone. A man drives to work; his attention, though, is not on his driving, which he does from habit, but on thoughts about his business. Thus consciousness has various levels. Attention is the work of the evaluative sense, which gives a definite direction or *intention* to the functioning of the secondary senses, so as to focus the data, especially that from the memory and imagination regarding what is relevant to the animal at the moment, although other data coming from the primary senses is still being used in habitual behavior. The dog is attentive to its master, yet as it runs toward him it habitually avoids bumping into whatever might be in the way.

But why does it run toward its master, and why is the man driving to work thinking about his business? The evaluative sense has stimulated affective drives; the dog wants food from its master; the man going to work wants to make more money. As has been explained, these affective drives as such are not cognitive and hence are unconscious, but they produce changes in the bodies of the dog or man of which they become conscious; recognizing their needs, they fix their attention on satisfying those needs. What Freud emphasized, therefore, is that we have unsatisfied desires that cause us such pain that we have tried to turn our attention from them (repressed them), but the changes they have produced in our affective state of affairs remain and they condition new experiences that have our attention and intention. For example, an animal suddenly turns on its master and attacks him, because it has become so hungry that he now sees his master as nothing but meat; or, the man going to work suddenly turns around and drives home because he is overcome with fear that his wife is with another man in his absence. Freudian psychoanalysis was supposed to enable persons to recognize such affective but repressed drives. It is certainly true that, besides the things that have our daily attention and which we pursue with conscious intention, there are affective drives and conditions of our bodies produced by these drives when they are stimulated yet frustrated that remain unconscious yet modify our conscious functioning.

What is the brain site of these affective drives? Since, as has been explained, the drives cause bodily changes in order to prepare human responses to varying life situations, and these changes involve not only the nervous system but the *hormonal* or *endocrine system* (ductless glands), this question cannot be answered without first saying more about that complex system.[26] At center of the brain between the two thalami is the *pineal* gland, which Descartes thought was the seat of the soul but which is now known to inhibit sexual development during childhood and is thought to regulate sleeping and waking and possibly dreaming. The *pituitary* gland is also in the brain on a stalk sticking out from the hypothalamus. Though only the size of pea, it is the master gland that controls the other parts of the endocrine system. It has three sections: the front section produces a growth hormone and stimulates the *adrenal* and *thyroid* glands, as well as the *ovaries* and *testes*; the middle section controls skin color; and the back section regulates the kidneys and produces the important hormone *oxytocin* involved in reproduction.

In the throat is the *thyroid* gland, which regulates the body's metabolism; the four *parathyroids* behind the thyroid regulate the cal-

26. See American Medical Association, accessed June 15, 2011, http://www.ama-assn.org/ama/pub/physician-resources/patient-education-materials/atlas-of-human-body.page?

cium of our body, which is so important for generating its electrical energy and building the bones. Under the breastbone is the *thymus*, which promotes the resistance of the body to infections. The *stomach* and *duodenum* contain cells that promote digestion and kidney functions. The very important *adrenal* glands sit on top of both kidneys, and their cores produce adrenaline that enables the person to respond to unusual situations ("fight or flight") and other hormones that maintain blood sugar levels, assist immunity, and control blood pressure, the amount of salt in blood, as well as *androgen*, a male sex hormone. The *pancreas*, between the kidneys, maintains several digestive hormones and, most importantly, *insulin* that regulates blood sugar.

Sexual emotions related to the complex male *testes* and female *ovaries* are of three types.[27] (a) Romantic attraction is located in the midbrain and basal ganglia (an area associated with autistic defects) and is in the right hemisphere of the brain, although sexual attraction stimulated by facial beauty is in the left hemisphere. Romantic attraction is more urgent than ordinary sexual desire and produces great mood swings, driven by high *dopamine* and *norepinephrine* levels and inhibited by *serotonin*. (b) Sexual attachment is also related to the basal ganglia but especially to its *ventral pallidum* portion, which secretes the hormones *oxytocin* and *vasopressin*. Oxytocin activity promotes interpersonal bonding and is much higher in females than in males, but in a male after orgasm it temporarily increases a sense of bonding that for him is very rewarding. (c) Desire for intercourse with arousal and orgasm is driven by *testosterone* in males and also in a lesser degree in females, but for females *estrogen* and *progesterone* incline her to accept and receive the male. For both sexes the neurotransmitter dopamine arouses sexual desire, but it is higher in men than in women, whereas norepinephrine from the adrenal gland excites them to

27. Michael Gurian, *What Could He Be Thinking? How a Man's Mind Really Works* (New York: St. Martin's Press, 2003).

actual sexual activity. *Serotonin* from central nervous system and digestive tract and *prolactin* from the pituitary can depress desire. *Testosterone* increases both a sexual and an aggressive drive, and is dominant in men, although women also have some. *Vasopressin* produced by the amygdala strongly supports aggression and seems very important for males and is connected with the anterior hypothalamus in the limbic system, which regulates hormone production; it somewhat inhibits females. Females are more concerned with attachment. Just as testosterone levels are much higher in males, oxytocin levels are generally higher in females. While men are aggressive in courting, they also send out signals that they need to be needed and to be trusted. Hence women attract by holding a man off in what can be called "intimate separateness."

Just as sexual emotions are fundamental to the survival of the species, emotions related to hunger and thirst are fundamental for survival of the individual. The thirst drive is controlled by the hypothalamus, but is stimulated by a dry mouth and by the condition of the blood. The hypothalamus also regulates hunger and has two areas with opposite effects: hunger and satiety. Specific hungers are stimulated by different deficiencies in blood chemistry and also visual stimulants. The hypothalamus and the visual retina regulate sleep, and the former regulates body temperature.

Conclusion

Modern research has made much progress in understanding how information about the changing material world and our own bodies as part of that changing world is cognitively received by the primary senses, recorded, processed, and evaluated by the secondary senses. It has also shown how the animal brain, as the primary organ acting on the evaluative senses' perception of a benefit or burden, guides the animal's bodily endocrine and motor system to react positively or negatively to the sensed environment or the state of its body. As the animal senses these changes in its body, especially through its somatosensory system (touch in the broad sense) its affective drives, for food and sex or for aggression or flight, are stimulated and lead to evident behaviors.

Although radical behaviorists claim that the notion of "consciousness" is irrelevant to this account, today the so-called "mind-body problem" about how to understand "consciousness" remains very urgent and often very confused. We will deal with that problem in the next chapter in which a distinction between animal and human intelligence will be verified and the necessary relation between them in human cognition, too often evaded by psychologists, will be explained. Clarification of this distinction is essential to the purpose of this book because, as will be shown in Chapter 9, it is precisely at the difficult borderline between comparative psychology and personal psychology that psychotherapy properly operates.

five

THINKING AND CHOOSING

Human Language Is Syntactical

Aristotle defines humans as "Animals that want to know" and Aquinas gives summary arguments to show that human intelligence is immaterial and thus properly has no material organ although, as already shown, it requires a material brain as its instrument to gain data.[1] Aquinas gives five arguments to show that our intelligence is not material: (1) animals cannot speak a syntactical language as do humans; (2) animals cannot form abstract concepts as do humans; (3) humans know truth, wisdom, and relations, which are not material; (4) we are self-conscious and animals are not; (5) human sense organs can be overpowered (for example, our eyes by a too-bright light), but our intelligence cannot.

The first of these arguments is that we humans have a true language (that can be used to make true, verifiable statements) and animals do not, although many of them have certain instinctual signals common to a species, and the higher animals, through imitation or

1. *Contra Gentiles* II, c. 66.

by conditioning, can learn many specifications in the interrelation of these signs. Now the noted psycholinguist and political activist Noam Chomsky (b. 1928) has developed a theory of "deep structures" or an innate grammar underlying all languages that is often cited as evidence that animals can learn to talk a true language.[2] Since he calls these deep structures "Cartesian," but also seems to think they are simply due to brain structures that developed after the hominids split from the other primates, his views remain materialist. Others, like Stephen Pinker in his book *The Language Instinct* (1994),[3] reject Chomsky's views and maintain that human communication is an evolutionary product that has rendered the brain much like a computer or "artificial intelligence."[4]

Certainly animal communication began quite early in biological evolution; for example, the lowly cuttlefishes communicate by changing their skin colors![5] Birds, also, whose brains have a structure quite different from that of mammals, through their songs communicate beautifully. But communication is not necessarily by true language, as has been thoroughly shown by the extensive, patient research done on primates.[6] For example: in the 1930s, W. N. and L. A. Kellogg compared the development of a young chimpanzee they named Gua to that of their own newborn son, but concluded that Gua was never able to use a true language. In the 1960s and early 1970s, Allen and Beatrice Gardner made a detailed study of a female chimp, Washoe,

2. *Cartesian Linguistics: A Chapter in the History of Rationalist Thought* (New York: Harper & Row, 1966).

3. (New York: W. Morrow and Co., 1994).

4. See Stuart J. Russell and Peter Norvig, *Artificial Intelligence: A Modern Approach* (Prentice Hall, Englewood Cliffs, New Jersey, 1995), and Richmond Thomason, "Logic and Artificial Intelligence," accessed November 22, 2012 (last revision October 31, 2012), http://plato.stanford.edu/entries/logic-ai/.

5. For excellent information on this subjects see Stephen Hart, *The Language of Animals* (New York: Henry Holt & Co., 1996).

6. For an excellent source on primate language, Lauren Kosseff, "Primate Use of Language," accessed June 15, 2011, http://www.pigeon.psy.tufts.edu/psych26/language.htm.

that they treated like a human child. She proved able to learn American Sign Language, which uses hand signals and which many deaf humans common employ to communicate. Washoe learned 250 signs, often by imitating her caretakers, but usually only when they taught her by repetition. Yet she also made use of signs spontaneously and combined some of them—for example, "water" and "bird" to mean a swan. Without specific instruction, Washoe could transfer signs; for example, she learned the word "more" when tickled and then spontaneously applied it to other actions or things; she also used signs in caring for a young chimp she adopted. She could name pictures as well as objects.

By purely laboratory methods in 1966 Sarah and David Premack studied a six-year-old female, Sarah, using plastic chips of different colors and shapes, each representing an English word. Sarah was reward with an apple to eat if she could identify the appropriate chip, and she learned to do this. Then they strung such chips in a series and Sarah learned to make "sentences" such as "Mary-to-give-apple." Ultimately Sarah learned to make such strings of as many as eight units. In a second stage, Sarah learned to use 130 signs and was able to string them together in a meaningful order, such as Mary/to/give/apple. Yet Sarah never asked questions.

Duane Rumbaugh and Sue Savage-Rumbaugh taught chimps and bonobos, notably a female bonobo named Kanzi, to use a computer keyboard on which each key was marked with a design corresponding to some object or concept; when Kanzi struck a good combination of signs, she was rewarded. She also combined the keyboard signs with meaningful gestures and was able to respond correctly to 70 percent of new commands given by a hidden speaker. To the command "Give the dog a shot," Kanzi respond by injecting a toy dog with a syringe.

Recent studies also show that chimps can form "categories" that they represent by a single sign or by combining signs; for example, one chimp called a watermelon "drink-fruit." Herbert Terrace taught a chimp called Nim to use signs such as "angry" and "bite" to express anger. The sets of signs that Nim produced, however, were in imitation of such sets previously produced by humans and did not combine signs to create truly novel ideas.

Monkeys have been shown to perform several arithmetic feats. For example, they have counted up to 9, learning by trial and error. They were also able to identify correctly a sequence of pictures within a series of 35 images differing in color, size and position; if the chimp touched four pictures in the right order it got a banana reward, whereas if it made a mistake it got nothing. These animals could also recognize that, for example, 7 is greater than 6. One of the researchers concluded that these chimps "share with humans the ability to master simple arithmetic on at least the level of a 2-year-old child."

Lower primates, such as the monkey called a "vervet," have been observed to give different cries on seeing a snake, a leopard, or an eagle, and their companion vervets make appropriately different responses to these different dangers. Birds also make signs and can be taught them, including series of colors like those the Rumbaughs taught their chimps to discriminate. Thus Otto Koehler showed a raven objects in sets of two to six and it learned to gain a food reward by matching these objects to black dots in sets of two to six.

Linguists, however, point out that these behaviors reduce to signals of warning or attraction and convey very limited information. In the case of bees, the correct direction in which to fly to find the right flowers can be communicated. We intelligent persons may see that this conveyed information is true, but there is no reason to conclude that the bee knows the difference between truth and falsity, and it is very easy for us to deceive a bee by a tricky signal.[7] In spite of the belief of some of these researchers that they had taught their animals

7. See the classical work of the pioneer in animal psychology, Jean-Henri Fabre (1823–1915), *The Mason Bees*, translated by Alexander Teixeira de Mattos (New York: Garden City, 1925, 1914). The rigidity of insect instinct becomes progressively loosened in higher animals, but even in the secondary senses of humans remains to a degree fixed.

true language, this research of many years has generally convinced psycholinguists and semanticists to the contrary.[8]

As we said in an earlier note, a true language, by contrast—one such as humans have invented in many different forms—can be used to make true, verifiable statements. When we look for the reason that this is possible, as semanticists have done, we find that animal signals lack *syntactical* signs such as "and," "therefore," "predicate," which do not signify anything in the extramental world, but only the mental relations that we form intellectually. A statement I repeat can be true or false, but only if I know its relation to the facts can I meaningfully assert that it is true or false. This relation of the conformity of the statement to the facts is a syntactical relation that exists only in the consciousness of the one making the statement and the consciousness of his intelligent hearer who also knows the language in which he makes it. Thus a dog may run to greet his master with a happy bark because it has been behaviorally conditioned to do so by the master's feeding or petting it, and the master may recognize that the bark is appropriate, The bark is not a linguistic assertion of a truth, however, because there is no evidence that the dog knows the logical relation between his bark and the master's identity.

In Chapter 4 I discussed the evaluative sense, common to animals and humans, that seems to account very well for the abilities shown by Washoe and Kanzi, whose learning of signs was largely the result of operant conditioning by food rewards. Such observations can contribute to the confirmation of Aquinas's third argument—that although subhuman animals communicate by signs, there is no evidence that they can communicate truth, since that requires syntactical language.

Like other animals, humans depend on their primary and secondary senses to carry on their life activities in their complex and changing environment. In the foregoing chapters I have sketched

8. See Thomas A. Sebeok, *Speaking of Apes: A Critical Anthology of Two-Way Communication with Man* (New York: Plenum Pub Corp, 1980).

out what today we know about their physical structure as organisms that makes this possible. Yet it is also obvious that human behavior, though it has much in common with the behavior of other animals, differs from it in striking ways.

Universals and Abstraction

Aquinas's second argument for the immateriality of human intelligence—that animals cannot form *universal* concepts as intelligent persons are able to do—seems to be called into question by some of the researches recounted here, since they show that animals can "categorize" objects so as to distinguish, for example, dogs from cats. This brings us again to the nominalism (or conceptualism) of William of Ockham (c. 1287–1347), which has recently been defended by Willard van Orman Quine (1908–2000). Quine claimed that human "universal" terms do not signify a collection of things that are essentially identical, but only ones that are "similar." We saw, in Chapter 4, that the secondary sense of imagination, common to animals and persons, can compare images, recognize their similarities, and even "abstract" from dissimilarities—as when an artist, matching colors, omits poor matches. This type of rough categorization possessed by animals, however, is not intellectual abstraction, since, contrary to the tenets of nominalism, abstraction forms *precisely* universal concepts. Research also shows that animals have a limited capacity to count;[9] but this does not prove that they know arithmetic. In fact, as we saw in Chapter 2, all scientific knowledge rests on at least some true statements that distinguish between *essential identity* and mere similarity.

The intellect *abstracts* from an image in one of the secondary senses (such an image is always of a singular) to form a *universal* concept;[10] for example, from an image of a hippopotamus seen in a

9. See American Psychological Association, "Researchers counting on animals for clues to math," *Monitor OnLine*, 30, April 1999.

10. The term "concept" has two senses: (a) the object known or *objective* concept;

zoo, one can form the concept of a special kind of animal that can be classified among even-toed mammals, such as the pig. No "universal hippo" actually exists (contrary to what Plato thought), since this concept omits everything that individualizes the hippo one actually saw and now remembers and imagines. The universality of the concept "hippopotamus," which makes it possible for a biologist to classify this animal taxonomically and study its properties scientifically, has been added by the mind and is the purely mental logical relation of "species" within a "genus," "two-toed mammal." Thus, this universal concept is not simply a "categorization" in the way that secondary senses of animals or small children nominalistically group together similar images, but it is truly universal by the process of abstraction.

Nevertheless, such truly abstract concepts are derived from images in the secondary senses, images that are less than precise and merely similar, yet these only serve instrumentally in the production of truly abstract concepts. Hence animals have been shown to be able to "categorize" objects so as, for example, to respond to red objects but not to blue objects.[11] In the last chapter we attributed this categorizing ability to the secondary senses of imagination and evaluation common to animals and human beings. No mathematician, however, will grant that "three" signifies three things that are only *vaguely* alike. The mathematician's "three" is made up of units that are absolutely and precisely equal parts of a whole collection of objects having no color, hardness, smell, or taste, or place, or change. For him, "three" is a purely *abstract* concept. While this is obvious in mathematics, all human languages also have signs for non-mathematical universal

and (b) the *species expressa* or the *subjective* concept, which is the sign formed by the mind through which we know the objective object.

11. Gerald Edelman's "Neural Darwinism" referred to in the last chapter recognizes the importance of "categorization" or ability to identify a group of somehow similar objects common to animal cognition and he also recognizes a higher kind of reflective "metacognition," yet although he gives a plausible theory of how the brain performs the first type of categorization, when he comes to higher, reflective knowledge his theory, as his critics have recognized, becomes very vague.

concepts or they could not be translated into each other. How could I translate "dog" into French *chien* if *chien* could also mean a "cat" since it is somewhat similar to a "dog"?

Precisely what is this difference between an abstract concept and a sense image? As Aquinas argues, the object of all the senses involves singular things, while human language and human sciences show that we can also think of universal classes of things by abstract concepts that classify not merely as similar but in certain respects *identically alike:* 3 is exactly 3 and nothing else is. We can think not only of five apples and five oranges but of the number 5, and this make possible the science of mathematics. Thus sense cognition is of singulars, whereas intellectual cognition is strictly of universal abstractions.

The significance of abstraction, however, is not just in the fact that it is universal, since what we want to know is reality, and nothing is real but singular things. The real importance of intellectual knowledge is that abstract thinking separates the *essential* from the accidental or superficial aspects of things. For example, for people who over-rely on the superficial qualities of things given by sense cognition, the color of a person's skin or whether they look like a male or a female is given exaggerated importance. But someone who really thinks about human beings knows that such differences are accidental (blacks come from sunny climates) or relatively superficial (males and females are equally intelligent). The existence of science depends on this search for the essential features of things amidst the chaos of chance and the existence of modern technology depends on the possibility of sorting out the means essential to achieving a certain goal.

Thus Plato was on the right track to scientific truth when in the *Republic* he portrayed Socrates as searching for the essential meaning of "justice," since, only if we can clarify that concept from a thousand irrelevancies and superficial substitutes, can we create a true science of what a society where the rights of all are respected must be. His mistake, corrected by Aristotle, was to seek the essential notion of justice in some idea innate to the mind (and thus to accept a dualism between mind and body that makes our specifically human thought essentially independent of the body).

Aristotle sought scientific, essential knowledge by studying actual political systems, to find in them what was essential to the welfare of all citizens and what was irrelevant or contradictory to this welfare. He showed that many forms of government are possible, each with its advantages and disadvantages in performing these essential functions of government, but all of them must be judged in terms of these essentials. Thus *essence* as the object that defines intellectual activity is nothing mysterious, nor need we claim to know the essence of anything exhaustively, not even our own essential nature as humans.

Essences are the *core reality* of the things that we experience or can infer to exist as causes of what we experience. Post-moderns are fond of making fun of every claim to know what is essential about anything; but the word games they play are just another proof of the human intellectual capacity to distinguish the essential from the nonessential. When these post-moderns claim that all human discourse is ambiguous, they are making universal and unambiguous claims about human discourse. To assert that a text can have many different interpretations, according to what one wants to do with it, requires sorting out from its possible meanings the meaning that is essential to our purposes and, unless it is simply arbitrary, corresponds to some essential features of the text. One can interpret the text of *Hamlet* in different ways, but to claim that it is aimless scratches produced by a chicken is to cluck less meaningfully than chickens do.

At the same time it is important not to neglect the role of *analogy* in human thought. Reality is immensely rich, and our thinking about it is relatively limited. Consequently, we often have to be content to extend signs (concepts or words) that mean one precise object (that is, are *univocal,* precise) to represent other objects to which they have only some similarity (that is *equivocal*, inexact). Seeing a giraffe in a zoo for the first time, I may refer to it as "a very long-necked deer," since it is related to a deer; but it is not exactly a deer, but only in some respects similar to a deer.

Analogies can be of several types. If the resemblance between two things represented by what my concepts or words pertain to what is *essential* in the two terms, it is said to be a *proper analogy* and can be expressed in the form "as *a* is to *b*, so *c* is to *d*" (a proportionality). For example: the circumference of a circle is related to the area within that circle as the sides of a square are related to the area within that square. A circle and a square are very different, but they have one essential similarity: they both enclose area. An especially important type of analogy is one between an effect and its cause (or vice versa).

As we saw in Chapter 2, all science is based on sense observation, but sometimes we have to reason from an observed effect to its unobservable cause. The effect and its cause may be univocal, but it is possible that they are not univocal, since a superior cause can have inferior effects. In that case, our knowledge of the superior cause through its inferior effects cannot be univocal but is said to be analogical by *attribution*, since what we know of the effect is attributed to its cause. Such an attributive analogy is also proportional (but not all properly proportional analogies are attributive, since we can compare things that are not related as effect to cause).

Furthermore we can have analogies that are not proper but merely *metaphorical* when a term that means one object univocally is used to indicate something that has a similarity that is not essential. Thus in poetic speech and often in slang we use words in a very loose way, as when we call a man a "dog" or a "rat," meaning that he is despicable. Scientific thinking avoids such loose metaphorical language and always seeks to be univocal, properly analogical, and preferably attributively analogical, because attributive analogy ties down the meaning of a term to some real, observable effect through which we can prove the existence of some cause that, though unobservable, can to a degree be known through its effect. Thus we today know that protons exist, although we cannot touch or see them, and we know some of their properties and that they are essentially different from electrons. As shown in Chapter 2 we also know that the First Cause exists and that it is non-material, and we can further arrive at some notion of its nature from the universe it creates and keeps evolving.

Therefore it is an error for scientists today to so quickly reduce the phenomenon of "consciousness" to observable chemical-electrical currents in the brain. These currents are observable effects, as are the behavioral responses of an animal to its environment, but we should not assume without further evidence that they have univocal causes rather than unobservable analogical causes whose nature must be explored.

Humans Seek Truth

The third reason Aquinas gives for the immateriality of the human intelligence is that animals cannot know immaterial objects such as "truth," whereas we humans certainly know the difference between truth and falsity, etc.—for example, in mathematics and as regards some conclusions in natural science. This is especially manifest in the use of human language: we can tell the truth or lie. It is also manifest in the diversity yet mutual translatability of human languages. Languages make sense only if they can convey truth (even though they can be abused by using them to deceive). We can test them by making simple statements about matters that both parties who communicate in a language can verify in their experience. For example, Einstein's statement "Motion is measurable only in relation to an observer" is true, but we know it to be true only from such *common* experiences as watching a train move by a station platform and wondering for the moment if it is not the train but the platform that is moving.

Reflective Consciousness

Aquinas's fourth argument for the immateriality of the human intellect is from the reflexivity of properly human consciousness as distinguished from animal consciousness; between these two types of consciousness there may be some analogical relation, but not univocity. As we stressed in an earlier chapter, the *materialist* tradition has always held that humans do not differ essentially but only in degree from other animals and that animal cognition, including consciousness, can be reduced univocally to some kind of brain states. The *idealist* tradition, on the other hand, holds that we can have a logically consistent view of material reality, but not its reality as such. For the idealist, the material world is only an imitation of the ideas we have in our minds. Is there any way out of this idealist dilemma?

In Chapter 2, I argued for the mediating position of Aristotle and Aquinas, which rejects innate ideas and insists that all our knowledge is based on primary sense information, which we process with our physical organs so as to arrive at conscious knowledge of our environment and our own bodies. Furthermore, in Chapter 4, I argued that animals, and human persons inasmuch as they are animals, have true consciousness, although there is no evidence that animal consciousness is anything but a function of material brains. Thus what we mean by animal "consciousness" is that the animal in sensing not only undergoes a physical change directly or through a medium caused by the object but also gains the power (*species impressa*) to unite itself to the object. In secondary sensing, the power is able to produce images of things that were first in the primary sense organ but which are now in the brain and can remain there even in the absence of the object imaged or after it has ceased to exist. Yet all animal thinking results only in a particular physical, material state of affairs.

The behavior of a dog running to pick up a ball and return it to its master is, however, too similar to the behavior of a small boy doing the same thing for us to seriously doubt that, since the child is certainly acting *consciously,* the dog is also acting *consciously*. Does that mean that if we invent a robot to imitate the dog's behavior that the robot is conscious? Some would say "yes," and there is no way to refute them except by showing that the robot fails to respond correctly to some cues to which the dog does correctly respond. So far, we have always been able to make that distinction! In the continuing mind-body controversy much confusion comes about through a failure to inquire whether the term "consciousness" is used to mean that kind of consciousness common to all animals or that kind unique to humans.[12]

Anyone with an animal pet knows that Descartes was absurdly wrong in claiming they are automatons without some kind of consciousness. But is it not equally absurd to suppose that human consciousness, manifestly displayed in the immense variety of human cultures and especially in the critical thinking of scientific investigation, can simply be reduced to that exhibited in instinctual animal behavior? Do we not observe a vast difference in the sort of consciousness required while driving to stop at a stoplight and our consciousness of how to answer the arguments that a companion in the car is making against what we have just said?

A second way to gain insight into the difference between intellectual cognition and sense cognition is to consider the two different kinds of *awareness* or *consciousness* they involve. Sense cognition makes us aware of objects but not of our awareness of being conscious. We cannot see ourselves seeing, or hear ourselves hearing. The reason for this is that the eyes with which we see are material organs, each located in a definite place. I cannot see the back of my neck. Even if I try to so process my primary sense data by using the images provided by my secondary senses of memory, synthetic sense, imagination, or evaluative sense, I cannot at the same time know an image and myself knowing that image.

By contrast, *self-consciousness* is precisely the ability to know myself knowing something; I can know that I know that I know. This was the element of truth in Descartes' *Cogito ergo sum*, namely, that human persons are self-conscious; but this does not mean, as Descartes seemed to think, that we can have a pure self-consciousness indepen-

12. Paul Thagard, "Cognitive Science," *Stanford Philosophical Encyclopedia* (Stanford, CA: Metaphysics Research Lab, 2010), accessed November 22, 2012.

dent of our primary and secondary senses. If you try just to think of yourself thinking you will find yourself thinking of nothing (as some practitioners of "centering meditation" discover) and suppose this to be a mystical experience. Human thought is not itself its own direct object. To know that I think, I must think about something. Even if I think about my thinking, that thinking must be about something other than my thinking it.

Human intelligence in this bodily life, therefore, is not perfectly transparent to itself in such a way that I can know the essence of my soul simply by introspection, as does a pure spirit. Insofar as I know who I am, it must be done in the same way I would know anything else, by seeing how I behave and gradually sorting out my core identity from the tangle of irrelevant and superficial aspects of myself. What introspection can reveal that is not available to others is what goes on in my internal imagination and other sense data processing powers. But that is not intellectual activity as such. Thus our self-consciousness is always background awareness unless we make an effort to objectify it, and then the content we find is the essential content discovered in our sense data.[13]

What makes this self-consciousness so different from some kind of sense cognition is that it cannot be an act of our external senses, nor of our introspective secondary senses, since those always present us with images that are *quantitative*. You cannot image a rose that does not have petals that occupy different places, nor imagine a sound that does not take time. Self-awareness, as I have described it, however, cannot be quantitative, since then we would be aware of only a part of our awareness, not of it as a single whole. Since, as we saw in Chapter 2, quantity is the basic property of all material things, my intellectual acts as well as the power that makes them possible and makes me truly human, unlike my sense cognition, is not primarily the act of

13. This is the error of what is called "Transcendental Thomism," which attempts to reconcile the epistemology of Immanuel Kant with that of St. Thomas by making our knowledge of the thinking, willing subject prior to our knowledge of sensible things.

my brain, which is, however, its primary instrument. The proper object of human intellection is the essences of material things, which we know only through our external senses and the data those senses supply to be processed in the brain. This processing by the brain begins the work of abstracting what is essential from what is not by collecting similar images in nominalist fashion; only our intelligences can complete that work, by producing truly abstract, essential concepts.

This processing can be partly unconscious, as is well illustrated by studies that have been made on "creative thinking." A famous example is the discovery by the chemist Kekulé of what is called the "benzene ring," an important feature of some molecules.[14] He had for many days tried without success to figure out what the chemical data seemed to be saying. Then one morning as Kekulé was waking up and was still half-dreaming, he seemed to see a snake run across the floor and suddenly seize its tail in its mouth and roll out of the room! At that moment he had the insight that the atomic units in the molecule form a closed figure. Evidently all the time, even when he was asleep, his mind had been working somehow, probing his secondary senses for an appropriate image, which finally emerged as the weird snake dream that supplied an analogy or model for the benzene ring. Such stories are told about many discoveries, and what they show is that an inventor works a long time on a problem without the intellectual insight that would solve it; then, often suddenly and during a time when maybe the inventor is thinking of something else, the right *image* pops up that makes possible his intellectual insight that answers his problem.

This process is the basis of the technique of "brainstorming" in which a group of persons trying to solve a problem keep proposing ideas without criticism, even ideas that seem wild and foolish, in the hopes that eventually someone will really see the answer.[15] This shows

14. John H. Lienhard, "Inventing Benzene," last modified 1997, http://www.uh.edu/engines/epi265.htm.

15. Daniel Kahneman, *Thinking, Fast and Slow* (New York: Farrar, Straus, and Giroux, 2011) and "A Perspective on Judgment and Choice: Mapping Bounded Rationality," *American Pychologist* 58, no. 9 (2003): 697–720.

that the sense data processing powers have a certain independence of the intellect and can continue to work through chains of association, analogies, and comparison of images even when the problem is not the focus of our attention.

That human consciousness, unlike that of animals, is *reflexive* and hence non-material is supported by the famous theorems of Kurt Gödel,[16] to which I referred in Chapter 2, according to which it is impossible to prove that any logically formal system is complete or consistent without adding further axioms in the terms of that system. Aquinas argues that through our senses we can consciously know material objects, but only through our non-material intelligence can we know that we ourselves are existent beings who are in the process of knowing these objects and we can know that we know that we know ... *ad infinitum*.

In brief, such perfect reflexivity is impossible for a material substance, even for our human brain, because material things have as their first property quantity, defined as "having parts that have only common boundaries," and hence a quantified object cannot have all its points present to each other, that is, cannot be self-conscious, since that is to be totally present to one's self performing an intellectual act.[17] It is this argument that is especially pertinent to refuting the possibility of artificial intelligence.[18]

16. See the essay of the English philosopher J. R. Lucas, "Minds, Machines and Goedel," last modified 1991, http://cogprints.org/356/00/lucas.html.

17. Note that the totality of reflective self-consciousness does not mean "totally self-comprehensive" since our human knowledge of objects is never perfectly exhaustive. Descartes was wrong to think that *cogito ergo sum* means that I am present to myself as a "clear and distinct idea." There are many degrees of self-consciousness, and in this life they are all very imperfect because of the dependence of the intelligence on the senses.

18. See also David Chalmers and David Bourget, *Contemporary Philosophy of Mind: An Annotated Bibliography*, last modified 2009, http://consc.net/biblio.html.

Comprehensivity

Aquinas's fifth argument for the spirituality of the intelligence is based on the fact that while the human sense organs can be overwhelmed, our intellect cannot. For example, a sense organ can be beset by the intensity of its object in contrast to the intelligence, which is perfected by more profound abstract, universal concepts. This is related to his discussion of angelic intelligence: the higher the angel is in the celestial hierarchy, the fewer—not more—ideas the angel has, because each idea is of such great comprehension.[19] This assertion is supported by the observation that the work of great geniuses often flows from some one insight they acquire early in their career, as for a eminent example, the fact that Aquinas, apparently when he was still a pupil of St. Albert the Great, who treated Plato and Aristotle as co-equal authorities, grasped the superiority of Aristotle to Plato. In Aquinas's own case it is often claimed that his original intuition, evident in his first philosophical work *De Ente et Essentia,* is the "real distinction of essence and existence." In my opinion, more fundamental still was his profound recognition that all our natural human knowledge rests on the senses, a point in Aristotle not clearly seen by earlier readings of the Stagirite, even by St. Albertus.

Intelligence and Reasoning

I have used the term "insight" (Latin *intuitus*, intuition, to see into something), but actually the term "intelligence" (Latin *intellectus*) has the same meaning. Aquinas makes the point that human intelligence is characterized by two types of function, *insight* and *reasoning.* What is basic is not reasoning but insight, the first act of the intelligence, which processes sense data so as to separate out what is essential to a problem and apply it abstractly to many instances of some general concept. For example, when a teacher draws several triangles on the

19. *Summa theologiae* I, q. 55, a. 3.

blackboard and then points out that although they differ in size and in their angles, all are "three-sided plane figures" and a pupil "gets the point" and becomes able to study the properties that all triangles—whether isosceles, equilateral, or scalene, and of any size—possess.

Reasoning, on the other hand, presupposes insight into at least two propositions (the second act of the intellect, which affirms or denies a predicate of a subject) and uses these as premises to *infer* other truths implied by these two propositions (a syllogism, the third act of the intellect). If we had perfect intellects, as Plato and Descartes supposed and as Aquinas thought angels have, all of our intellectual thought would be independent of sense data and based on innate ideas, and reasoning would be unnecessary. In fact, however, human intelligence depends on sense data and has to move intellectually from very general and vague truths to more and more specific truths about things.

It is a common error to suppose that Aristotle and his followers, such as Aquinas, based their thinking on *deduction.* Modern scientific thought began with Francis Bacon (1561–1626), who emphasized *induction.* In Aristotelian logic, however, deductive reasoning must proceed from two premises, each of which must be known to be true. They may be known to be true because they are conclusions of some previous deduction, but ultimately they must all be based on abstraction from particular cases known *inductively* from sense data and known intellectually by insight into this data. Thus all reasoning ultimately rests on induction, not inductive *reasoning*, but intellectual *analysis* of the essential, universal features of particular cases known empirically. Moreover, in deduction, the minor premise cannot be deduced from the major premise but must be known independently. Even in mathematics, conclusions are not known simply through deduction from a few axioms. The axioms state some truth about a very large class of things, but to know that some true statement applies to some smaller class of things, one must first know, either directly from the sense data, or by intuition, or by some other proof that rests ultimately on direct intuition from sense data, that this smaller class is included in the larger class. This requires a definition of the smaller class that can be obtained only by intuition.

To take another example, I can know that a crocodile is an animal because it lives and moves, but I cannot deduce from this that it is carnivorous. I can find that out either by watching it eat meat, or by reasoning that it would not have the kind of teeth it has if it were not carnivorous. But that reasoning is based on the premise that only certain kinds of teeth are appropriate for meat-eating, and the truth of that premise I also have to find out by empirically examining the teeth of other carnivorous animals. Thus all our knowledge ultimately traces to intellectual insights derived from sense cognition.

As Francis Bacon and modern logicians influenced by him use "induction," it means not such direct insight based on empirical data but a kind of reasoning, opposite to deduction, in which one examines various cases and then reasons to the conclusion that they belong to the same class of things. To be certain, such an inductive argument must apply to all member of a class, which can seldom be achieved. For example, to be sure that all cats have claws, we would have to examine every cat that exists. Although such reasoning is of some use in arriving at the analytical insight that some features of a thing are essential and others not, it cannot replace direct intuition, because it presupposes intuitions.

Therefore, human intellection is not what logicians call a "formal system" of logical deduction from a small set of arbitrary axioms. The mathematician David Hilbert (1862–1943) in the last century proposed the model of such a formal system and thought that mathematics could be reduced to it. Bertrand Russell (1872–1970), in turn, proposed the idea that mathematics itself could be reduced to pure logic.[20]

20. See A. D. Irvine, "Bertrand Russell," *Stanford Encyclopedia of Philosophy,* last modified Mar. 29, 2010, http://plato.stanford.edu/entries/russell/, and A. D. Irvine, "Russell's Paradox," *Stanford Encyclopedia of Philosophy,* last modified May 27, 2009, http://plato.stanford.edu/entries/russell-paradox.

For a time the school of logical positivism, which originated with the so-called "Vienna Circle," of which Rudolf Carnap (1891–1970) was a leader, thought that all of objective knowledge, which they held was limited to empirical science, could be formulated as such a formal system.[21] These philosophers thought that such a formal system would eliminate all ambiguity of language and at last realize the Cartesian ideal of "clear and distinct ideas." Gödel's theorems, mentioned above, radically eliminated logical positivism.

For Aristotle and Aquinas the psychological reason for rejecting purely formal systems is that human concepts, even mathematical ones, since they are derived from sense data that is always inadequate to the totality of reality, are not perfectly "clear and distinct."[22] A concept taken apart from its grounding in sense data has a vagueness that results from its processing by the internal senses, and we can never be sure that on further inspection it may not turn out to be a contradictory notion like "square circle." If it is contradictory, nothing can be known from it. For an insight to provide certain knowledge free from contradiction, the images from which it is derived must be grounded in the reality of sense objects, a reality that cannot be contradictory since it is real.

Therefore, although every science is a logical system, it is always incomplete. This does not mean that its axioms are incomplete, but their full significance is made known only by a continuing process of applying them to sensible reality, which they illuminate. Thus, for example, the principle of causality ("Whatever changes is changed by

21. See Mauro Murzi, "Vienna Circle," *Internet Encyclopedia of Philosophy*, last modified Aug 28, 2004, http://www.iep.utm.edu/v/viennaci.htm, and Mauro Murzi, "Rudolph Carnap," "Vienna Circle," *Internet Encyclopedia of Philosophy*, last modified April 12, 2001, http://www.iep.utm.edu/c/carnap.htm.

22. For example, pi, the ratio of the radius of any circle to its circumference, is "irrational"—that is, it can never be expressed by a whole number and in its decimal form the numbers to the right of zero never repeat the same pattern. The legend is that when the Pythagoreans discovered this, they were so shocked that they require all members of their society to take an oath never to reveal it to outsiders!

another entity that is its cause") is true in natural science for all time, but what it can tell us about our world can never be exhausted as long as we continue to observe new things about the changes in the world.

Since mathematics is the logical model for other sciences, then, Gödel's theorems show us that human intelligence cannot be an action of the brain as such. Any computer is a logic machine whose program is actually a formal system. If human intelligence were based on a purely formal system (actually a processing of information like that done by the internal senses in the brain), a computer program could be made to do what human intelligence does.[23] But no matter how good our computer or how elaborate its program, a human inventor could improve on them. Our intelligence, therefore, cannot be the work of the brain but must be an immaterial power. To be immaterial is to be real but non-quantitative, since quantity is the first property of material things.

From Comparative to Personal Psychology

By these five arguments of Aquinas it can be established empirically and with certitude that human intelligence is specifically different from animal "intelligence" and cannot be a proper act of the human body, not even of the remarkable human brain. This brain is the seat of the secondary senses, which, together with the sense organs that are the seats of primary senses, are the material instruments of the human spiritual intelligence. That intelligence is a power of the human spiritual soul. We humans, therefore, are primarily spiritual beings and only secondarily, although essentially, part of the material universe. As spiritual we, along with pure spirits, form the superior part of the total universe, although we humans are the least members of that self-conscious community of spiritual *persons*.

During the twentieth century, the terms "person" and "personal-

23. Unless Gerald Edelman's *Neural Darwinism* is true; see Chapter 4.

ism" were given much attention, especially in the face of the "totalitarian" doctrines of Marxism and National Socialism that subordinated the members of a state to the military, economic, and racialist views of its leaders and their personal ambitions. In recent times, in the context of the abortion controversy, some have denied the personhood of unborn children and even of defective infants; further, some have ascribed human rights to animals, as if they were persons. The views of Aristotle and Aquinas on when human personal life begins—so-called "delayed hominization," based on the sound principles I discussed in Chapter 2 but whose application must be corrected in view of modern embryological findings—have also been widely debated. Proponents of a "freedom of choice" to use direct abortion have claimed that a "human being"—an organism with a human genome and as such a member of the human species—is not necessarily a "person" having "rights." They think that "person" should be taken to mean someone actually capable of intelligent and free acts. This would logically mean, however, that children are not true persons until they are six or seven, that the mentally defective may not be persons, and that the comatose (and we ourselves when asleep!) are not persons.

As I have argued at length elsewhere,[24] the human organism begins with the completion of the fertilization of the ovum and the constitution of the unique genome of a human person. The nucleus containing this genome is the physical prime mover of this new organism,[25] which then produces the so-called "pre-embryo" that implants itself in the mother's uterus and becomes the fetus with the beginnings of a brain, and finally the born infant. All these are the identically same human organism at different stages of its self-development guided by the same prime mover. Although identical twinning can occur in this pro-

24. "When Does a Human Person Begin to Exist?" *The Ashley Reader: Redeeming Reason* (Naples, FL: Sapientia Press, 2006), chap. 20, 329–68.

25. See Chapter 2 on the notion of prime mover.

cess, producing a second self-developing person, this second person began when one or a few totipotential cells became abnormally separated from the original organism.

When then did the original organism and afterwards its twin become ensouled? Since by the term "soul" (*psyche, anima*) Aristotle and Aquinas mean simply the form or actuality of correlative potentiality of the body, this ensoulment is a process determined to be the term of the natural process of reproduction. But what agent is capable of producing a spiritual being? Physical causes act by actualizing a previous matter, and hence the father of the child is a physical cocause with the mother of the production of its body, but he cannot be the proper cause of the production of its spiritual soul, because such a soul, as such, has no material potentiality. To explain this remarkable human procreation, therefore, we must have recourse to the First Cause of the universe, who alone can create *ex nihilo*. This solution is not to resort to a "God of the gaps" but, as we showed in Chapter 2, is established as part of the foundations of natural science, and to reject it would be to make natural science contradict itself.

Nor is this direct creation by God of each human soul a miracle or divine intervention in the order of nature. As part of the natural order of the universe, the First Cause produces animals using the instrumentality of their natural parents, as he does for the whole human species, but in the special case of the human species the First Cause completes a natural process by a direct act of creation of the spiritual soul, just as the First Cause creates the universe as a whole. If pure spirits exist they too have been created *ex nihilo* and their intelligence is of such a power that it has no need of a body, as does the intelligence of human persons, to supply it with information, but possesses this information innately.[26]

Up to this point, our discussion of the human person has per-

26. This is why Jacques Maritain said that Plato and Descartes "angelicized" the human person by their idealistic dualism.

tained to natural science and is part of comparative psychology. We have discussed the differences between the human animal and other animals, but in terms of information that is gathered from their empirically observable behavior. *None of comparative psychology's claims depend on metaphysics or on religious faith.* To obtain a more positive understanding of the nature of human intelligence, and the free will that flows from it, we must transcend natural science and comparative psychology and enter into a properly metaphysical analysis.

Metaphysics presupposes that natural science has established the existence of a spiritual First Cause; the part of metaphysics that treats of the human soul as spiritual, which I have called *personal psychology*, presupposes that comparative psychology has already shown how and why human persons differ from other animals by having spiritual souls. To continue this analysis, therefore, we must follow the method proper to metaphysics, which is to use analogies between the material effects and their spiritual causes so as to extend empirically derived concepts to include spiritual realities.

In reverse order, owners of pets often treat these animals as personal friends. A researcher on dog psychology concluded, "Your pet loves you because he thinks you are a dog." Conversely, in treating of animal psychology, we can understand them to a degree from our own self-conscious experience, because we are in part like them, although ultimately we are quite different. Thus any metaphysical discussion, which is always rooted in the empirical, ought to be rather modest in its attempt to transcend those roots. And yet, since in fact our intelligences *are* intellectual, they are not limited to reflection on material things but can reflect on themselves in analogical terms derived from material things and arrive at some genuine certitudes.

Thus we can be sure, that we are each a single substance—not, as Descartes thought, two substances, a body and a mind. There is no reason that a single substance cannot have higher and lower powers (pertaining to the category of quality). For example, animals have sensory powers that are of a higher order in evolution than their vegetative powers of nourishment. Hence the fact that a human soul is spiritual does not contradict the fact that it has, not only the spiritual powers of intelligence and free will, but also the lower animal powers that require a body. The correlation of the two levels of powers (spiritual soul and animal body) maintains the unity of the human substance: our spiritual powers are of such a low rank that they need the instrument of the sense powers and hence of a material body to operate. Again this correlative dependence resembles the way our brain depends on our limbs and muscles to carry out its orders and would die if it could not get these orders executed.

Aquinas's analysis of the power of the human intelligence goes well beyond that achieved by Aristotle who in his *De Anima* proves the existence of human spiritual intellect and simply quits there, without ever taking up the question in his *Metaphysics*; his later Greek and Muslim commentators tended to fill this metaphysical gap with Neo-Platonic dualism. Aquinas shows that the human intelligence is twofold: the "agent intellect" and what (rather confusingly) he calls the "possible intellect,"[27] meaning that it is able (*posse*) to actually know any object, but must be activated to do so by the agent intellect. The agent intellect of each person is the prime, or unmoved, mover of the person and is always in act, because it is kept in act by the First Cause, who created the human soul in act, like a light that never goes out. It acts analogously to the way a light makes a visible object visible: the agent intellect makes objects intelligible to the possible intellect. This relationship between the agent and possible intellects presupposes the existence of an image perceived by the secondary senses in the brain, which has been derived ultimately from the primary senses in their primary sense organs. When such an image is not presented to the possible intellect, it remains merely potentially knowing, and the agent intellect, although it remains in act, remains unconscious be-

27. On the history of this terminology see http://nd.edu/Departments/Maritain/etext/gc2_59a.htm (accessed June 15, 2011).

cause it has nothing to actualize. Only after death can our spiritual intelligence, freed from dependence on the body, know itself directly, both as to its power of intelligence and as to the substance on which that power depends, as do pure spirits.

Jacques Maritain, in a very original essay,[28] showed how this Thomistic analysis of intelligence can be used to explain "natural mysticism," a phenomenon so widely reported and so basic to long-enduring religions such as Hinduism, Buddhism, and Taoism that it can hardly be an illusion. By techniques such as yoga, the natural mystic, while remaining awake, gradually suppresses the activity of the secondary senses, thus emptying the mind of images and with them the intellectual concepts that depend on them. What remains in our intellect is the indirect awareness of our spiritual existence that is always present in our direct knowledge of abstract concepts, including in the reflexive knowledge of one's self. This awareness is "dark," that is, indistinct, but, with fixed attention on it, can be very intense.

Sometimes, also, this self-awareness can be spontaneous and occur in the midst of other activities, but because of its indistinctness it can be interpreted in many ways and may become the object of delusions that lead to a false mysticism. For instance, the poet Edgar Allen Poe, who had such experiences frequently, interpreted them to mean that he was God, a notion that so terrified him that it confirmed him in his alcoholism!

One of the intellectual tasks proper to metaphysics, because it embraces the whole of knowledge, is to classify our knowledge into different but related sciences. Aquinas, therefore, explains that in ordinary thinking and speaking and in natural science we have four types of abstraction that underlie the ordering of the sciences:[29]

28. "The Natural Mystical Experience and the Void," in *Redeeming the Time* (London: G. Bles, The Centenary Press, 1943), 225–55. The American edition (New York: Charles Scribner's Sons) has the title *Ransoming the Time.*

29. On the ordering of the sciences, see St. Thomas Aquinas, *Commentary on Aristotle's Metaphysics* translation and introduction by C. I. Litzinger, OP; foreword by

1. We can omit from what we empirically observe only what individualizes the object known. This is true also of practical knowledge, whether ethical or technological, since these disciplines state general rules but must consider all real aspects of human behavior or technological construction.
2. We make a very different type of abstraction when we think mathematically, because then we not only universalize our concepts as in natural science but also leave out all the properties of the object, except that we retain its quantity and, in continuous quantities, its correlative quality of figure—for example, that it is a circle or a square, etc.; or, in the case of discrete quantities, its correlative quality of limit—for example, the last unit counted in a number that limits a number so as to distinguish it as greater than the preceding number but less than the one that follows. This type of abstraction is legitimate because, as we saw in Chapter 2, quantity is the first property of material things.
3. In metaphysics, we not only universalize, we also abstract from the distinction between material and spiritual things and thus use only "transcendental" concepts, which include what is analogically common to the spiritual causes of things and their material effects, such as "one," "true," and "good."
4. A fourth type of abstraction is found in logic (taken in its broad sense and including linguistics and semiotics). Unlike natural science, practical knowledge, mathematics, and metaphysics that all concern real, existent objects, logic abstracts from real existence and considers only the mental relations we construct in our minds to order our thoughts or the linguistic signs that are equivalent to these syntactical relations. Like

---

Ralph McInerny, revised edition, 1995, *Proemium* and *The Division and Methods of the Sciences, Questions V and VI of the Commentary on Boethius 'De Trinitate,'* translated by Armand Mauer, 4th ed. (Toronto: Pontifical Institute of Medieval Studies, 1984).

> metaphysics, logic transcends the material and this led Plato to confuse logic with what Aristotle was to call *metaphysical objects*. (Later, and similarly, Bertrand Russell too would confuse mathematics and logic.)

The history of Thomism has been greatly affected by the work of Tomas de Vio, Cardinal Cajetan (1469–1534), the great commentator on Thomas's works. It was he who introduced the term "three *degrees* of abstraction": first, that of natural science; second, mathematics; and third, metaphysics and logic. Although he understood the degrees correctly, some writers have been led to treat these "degrees" as three levels of the same sort of abstraction, and a certain confusion between metaphysics and logic has resulted. It is important to keep clear that all these sciences use the first type of abstraction, namely, universalization, or they would not be *scientiae*, since *scientia* is of the universal. Furthermore all are about reality, except logic, which concerns only mental constructs. Again, mathematical abstraction (which is the only abstraction for which Aristotle himself used the term "abstract") is not (as Plato thought) a step toward metaphysical thinking but concerns only the property of quantity, which pertains to the objects treated in natural science. Finally, metaphysics divides and orders all the sciences, and thus it does not exclude any of the objects that they study. It also includes the real, spiritual objects that we can explain only by analogy from their empirically observed material effects.

The distinction of the sciences is established only by critical thinking that carefully seeks the basis and validity of our different kinds of knowledge. According to Aristotle and Aquinas, metaphysics is so eminent a science that it should be studied only by the mature. It might therefore seem that ordinary people never think metaphysically. But ordinary people know that they are self-conscious persons, even though, as we have been arguing in this chapter, the study of self-consciousness pertains *properly* to personal psychology, and that is properly part of metaphysics, since it treats of a spiritual reality.

Now, someone can make change of money without having critically studied mathematics; in similar fashion, one can think about the First Cause, which is supremely personal and spiritual, without being a metaphysician. This "common sense" sort of knowledge, however, because of its lack of precision can often lead to errors in reasoning. Thus when the Bible calls God "the Rock" or "Spirit" (which literally means "wind"), one might think He is material.

On the other hand, it is inadequate to say that metaphysics as a science rests on common sense, since a bare common sense notion of metaphysics has caused some analytic philosophers to reject it as "nonsense." Thus for personal psychology we must be careful to treat human thought with scientific, and therefore metaphysical, rigor, although it is also sound "common sense." This becomes particularly clear when we consider how the spirituality of the human intellect makes it possible for us to transcend the material determinism of the brain and make *free* decisions.

Human Freedom

Subhuman animals, as we have seen, are not free, because they live by innate instincts or routines (which are instincts that have been modified by learning but that do not result in the remarkable variety of cultural inventions that human animals exhibit). Humans, however, have manifested that they are free: if they were not free, how could they have invented new languages or developed such a variety of technologies and cultures? And why, if humans were not free, would we all condemn some human behavior as bad and commend some as good? Therefore, just as we empirically identified a number of affective powers that depend on our senses and which, when we become aware of the changes they work in our bodies, we call "emotions" or "feelings," so also we must infer from human behavior that we have an affective freedom that depends on our intellectual cognition. This driving power that follows on intellectual knowledge is called the "will," which cannot act until the intelligence presents some good (goal, value) to be sought by willed actions.

The term "freedom" of the will—freedom of decision—that we use so often but sometimes confusedly, has three main senses: (1) Freedom *from coercion.* Often our choice of means to an end is limited by external forces that prevent us from taking the means we would prefer. It is an unfortunate aspect of modern culture that too often this meaning of freedom is regarded as the most important or even the only meaning of freedom. Yet Robinson Crusoe on the desert island can hardly be the epitome of a free man. (2) *Ethical* freedom is the freedom to do what our reason tells us is realistically good for ourselves and for others. We will be discussing ethical freedom in the next chapter. (3) *Psychological* freedom is, the power to intellectually understand that there are a number of alternative means to attain a given end, each of which means is perceived to have advantages and disadvantages, so that in order to seek that end effectively we must choose among these means those which, in a given situation, are at least reasonably effective. *Mental illness is predominantly a defect in such psychological freedom, just as physical health is commonly a defect in regular bodily functions.*

Freedom of decision in senses 2 and 3 ultimately rests on some theoretical truth about the nature of what we choose or refuse; flowing from *theoretical* truth (what is), freedom of decision is proximately *practical.* It concerns two kinds of choices: *ethical* or absolute (doing) and *technical* or conditional. Ethical truth is about human actions with regard to the means that lead to the goal of true human happiness. The ethical judgment "I should choose to do this because it will lead me to genuine happiness" is absolute, since it can never be reasonable to do what will make one unhappy. Technological truth, on the other hand, is conditional, since it concerns actions that produce something that is not directly itself an element of happiness but only an instrument that can be used (but also may be abused) to help me attain happiness. The most obvious example is food, which I need to live, yet which can be consumed in quantities (too much or too little) that compromise the bodily health that is an important element of human happiness.

Technological truth can produce *useful* objects—a hamburger, a computer, an automobile—or objects of *contemplation*, such as music or sculpture, or a mixture of these, such as architecture, which houses us but is also beautiful, or football which serves health but also entertains.

Since freedom is the means to a goal, it has a certain order of choice. First, one must choose a "value system," that is, a logically ordered set of goals that will make one truly happy because they satisfy one's innate needs in a fitting way. The failure to set such unified goals in a realistic manner can only lead to contradictory and destructive results. Second, one must make a reasonable choice of the means that will agree with this value system, in the vicissitudes of one's life, always sacrificing lesser to more important values.

An important fact about psychological freedom of the will is that it cannot be completely eradicated by external coercion. Martyrs suffer torture, dismemberment, and death at the hands of those who attempt to coerce them to deny what they believe—and they still refuse. Moreover, even persons who are drug-addicted can seek treatment and thus become free of their addiction; similarly, persons with a vice, such as laziness, can succeed in overcoming it by constant effort. Yet psychological freedom can be limited by external and internal conflicts, and it can be entirely overridden by psychoses or by physiological compulsions that prevent the person from perceiving alternative ways of acting and that therefore make free choice impossible. A drug addict, at a time when he is desperate for a fix, may be able to think of nothing else and so is no longer free, although when he is feeling better he may be able to choose to get treatment. Schizophrenic or severely depressed or manic persons may behave irrationally at times yet at other times be able to understand their condition and take medications to help them remain sane.

Only severely demented or unconscious persons lack all psychological freedom. All of us when we are asleep lack such freedom because, though our secondary senses may produce dreams, our intelligence that gives us contact with reality is not functioning or is functioning only in a borderline state. It is unfortunate, as is apparent from certain criminal trials, that persons can commit very terrible crimes yet not be morally responsible, because they are not free by reason of one of the conditions just mentioned. Our present laws count as crimes acts by persons who can "tell right from wrong," but a person may know that something is wrong and yet not have the freedom to choose not to perform that act, or at least to have very much diminished freedom and therefore diminished responsibility.

It should also be recognized that, since we all live within a particular culture and in a particular social situation, even when our intellect is operating well and we have basic psychological freedom, that freedom is limited by the understanding of the alternatives of life open to us recognized in that culture. Although some can get free of the limits of their cultural perspective, that is not easy.

Cognitive psychotherapy is based on the clinical observation that many people are caught in certain habits of thought that blind them to alternative ways of thinking and acting. For example, adults who were raised by parents who criticized them for every mistake and never praised them for their achievements may have grown up with the habit of thinking of themselves as failures. When faced with any problem, such adults, instead of thinking how they can meet the challenge, are preoccupied with fears of failure and what excuse they must make when they fail, as they are sure they will. Cognitive therapy aims to help people recognize that such patterns of thought, although based on real failures, ignore equally real successes. As we will see, a good deal of confusion of thought arises in our culture from the idea that freedom is the ability to do whatever one feels like, rather than the ability to do what one knows to be really constructive. In a permissive, hedonistic, and impulsive society, people lacking adequate discipline and foresight become enslaved to their sense drives, and self-destructive.

The existence of human freedom has often been questioned. Even in ancient times the Stoics, as determinists in science, maintained that human behavior follows rigid laws just like the rest of nature; they also, however, proposed a severe code of morality. This sort of determinism has been favored by radical behaviorists, such as J. B. Watson (1878–1958) and especially B. F. Skinner (1904–90), who argued that human actions can be explained, just as one explains animal behavior, by innate instincts modified by "operant conditioning." Although radical behaviorism dominated much of twentieth-century psychology, it was largely discredited by the end of the century. Replacing behaviorism, the recent development of sociobiology under the leadership of E. O. Wilson (b. 1929)[30] is based on Darwinian evolutionary theory and so ascribes much of human behavior to instincts derived from our non-human ancestors.

Neither radical behaviorism nor sociobiology does full justice to the great difference between human and subhuman animal behavior that I have analyzed in this chapter. Nevertheless, behaviorism and sociobiology can be credited with uncovering a great deal about instinctual patterns that humans share with animals at the level of sense cognition and sense drives. As I have argued, there is such a thing as human nature, which is a given, and human freedom must operate within the limits of our fundamental human needs or it will be destructive. We need to eat and we have a normal drive to eat, but unless our learned eating habits supply us with certain kinds and amounts of food, we die of anorexia or morbid obesity.

30. See E. O. Wilson, *Sociobiology: The New Synthesis* (Cambridge: Harvard University Press: 1975); and Ullica Segerstråle, *Defenders of the Truth: The Battle for Science in the Sociology Debate and Beyond* (Oxford: Oxford University Press, 2000). Wilson's critics accused him of racism and sexism because of what they thought were the political implications of his views, but some of those critics could be accused of Marxist tendencies.

Conclusion

The facts of human and animal behavior show that animals and human persons have much in common, yet they also differ remarkably. The human brain has so evolved that it makes possible ensoulment by a spiritual soul directly produced *ex nihilo* by the First Cause. This spiritual soul directs its physical powers that are required for the unified function of its body and the acquisition of information from its bodily primary and secondary senses. Moreover, through the spiritual intellectual and will powers, the soul can analyze and freely use this information to satisfy human needs. The human person thus exists on the borderline between the physical and spiritual parts of our universe, and so it must be studied first by comparative psychology (which is part of natural science) and second by personal psychology (which works by analogy from the results of comparative psychology).

six

SEEKING PERFECTION

The Nature of Morality

Presumably psychotherapists have it as their aim to help people become optimally functioning human persons with skills to cope with the major problems of life. They realize, no doubt, that psychotherapy cannot do this whole job but can at best only help people overcome certain conflicts within themselves that are holding them back from developing their full potential. Yet even to attempt such first steps in helping persons become fully functioning, it is necessary to have some model of what is the ultimate goal: what it is to be a really good human being? Amazingly enough, one can read innumerable works on psychology and psychotherapy without ever running across any such model. And so in this chapter I will try to present such a model, based on what we have learned about human persons throughout history and in present research. To construct such a model we must first ask, what do we mean by humanly good or moral behavior? In attempting to respond to that question, we shall consider first the nature of ethics.

Ethics is a practical kind of knowing that guides free choices of means to some good end or goal. As we saw in the last chapter, ethics is distinguished from the theoretical disciplines of natural science, mathematics, and metaphysics and so also from comparative psychology (which is part of natural science) and from personal psychology (which is part of metaphysics). It is also to be distinguished from the *technologies*, which produce instruments for good human living but do not make life decisions, as the ethical sciences do.

Actually, because of a person's three main goals in life, ethical science is three closely related yet distinct disciplines: individual ethics, family ethics, and social ethics or politics; the latter two will be the concern of the next chapter. As will be seen in the course of the present chapter, individual ethics presupposes important truths from natural science and the comparative psychology included in it. Individual ethics also provides a necessary reason for seeking to know metaphysics and the problems of personal psychology that metaphysics includes.

The practical goal that ethics guides persons to achieve—what ancient and medieval ethicists have called in Greek *eudaimonia* (spiritual good) and in Latin *summum bonum* (supreme good)—is the *integral fulfillment* of their natural needs, in the order of importance of those needs. Because the purpose of ethics is practical guidance, it begins with principles that are *universal* rules, and this gives it the appearance of a theoretical science; it ends, though, in free, *individual* decisions that are not universal but take account of the unique circumstances of practical decisions. Each of the three kinds of ethics belongs to the type of knowing called "prudential," and so, taken as a whole and in spite of its theoretical part, ethics is a thoroughly practical skill, and its value is practical, not theoretical.

Moral Development

We all make choices about what to do and not to do, and we debate within ourselves and with others what is the "right" and the "wrong" kind of behavior. Human language is filled with imperatives: "Do this, don't do that." The psychologist Lawrence Kohlberg (1927–87)[1] developed a theory of normal moral development for which he claimed empirical evidence based on observing how people think when presented with ethical decisions. According to this theory, six stages can be distinguished.

The first stage is "pre-conventional" and has two phases. In the first the child thinks only in terms of rewards and punishment dealt out by an authority figure for its obedience or disobedience. This stage corresponds to Freud's notion of the superego or a set of unreasoned norms learned by the child that later become unconscious but remain a source of guilt. In the second phase of this first kind of moral reasoning, the child begins to think for itself, but only in terms of individual self-interest.

The second major stage moral thinking is "conventional"—first a phase in which the child looks for approval or disapproval from an authority figure or peers, then a latter phase, in which he conforms to some notion of "law and order."

The final or mature stage is "post-conventional" and in this the adult (according to Kohlberg) thinks either in terms of a "social contract" or still more maturely in terms of a "principled conscience."

This theory has been strongly criticized because it is too rigidly schematic to fit every individual's development. Kohlberg's description of the post-conventional, mature conscience, moreover, reflects his own Kantian understanding of morality, which is very questionable. Nevertheless, the main lines of the theory correctly describe the progress from a child's concern about being rewarded with candy or avoiding punishment through a maturing consciousness of what is socially acceptable by one's community, to a mature stage of understanding why some kinds of behavior are personally and socially de-

1. *The Meaning and Measurement of Moral Development*, Heinz Werner Lecture Series 13 (Dorchester, MA: Clark University, 1979).

structive whereas others are constructive and fulfilling. It is obvious, both historically and from everyday observation, that many people—perhaps most people—judge what is right and wrong pragmatically by its immediate consequences, whether these be pleasant or painful consequences, or by social pressure or commendation. But when pressed to explain why we consider something moral and praiseworthy or immoral and blamable, even mature people give various answers. Plato, in the *Republic,* begins the dialogue about "What is justice?" by picturing the wise and religious Cephalus, who knows what is just in his own life but cannot explain how it is to be determined and quickly escapes the discussion.

Conscience and Truth

One of the weakest of the answers to ethical problems is that moral right or wrong should be determined by the popular opinion of most people in one's time and place. This is *cultural relativism,* which makes morality a matter of custom or majority opinion. It was taught by the ancient Sophists, against whom Socrates and Plato so strongly objected, and it has been revived today in a radical form by postmodernists. Its weakness is evident when we think of Hitler's Germany. Most of the German people seem to have supported Hitler. Does this mean that what Hitler did was moral? Today when we talk about international justice for war crimes, we evidently must hold that the norms of morality transcend particular cultures.

One way of defending this transcendence was taken by Jean-Jacques Rousseau (1712–88), who argued that all persons have a "moral sense" or instinct that transcends the distortions of culture and even of civilization. He thought that we should be guided by "natural feelings" that are revolted by what is evil but admire what is good and noble. This theory is reflected in much of American political rhetoric that appeals to what "the American People feel" about some issue, on the assumption that the "common people" have sound moral instincts. Again, this theory fails to give us a way of distinguishing between the moral sense and its corruption—take the case of the United States citizens of the Old South who accepted without question that slavery is moral, or the case of all the citizens of our whole nation who accepted the despoiling of the Native Americans. It seems that resting morality on a "moral sense" makes it a matter of animal instinct—but animals are amoral.

Yet for St. Thomas Aquinas there is an element of truth in this notion of natural instinct, for two reasons. First, both the fundamental principles of morality or "primary principles of the natural law" and the secondary principles immediately derived from them, such as fairness or justice, are directly known to the intuition of our practical intelligence and do not need reasoned proof, since we experience their consequences in daily life. For this reason, the Catholic Church often speaks of "the voice of conscience born in every heart."[2] For most people, these principles are obscured only in extreme situations such as occurred in Germany in the wake of the troubles their country experienced following World War I. On this account it would probably be better to speak of the primary and secondary moral principles as "moral insight" rather than "moral sense."

A second element of truth in Rousseau's theory is that the power of processing sense data (which in Chapter 5 was called the "evaluative sense" in animals and the "cogitative sense" or "animal intelligence" in humans) prepares our intellectual acts of free decision by presenting images as pleasant or unpleasant. For instance, to most

2. John Paul II, in his encyclical *The Splendor of Truth* (*Veritatis Splendor,* n. 54), wrote: "Man's sanctuary: The relationship between man's freedom and God's law is most deeply lived out in the 'heart' of the person, in his moral conscience. As the Second Vatican Council observed: 'In the depths of his conscience man detects a law which he does not impose on himself, but which holds him to obedience. Always summoning him to love good and avoid evil, the voice of conscience can when necessary speak to his heart more specifically: 'do this, shun that'. For man has in his heart a law written by God. To obey it is the very dignity of man; according to it he will be judged (cf. Rom 2:14–16)."

people, talk of "murder" first calls up an image of blood and death that is horrible, even before their intellect judges it as a crime. Similarly, the image of "care for a child" brings up an image of tenderness and charm even before one intellectually decides one ought to do something for the child. In these examples we can see that humans need feelings at the sense level that support their moral judgments at the intellectual level. Evidence of the great importance of such natural feelings is found in the abnormal behavior of the *sociopath*, that is, a person who seems to have no empathy for others or emotional reaction to situations of moral decision.[3]

Another form of Rousseau's theory, which is defended by arguments different from those he used, is the "emotive theory" of morality (or "emotivism") favored by G. E. Moore (1873–1958) and many British philosophers of the analytic school.[4] They were struck by the logical gap between "is" statements such as "Smoking causes cancer" and "ought" statements such as "Do not smoke!" Since the latter kind of imperative statement cannot logically be deduced from the former indicative statement, they argued that, whereas the former can be established on objective evidence, the latter is merely an expression of subjective attitudes and means "I don't like you to smoke."

Oddly, this difficulty has been accepted even by some distinguished and orthodox Catholic moralists such as Germain Grisez,[5] William E. May, and John Finnis, with the result that they attempt to construct ethics on a set of eight or nine intuitively evident, "incommensurable" goods (plurifinalism), rather than on empirically observed human nature and its ordered needs, as did Aristotle and

3. See M. F. Mendez, "The Neurobiology of Moral Behavior: Review and Neuropsychiatric Implications," *CNS Spectr.* 14, no. 11 (November 2009): 608–20.

4. See G. E. Moore, *Principia Ethica* (Amherst, NY: Prometheus Books, 1988, original 1903), and J. O. Urmson, *The Emotive Theory of Ethics* (Oxford: Oxford University Press, 1968).

5. *The Way of the Lord Jesus*, with the help of Joseph M. Boyle Jr. et al. 3 vols. (Chicago: Franciscan Herald Press, 1983–97).

Aquinas. Grisez has also argued that Aquinas's consideration of contemplation as the ultimate goal of human life is too "clerical," since laypersons cannot devote themselves to contemplation, as can the clergy. He also attempts to correlate these ultimate goods with the eight Beatitudes with which Jesus' Sermon the Mount (Matthew, chapters 5 to 7) begins.

I have argued against this view at length elsewhere.[6] Here let me only point out a simple case in which the notion of an "incommensurable good" clearly does not hold. One of Grisez's eight goods is "physical health." How then can a soldier sacrifice his life for his country? Aquinas's view is that, in the natural order, even things that are morally good goals (*bona per se*) are ordered as more or less good, and thus these goods are "commensurable" goods. He and Aristotle did not hold that natural contemplation is the only such good required for happiness, but that other goals can and should, if necessary, be sacrificed to it. Aquinas furthermore identifies as the supreme good the contemplation found in the beatific vision.

Actually G. E. Moore's logical difficulty about the relation of the "ought" to the "is" that has influenced these authors is easily solved. "Ought" or imperative statements cannot be deduced directly from indicative "is" statements. Yet imperative statements have to do with the choice of means to an end or human need, and such needs are not chosen but are fixed by human nature. Thus we can reason from the scientific, theoretical truths that smoking *is* the cause of cancer and cancer *is* a deadly disease, to the conclusion, if the patient wants to live longer he *ought not* to smoke. There is nothing "subjective" about such an imperative. Technological statements such as a doctor's prescription are *conditional,* since the command "Don't smoke" holds only *if* the patient wants to live longer. Moral prescriptions, however,

6. See my essay "What Is the End of the Human Person: The Vision of God and Integral Human Fulfillment," in *Moral Truth and Moral Tradition: Essays in Honour of Peter Geach and Elizabeth Anscombe*, ed. Luke Gormally (Dublin and Portland, OR: Four Courts Press, 1994), 68–96, which is included in my *The Ashley Reader,* 225–70.

are *absolute,* since, if the smoker asks his confessor whether it would be a sin for him not to follow the doctor's prescription, the question cannot be answered by an "if" but only by "yes" or "no." All practical decisions presuppose certain factual truths, although the facts do not of themselves settle the question. Thus, practical moral decisions presuppose human nature and its absolute needs; but, since they concern the choice of means to satisfy these needs, they are not merely factual but are normative. Further, their normative character does not reduce practical moral decisions to mere subjective preferences.

The weakness of cultural relativism and emotivism as moral theories has led other philosophers to ground morality in more objective and universal truths. Traditional moral instruction, such as that given by the Ten Commandments in the Bible for Jews and Christians or in the moral code of the Qu'ran for Muslims, is usually stated in terms of laws or rules made by an authority whose has the power of enforcement. Persons subject to these laws and rules, whether they understand or agree with them or not, must obey without question or be punished for disobedience. This is the legalistic conception of morality, or *voluntarism,* so called because the ultimate criterion of right and wrong is the *will* of the lawmaker. This type of ethical thinking can also be called *deontological* (from Greek *deontos,* duty or obligation) or *command* ethics.[7]

Obviously this mode of moral decision, which corresponds to Kolberg's final, mature phase of moral development, cannot really be mature, since a little experience teaches us that human authorities can sometimes make laws that are unjust and that our consciences tell us we must disobey, and there can sometimes be no law to guide us to do what our consciences will approve. Even if we know that there is a law of God, such as the Ten Commandments, that cannot be other than just, yet if we are to apply these laws in the most intelligent and effec-

7. Thus Kai Nielsen, *Ethics without God*, revised edition (Amherst, NY: Prometheus Books, 1990), argues that a good act is good whether God enforces it or not; hence, God is unnecessary for ethics. This argument presupposes a voluntaristic ethics.

tive way to the constantly changing situations of daily life, we must have at least some understanding of the reasons for which God or human authorities made the law, or our obedience will be so blind as to frustrate the legislator's purpose.

Furthermore, the philosopher Immanuel Kant pointed out that if we are good simply because of fear or coercion by some lawgiver, our morality is *heteronomous* rather than *autonomous*.[8] He argued that, since coercion takes away freedom, heteronomous morality, since it is not free, cannot be genuine morality. He then tried to solve this dilemma by arguing that, in acting morally, we do not obey the will of another but our own will, provided that will is good. The question for Kant then became: "What makes the human will good?" This he answered by saying that our will is good when we act not from motives of our own happiness or welfare but in accordance with universal human reason. Thus, for Kantians the moral categories of "right" and "wrong" are not derived from human experience but are imposed on human experience so as to obtain an ordered society that makes possible a consistent, disciplined personal life. Therefore Kant tried to reduce moral norms to a single principle called "the moral imperative": "So act that your action can become a universal norm for everyone." For example, we should not lie, because only if all people tell the truth can human relationships be maintained. Kant had difficulty in showing how a concrete set of norms could be developed from so general a principle, and it seems that he was inclined to go along with Rousseau and fill out his empty general norm with other norms derived from an emotional "moral sense."

Both of these thinkers, in fact, derived most of their concrete morality from traditional Christian morality, although both had deserted that faith for the secular humanism of the Enlightenment, which rejected biblical revelation in favor of unaided human reason. Kant's no-

8. See Roger J. Sullivan, *An Introduction to Kant's Ethics* (Cambridge: Cambridge University Press, 1994).

tion of a totally disinterested morality of duty, however, has been deeply influential on modern thought and can still be found in such thinkers as William K. Frankena (1908–94)[9] and John Rawls (1921–2002).[10] It shows up among some analytic philosophers who have moved from the emotivist theory of morality (emotivism) to talk about "good reasons." This trend is explained by Kant's notion that truth is not conformity to reality but *consistency* in one's view of the world and one's "integrity" of life. In this view, the moral person is one who consistently lives by his or her "principles." One might raise the problem that Hitler and Stalin were consistently tyrannical! It does seem, then, that deontological theories of morality are inadequate to the task of transcending custom and culture or individual idiosyncrasy.

A more adequate ethical theory must be *teleological*, that is, aimed at an end that involves the ultimate flourishing of the person and mankind. It must be based on the view that in human nature there are certain basic needs or goals to be achieved by free human persons if they are to be happy and contribute to a just society in which they can live, although (contrary to plurifinalism) some of these needs and goals are more important than others. Mature persons have the intelligence to discern the possible ways to attain these goals and to attain them all in a unified way that respects the hierarchical order of their importance. In considering the relation of these possible means to the end, persons must first always exclude any means that are contradictory to achieving that goal. Such means are *intrinsically wrong or sinful and can never be justified by circumstances,* although they may be either venial or mortal sins. On the other hand, if an act is possibly a true means to happiness, persons prudently consider the relative advantages and disadvantages for their purpose, within the concrete circumstances, and then in this freedom make a decision.

Such a prudential ethics, however, does not reject the need for moral laws or norms, since each of us has limited knowledge and ex-

9. *Ethics,* 2nd ed. (Englewood Cliffs, NJ: Prentice Hall, 1973).

10. *A Theory of Justice,* rev. ed. (Oxford: Oxford University Press, 1999).

perience of our own needs and the possible effects of various means to satisfy them. Consequently we need the help of moral guidance. This is obvious in the case of children and adolescents, but even mature persons find that they sometimes very much need to obey the guidance of more expert moral persons, as patients do well to obey their doctors. We cannot, though, obey authority or set laws merely mechanically. Sometimes we perceive that human laws are unjust and must be disobeyed and sometimes we come to see that what we understood to be the laws of God were misinterpreted.

Yet a sound teleological ethics cannot be rooted merely in what Pope John Paul II in his very thorough encyclical *The Splendor of Truth* (*Veritatis Splendor*, 1993) called "teleologism" or "proportionalism."[11] This theory, which arose after Vatican II in reaction to the legalistic presentation of Christian ethics that was sometimes given in Catholic catechesis, distorted a traditional formula of St. Thomas Aquinas, usually stated as saying that the morality of an act was determined by its "object, circumstances, and intention." From this, proportionalists argue that until all three determinants are taken together one cannot say that an act is morally good or evil. Hence, it would seem, no concrete negative norm of morality can be formulated that does not have possible exceptions, since one could always imagine some combination of these three determinants that would make its good values outweigh its evil ones.

When the proponents of proportionalism were accused of saying that "the end justifies the means" or that it is sometimes right "to do evil for the sake of a greater good," they distinguished between dif-

11. Proportionalism seems to have originated with Josef Fuchs, SJ (1912–2005) as a product of his participation in the consultation on contraception under Pope Paul VI. In his encyclical *Humanae Vitae* (1968), the pope rejected Fr. Fuchs's advice as contrary to Catholic tradition and to reason. Proportionalism was popularized in the United States by Richard A. McCormick, SJ; see the book *Doing Evil to Achieve Good: Moral Choice in Conflict Situations* (Chicago: Loyola University Press, 1978), which was edited by Fr. McCormick and Paul Ramsey, who debated the virtues and vices of proportionalism.

ferent "pre-moral or ontic"[12] values that are weighed to determine whether for a certain object, intention, and set of circumstances the positive values outweigh the negative ones. Then, granted that this was the case, one could judge that the act was "ontologically" moral.

Their critics also accused them of being *consequentialist* or *utilitarians* or *situationists*, all ethical theories with a bad name in Christian tradition. But the proportionalists answered that, unlike consequentialists, they considered all the values in an act, including the nature of the act (i.e., the object) as well as its consequences. Nor were they utilitarians since, unlike them, they do not reduce the calculus of right and wrong simply to the amount of pleasure versus the amount of pain to oneself and the community, but include in their calculus all types of value. Finally they were accused of being relativists, since they denied any absolute moral norms, since for them not only positive norms admit of exceptions (as classical moralists had always admitted) but even negative norms concerning acts that are *intrinsically evil* could have exceptions. For example, they were accused of teaching that the positive value of lying in certain circumstances could outweigh its evil.

To this latter charge they answered that some moral norms are always obligatory but these are only *formal* norms, such as "Do good and avoid evil," or "Always act out of love," which in different circumstances and with different intentions can be understood in different ways. As for the accusation that they were situationists, proportionalists point out that they weigh not only the circumstances of an act but its intention and object as well.

12. The distinction between "ontic" and "ontological" betrays the Kantian context of this thinking, since "ontic" refers to the bare "is" or description of reality, while "ontological" refers to the human "meaning" that bare facts acquire through our interpretation of them in view of human purposes and concerns. If, however, we consider only the bare facts of a moral situation without considering its relation to human purposes, how can we weigh them in any manner that is morally significant? Consequently, when we weigh them in a manner relevant to human purposes, we are already weighing them ontologically, not ontically, and they cannot be called "pre-moral."

The lively controversy over this theory showed first of all that it misrepresented the thought of Aquinas, who actually said that the morality of an act has only two determinants.[13] The first and essential consideration is whether the object of the act is a suitable means to attain an intended good end. If the end intended was not good, then the act was evil and could not be made good by any circumstances, and if the means was contradictory of a good end, then the act was also intrinsically evil, since it could not lead to good and could not be made good by any circumstances. The second and accidental consideration presupposed that the act had been proved to be good; when the act, however, was further related to its circumstances—such as where and when and by whom and for what intention it was performed—these circumstances could render an act that by its object was good to be accidentally bad, less bad, or less good. For example, giving alms is good, but not when your own children need the money for food. Or it could accidentally make a bad act less bad as when one lies to help a friend. Yet no circumstances, not even a good intention, can make an act good if it is essentially bad as regards its object. For Aquinas there is the *intention of the object*, namely, we choose a means to reach an end, and in this sense the intention is the essential determinant of morality, and there can also be *secondary intentions,* which are circumstances and which can modify the intention of the object for better or worse but not replace its primary role.

Thus the Pharisee (Mt 6:1–6) gave alms to the poor, an act whose intention of the object (helping the poor as a religious duty) was essentially morally good, but he also took care to do this publicly (a circumstantial intention) and thus accidentally lessened the goodness of his act and made it hypocritical. If he had done it *only* to be seen by others and with no concern for the poor, that would have been his essential intention *of the object*, not a circumstance, and the act would have been simply bad, a sin of pure hypocrisy.

13. *ST* I-II, q. 18, aa. 2–4.

Even more fundamentally, proportionalism was a wrong theory, in spite of its seemingly teleological character (actually it historically had its roots in voluntarism and the concern "to find a loophole in the law"), because of its two weaknesses as a practical guide to moral decision. First of all, in execution proportionalism tended to be arbitrary, since the term "value" is very vague and a creative imagination can always think up enough positive values in any act and minimize the negative values so as to justify it. For example, Harry Truman thought that the possibility of saving the lives of a large number of American soldiers outweighed the evil of actually killing what might be a smaller number of innocent Japanese noncombatants.

A second and fundamental error in proportionalism was that this arbitrariness arose from the fact that the theory itself was self-contradictory. Its claim to first weigh pre-moral evils and only then to make a moral judgment would mean that in the pre-moral calculus one would have to consider the relation of the act as a means to the end, but in that case one would already be judging it morally, since that relation of means to end is the very essence of morality. Thus, in the proportionalist system, the same judgment would be both pre-moral and moral, that is, both not moral and at the same time moral.

Therefore, the best system of moral judgment is that proposed by Thomas Aquinas: to rightly judge whether act is an appropriate means to attain true human happiness, one must first consider the *moral object directly intended by that act*. The moral object differs from the physical object in that it is viewed in relation to the end for which it is being considered as a means. For example if one is forced to kill another in self-defense, the act of killing is the same physical act as if one killed the person out of revenge, yet the two acts (self-defense and murder for revenge) differ morally because they are intended as means to different ends.

Similarities in the physical nature of the act should not be understood, however, to imply that the intention of a good end justifies any physical means. There are those who denounce as "physicalism" or "biologism" the condemnation of acts on the grounds of their physical character no matter for what good intention they are done. This denunciation again overlooks the fact that the primary intention is the intention of the object whose physical character may make it an intrinsically wrong means, while any other intention is only a circumstance that cannot make a wrong object good. For example, one cannot defend sadistic acts even if they are intended to express love, since the physical character of the act, by its nature and by the nature of the person, cannot express love even when done with that purpose in mind. Therefore, after one has first considered the moral object of an act and found that it is good or at least not intrinsically bad, one must then consider the circumstances in which it is to be performed, including any intentions besides the intention of the object. I have already discussed how such circumstances can modify the essential moral character of an act.

The Goal of Life

While it is often said that the first principle of ethics is "Do good and avoid evil," this states the matter only abstractly. In a teleological ethics, to do good is always to choose as means those acts that lead to the true goal of human life, namely, happiness, and to avoid what will lead to unhappiness. But what concretely is this true goal of human life inherent in human nature itself? Aquinas broadly characterizes the basic needs of human nature whose harmonious satisfaction constitutes natural happiness as (1) physical health including security and necessary external property; (2) family life for the education of all children and for the sexual fulfillment of those who freely choose to marry; (3) participation in a good human community; (4) true knowledge.[14] These goods, though good in themselves (*bona per se*), are hierarchically ordered and unified by the supreme good of true knowledge.

Aristotle, in the last book of his *Nicomachean Ethics,* argued that

14. *ST* I-II, q. 94, a. 2.

since things are specified by what is best in them and human nature is specified by intelligence, the supreme element in human happiness is the achievement and enjoyment of true contemplation, that is, knowledge of the highest truths accessible to human beings. The Latin *contemplare* etymologically refers to the observation auguries (prophetic signs) in a temple that show the will of a god, and it translates the Greek *theorein*—to know what it is valuable to know for its own sake.

As I indicated above in criticizing Grisez's views, this does not mean that for Aristotle contemplation is the *exclusive* goal of human life.[15] Aristotle, a thorough realist, is quite clear that the other needs must also be satisfied, since one who lacks adequate material goods and health, family support, and society cannot engage in contemplation. Nor should we think of this "contemplation" as mysticism or some rarified kind of knowledge possible only to a few. In modern terms, what Aristotle had in mind was what today we might call "the search for meaning in life" and, more specifically, the wisdom of "first philosophy," metaphysics.

It follows that the lesser goods of physical life, family, and society are necessary conditions of the highest good of knowledge; they are subordinated to it and can in a measure be sacrificed to it, and yet they may never be totally neglected. Hence Aquinas follows Aristotle in insisting that a certain amount of material possessions, but not many, is necessary for the contemplative life, and that for these to be readily available there must be some private property, though its use must be regulated for the common good. They both also recognize that many persons are so occupied in the practical life of society that the "contemplative life" devoted principally to study is impractical for them. Hence to them Aristotle assigns a genuine but secondary kind of happiness, in which the practice of the active virtues predominates—the "active life."

15. See the essay of Daniel T. Devereux, "Aristotle on the Essence of Happiness," in *Studies in Aristotle*, ed. Dominic J. O'Meara (Washington, DC: The Catholic University of America Press, 1981), 247–60.

Today it may seem to psychotherapists quite unrealistic to claim that human "happiness" above all consists in "contemplation" or in "metaphysical wisdom." I will discuss this further in Chapter 9, but I believe this position makes good psychological sense, if we note that human unhappiness is "conflictual," that is, a war between a person's inconsistent values. The only way this conflict can be ultimately resolved is by a reordering of values that subordinates less important ones to more important ones. This requires that we find "meaning" in our life events and in our actions that respond to those events; this "meaning" is a worldview that is truly a "wisdom" that makes our life rich and worthwhile as it moves to fulfillment. That is what Aristotle and Aquinas meant by "contemplation."

The Formation of Personal Character

To attain this contemplative fulfillment, we have to have behavioral skills that enable us to act consistently so as to move toward our goal. These skills were traditionally called "virtues." They are not routine *habits* which are rigid and instinctual, but flexible skills by which we can meet ever-varying circumstances. To achieve that consistency of good behavior that we call *character* requires the development of skills, just as an athlete or a musician can perform well consistently only if they are thoroughly trained and practiced in their art.

A skill in good moral decision and behavior is called a *virtue* (from Latin *vir* a man, that is, a *real* man or a *real* woman, someone who lives up to the human potential). Thus good character is the possession of all the necessary moral skills or virtues; its opposite, bad character, consists in *vices* or consistency in doing what is evil. As a person is disciplined in good behavior, it becomes easy for them and even pleasant to do what is right, although at the beginning doing right was difficult.

For Aristotle and Aquinas, the fundamental life problems that require virtues to solve are: (1) control of biological drives for pleasure, especially for food and sex (*temperance* or moderation); (2) control of biological drives for aggression against danger or for flight in the face of danger or for endurance in inescapable, painful situations (*fortitude,* or courage, and patience); (3) control of the will to respect the rights of others as well as one's own needs (*justice*); (4) control of intelligence so as not to act on impulse but to make thoughtful and informed decisions (*prudence* or practical reasonableness).

In difference from Plato, Aristotle and Aquinas did not consider these four virtues (called "cardinal" from Latin, *cardo,* hinge) to be merely qualities of any moral act; instead they held that the objects of the cardinal virtues were especially difficult problems of human living. Thus the practical science of ethics is not simply about particular moral decisions, but more fundamentally about the formation of a virtuous character.

As noted above, the first two cardinal virtues are *temperance* (moderation) and *fortitude* (courage), because at the level of our sense cognition and sense drives there are two basic drives that explain behavior, namely, the pleasure-pain drive and the aggressive drive that enables us to deal with difficulties. These skills are actually in our bodies; they arise from sense cognition and prepare our bodies for a certain kind of physical behavior, but although the cardinal virtues exist in our bodily drives, they participate in the guidance of reason. They help us act reasonably about physical matters that in a person who lack these virtues often get out of control and end in self-destruction.

The specific major problems that the virtue of temperance or moderation enables us to handle well are the two pleasure drives that are strongest: (1) the pleasure of eating and drinking (to which, also, chemical dependency can be reduced); (2) the pleasure of sex. These drives are themselves good and necessary for the human species, yet experience shows how easily they get out of control and cause endless damage. The opposite vices are *gluttony* (lack of moderation in food and drink) and *lust* (lack of sexual control).

The specific major problem that fortitude or courage strengthens us to face is death, and especially when we see we are obliged to give our life for our country, our faith, or some other great good.

Traditionally it was thought that the importance of these virtues differs for the two genders, in that it was especially disgraceful for a man to lack courage (since it was his duty to defend his family and his country) and for a woman to lack chastity or sexual control (since a mother had to be devoted to her family), while lack of sexual control seemed less disgraceful in a man and lack of courage less disgraceful in a woman. Although, considering the difference of the man and the woman's role in family life there is some truth to this traditional notion, it has often been much exaggerated, since both men and women need both virtues, and without them will certainly fail in life, that is, men must also be chaste and women courageous.

Besides our control of our sense drives, we also have problems to meet that are specifically at the human level of intelligence and will. While each of us confronts our problems in satisfying the needs of which we are usually so keenly aware, we may think little of the needs of our neighbors, and yet we are intensely social animals who cannot satisfy all our needs except through a community with others and we also take pleasure in sharing our life with others, even when we do not need them to satisfy our own goods. Who does not know the joy of a feast, in which not only do we have plenty to eat and drink but we have delight in the presence of those with whom we share our food? Anthropologists note that we humans are by nature food sharers in a way far more *convivial* (from Latin for living together) than are other animals. We need therefore to have the will to think not only of ourselves but also of others of our community. Aquinas does not picture this as *altruism,* in the sense of "thinking only of others," because for him that would contradict our legitimate responsibility to seek our own happiness. Instead, he holds that human goods are of two kinds: private and common. Private goods are such that if I possess a good, you cannot also possess it. For example, you cannot eat my piece of pie. Such goods are principally material, since matter is divided into parts. Common goods, on the other hand, are ones that we possess in common, so that my having them does not prevent your having the same good but rather enhances it. Thus at a feast, the food is divided up, but the entertainment and conversation are shared and are all the better for being shared. Thus common goods are primarily spiritual, because they unite rather than divide.

There have been philosophers—the Italian Machiavelli (1469–1527) and the Englishman Thomas Hobbes (1588–1679) are notable examples—who so exaggerated private goods at the expense of common ones that they held that each of us is motivated only by his or her self-interests. Hobbes claimed that people obey the ruler only so that he will protect them against their fellow citizens, who otherwise would attack them and take away all they possessed. At first sociobiologists, influenced by Darwin's notion of the survival of the fittest, agreed with Hobbes, but now they have come to see that human survival depends on the social nature of people cooperating with each other for the common good. Thus it is a life problem for each of us as individuals to learn to be concerned about others and to be fair to them.

The virtue that makes consistent fairness is *justice*, the will to respect others rights, and it has three species. First there is justice between individuals, for example, in buying and selling, and this is called *exchange* (commutative) justice. It is based on exact equality, since, if I buy from you, you should give me full value for the price. If we make a contract, each of us must fulfill it to the letter. The second kind of justice is traditionally called *legal* justice, because it is the will of individuals to do their part for the common good, for example to pay taxes, to vote, to obey the law. The third kind of justice is that which is in contrast to legal justice, since it is the will of the leaders of a community to give to the members their due share in the common good, and that is called *distributive* justice. These last two species of justice, since they are reciprocal, today are commonly taken together under the name of *social justice*, the obligation of the members of a community to the common good and of those in charge of the common good to its members. Just distribution demands that every citizen of a community has what is required for his or her basic needs but also that those who do more for the community than others should be properly honored and rewarded.

The fourth and most important of the cardinal virtues is *prudence*, skill in making good ethical decisions. In fact, ethics is simply the more theoretical, universal, and scientific aspect of the virtue of prudence, since prudent (i.e., practically wise) persons are first of all concerned to perfect their own characters by striving always to act in the light of reason, that is, of the general truths about right and wrong provided by ethics as a practical science.

Aquinas shows that when we are faced with a moral decision, we need first to use our *memory* to supply us with the information we need; we must also be open to new information (*docility*); and we must be *careful* to study all aspects of the problem, *seeking good advice* about what we do not ourselves know, trying to look to the possible *consequences* of our acts as well as to the *circumstances* in which we are acting. Finally, we must be *cautious about the risks* we are running and what may interfere with our success.

The virtue of prudence, which requires much experience and is not often found in young people, is of several types. First there is the prudence we need to manage our own individual lives. Second there is the prudence needed to manage a family. Third there is the prudence needed to lead a community, or some considerable organization within the community. Fourth, there is the prudence needed to lead an army or other organization that calls on people to be willing to give up their lives for the common good. Then there are various kinds of prudence that underlie professional ethics, which enable a businessman, a physician, a lawyer to work with others in his profession. More discussion will be given to social justice in the next chapter.

Aquinas shows that besides these four cardinal virtues there are a number of lesser virtues, which deal with less difficult problems. The virtues that resembles moderation are *humility* (as against the vice of pride) in controlling our desire to be superior to others; *docility* (as against being self-opinionated) that makes us teachable by those who know more than we; *politeness* and *gentleness* in respecting others feelings (as against rudeness and harshness); and *frugality* (as against greediness) in not seeking too many possessions. The virtues that resemble courage are *patience* and (when the need for the virtue is long drawn out) *endurance* on the more passive side, and *courage* and (when great deeds are to be done) *nobility*. I emphasize that such virtues are given many different names, often with different shades of meaning. What is important is get some idea of the human problems that each of them enables us to cope with realistically and consistently.

Along with justice, Aquinas lists the lesser virtues of *religion, obedience,* and *patriotism,* because we have a debt to God, to legitimate human authorities, and to our country, in each case a debt that is too great to fulfill perfectly. Also he lists *truthfulness, gratitude,* and *leniency,* because they imply a certain debt, although not a strict one: not every one has the right to know all that we know; gratefulness for gifts does not require an equal repayment; and those who offend us cannot expect us not to demand full recompense.

The lesser virtues that go with prudence are *eubulia* (deliberating well), *synesis* (judging by the common law), and *gnome* (judging by general laws or principles). The virtues enable us to be consistent in our actions, as the vices tend to make a criminal insistently bad. Yet, because we are very complex persons who are often subject to internal struggles and subject to changing situations and pressures, it is not easy for us to be *consistent* in our good behavior. I may act kindly when in a good mood, but watch out when I get annoyed! Hence little children are good one moment and naughty the next, and adolescents are still very inconsistent in good behavior.

Grace and Original Sin

In Chinese Confucianism there was much debate as to whether human persons naturally tend to evil or to good. Empirically we have to face the fact that everybody, or almost everybody, does wrong things and that the weight of moral evil in the world is immense. This is all too true, in spite of the fact that it seems contradictory to suppose that anything has a natural tendency to moral evil, since the very definition of a wrong act is that it is one contrary to one's nature.

Christian theology escapes this dilemma by the doctrine of *original sin,* according to which humankind got off on the wrong track at the very beginning of its history and the effects of this misstep have influenced all of subsequent human history as the consequences of one wrong act after another have accumulated and have not yet been historically completely overcome. In any case, that human nature as such, whatever its historical situation, is essentially good and tends to good rather than bad behavior must be taken as necessarily true, since evil is not something in itself, but a lack of some goodness appropriate to a thing.

The human race's fall into original sin did not "totally corrupt" human nature, as the Protestant Reformer John Calvin (1508–64) maintained, but by removing its actual relation to our ultimate end, it disordered our faculties, so that they are at war with each other. Furthermore, it removed from human nature an elevation through what the New Testament calls "grace" (free gift). God willed to raise spiritual beings through grace to a union with him that would not be merely an imperfect one through a knowledge of God as creator, but rather would culminate in the perfect happiness of the Beatific Vision of the Triune God.[16]

Through original sin, all of our race except Jesus and his mother, the Blessed Virgin Mary (who was freed from original sin in the very moment of her conception—the doctrine of the Immaculate Conception), are born with disordered natures. At birth, we lack the elevation by grace which God restores only by the sacrament of Baptism or by a desire for the effects of this sacrament inspired by the Holy Spir-

16. On a fuller treatment of the grace of faith, see Romanus Cessario, *Christian Faith and the Theological Life* (Washington, DC: The Catholic University of America Press, 1996).

it. Persons not in the state of grace can perform good acts, but they soon fall into mortal sin again. As long as we are able to use our intelligence, we are free to make choices that are good as well as bad in our lives, and in any given situation we can do what is good and avoid what is evil.

In addition to the four cardinal virtues, grace confers the far superior theological virtues, which are skills in moving beyond natural imperfect happiness to that of eternal life in the beatific vision. The first theological virtue is Faith in God and his guidance through Sacred Scripture and Tradition that is the teaching of the Catholic Church. The second is Hope, which, in spite of our own defects and the misery of a fallen world, makes us confident we can reach our goal in God. Often people understand Hope as simply "I hope I will make it," but this virtue goes much further. It is the *certitude* arising from Faith; that is, we continue to trust God, that he will certainly bring us to our goal, just as the Good Thief even on his cross put his trust in the Crucified Jesus at whose dying side he was dying. The third, greatest of all the virtues, is Charity or love, not erotic love but agape love: "Love God, and your neighbor as yourself." Note that this implies that we should love ourselves (that is, seek true happiness), but in a way that includes our God and the whole human community. St. Thomas Aquinas points out that "charity begins at home," that is, with those whom we are actually able to help toward their true happiness, and that happiness is union with God in love.

Along with the moral virtues there are also other practical virtues, the *technologies,* which are only *conditional,* since they guide us in how to do something that is not absolutely necessary for us. For example, the technology of making computers tells us how to do that well *if* we want to make a computer. Each of us needs all the virtues, but we do not need to have all the technical skills.

Along with the technologies are the *fine arts* and the sports, which, from a constructive or performance point of view, are technologies. Unlike other technologies, these have as their purpose not the making of something useful for life but the making or doing of something to be enjoyed contemplatively or participatively. Thus the fine art of making a movie is highly technical, but the maker hopes we will not "use" it, but simply enjoy it, while the sports—including spectator sports—are an exercise of aggressive affectivity.

Besides these practical skills and fine arts and sports, there are also skills whose purpose, somewhat like the enjoyment of works of fine art, is not to make something (technology) or do something (morality), but simply to know something. These are the intellectual virtues, which are either theoretical or practical. Theoretical knowledge aims simply at understanding reality and, as we noted in an earlier chapter, is of three types: insight, reasoning, and wisdom. Every *science,* in the broad sense of a discipline that is logically organized in order to explain phenomena in terms of cause and effect, also presupposes *insight* into the basic truths derived from experience from which it reasons to its conclusions. Wisdom, however, is knowledge that embraces and unifies the other sciences, while protecting their proper autonomy.

By Aristotle, wisdom was called "First Philosophy" or, as relating all knowledge to the First Cause of all things, "Theology." However, First Philosophy came to be known as "metaphysics," that is, "after physics" or after natural science, because it is studied after the natural sciences, each of which presupposes or give indications of the First Cause of all being.[17]

The human virtues both moral and intellectual have to be achieved by practice and experience and ordinarily require a teacher or a guide in their formation. We must, therefore, inquire how we get such guidance. In the next chapter I will discuss the social aspects of human personhood and how this contributes to the development of the person. Before concluding the present chapter, however, it is necessary to emphasize that free moral decisions are sometimes very

17. See my *The Way toward Wisdom: An Interdisciplinary and Intercultural Introduction to Metaphysics* (Notre Dame, IN: University of Notre Dame Press, 2006).

difficult to make honestly because the concrete situation presents a "borderline case." It was this fact that led proponents of the erroneous theory of proportionalism to deny that any kind of concrete act can be intrinsically evil and therefore to claim that no concrete moral norm can hold without exceptions.

We can, therefore, concede the usefulness of a duty ethics (made up of an ethical code or set of moral norms). For once specialists have worked out an ends-means ethics, it is helpful to formulate, on the basis of its conclusions, a set of norms to guide persons in their prudent decisions in particular cases. Without such a set of norms it is very difficult for any individual to work out the foundations of the whole of ethics every time he or she makes a decision.

Yet one cannot simply deduce moral judgments from general rules by introducing "middle principles," as some ethicists call them, in a mathematically deductive system. Instead ethical norms are only general guides to prudent reflection on concrete moral questions. Even when a norm declares that some type of action is intrinsically evil, so as to exclude it from further deliberation, this still leaves it up to prudence to determine whether in fact a particular act under judgment actually involves the intrinsic evil that the norm absolutely forbids. Thus, one can formulate the true norm, "Lying is intrinsically evil, because it always violates our need for membership in a community of mutual trust," but this still leaves open to prudence the determination of whether a certain apparently communicative act is in fact a lie.

To formulate all of ethics in a series of norms is an impossible task. The Ten Commandments are valid and universal norms, but even they are not exhaustive. Sometimes, even after much reflection, we find ourselves faced by what seems a moral dilemma. "I am damned if I do and damned if I don't!" Here ethical theory can help, because over the centuries ethicists have worked out two important norms for prudent reflection when we are faced with ethical dilemmas. These especially concern (1) decisions that have some evil effects and (2) cooperation with wrongdoers.

The first type of moral dilemma arises in situations where the moral object intended is good and thus has ethically beneficial results, but it is foreseen that the action may also have some physically harmful effects. Such an action should still be performed if the following conditions, usually called the "principle of double effect," are met:

1. The directly intended object of the act must not be intrinsically contradictory to the true ultimate goal of human life.
2. The intention of the agent must be to achieve the beneficial effects and as far as possible to avoid the harmful effects (that is, the agent may only indirectly intend the harm).
3. The foreseen beneficial effects must be at least equal to the foreseen harmful effects.
4. The beneficial effects must follow from the action at least as immediately as do the harmful effects (otherwise the harmful effects are the real means chosen to obtain the good end).

Sometimes a fifth condition, "There must be a grave reason for permitting the evil effect," is added, but this is already covered by condition 3.

Since in some situations it is not possible to avoid all harmful side effects and at the same time to fulfill our obligations to do the good from which these harmful effects may also result, we need a principle to guide us through such moral dilemmas. For example, to save someone's life, a physician may perform an amputation. Although the disablement caused by the surgery is foreseen, it is not what is desired or chosen as such, and would be avoided were it possible to heal the person in a better way. Thus it is not a moral effect, but only a physical effect, since morality always pertains to *free* choices (nor is it "premoral," as proportionalists claim, since it is the physical effect of a moral decision). In this case the effect that is freely (directly) chosen is *morally* good, while the other effect is *physically* harmful but of itself neither moral nor immoral, because it is not freely chosen (it is only indirectly "chosen").

Only the first of the four conditions listed above is it really essential to a good decision. The other three merely suggest prudential tests by which one can better determine if the first condition is actually being fulfilled. Consequently, what the third condition demands is not the precise, determinative weighing of values on which the entire methodology of proportionalism depends, but merely that an action, already determined to be intrinsically moral (first condition), is not vitiated by circumstances that produce obviously greater evils than the good intended. The second and fourth conditions are required for the same reason, to ensure that the agent directly intends only the intrinsically good effect.

A psychotherapeutic example of the application of double effect is the great distress and anxiety ("abreaction") that clients may experience in therapy as they recall and express to the therapist some traumatic experience in their life. Yet unless these traumas are recalled, and as it were "relived," it is difficult for the therapist to know what they were or the client to face up to them. Like surgery, this healing is at first seriously wounding. Is it prudent, that is, moral, for the therapist or the surgeon to cause such pain, especially since it might leave the patient worse off than ever?

The therapist can prudently decide that causing this abreaction is ethical if (a) the therapist's direct intention is to improve the client's mental health (the first condition), (b) the therapist avoids causing unnecessary or badly timed suffering to the patient (second condition), (c) the probable value of the healing is greater than pain of the abreaction and of any danger of the patient "acting-out" anger, despair, or immoral sexual or other impulses, (d) the purpose of the abreaction is to understand the client's neuroses and help her or him to overcome these neuroses, and not some sadistic pleasure on the therapist's part in dominating the client (fourth condition). The delicacy of such decisions is evident from the notorious cases of false recollections of abuse stimulated by imprudent, suggestive therapy, especially hypnosis.[18]

A second type of borderline case involves *cooperation* for a mor-

18. C. J. Brainerd and V. F. Reyna, *The Science of False Memory*, Oxford Psychology Series (New York: Oxford University Press, 2005).

ally legitimate purpose with some other person or organization that one knows may use this cooperation to further some immoral purpose. Such moral dilemmas frequently arise when, to fulfill our responsibilities, we have to seek the cooperation of others. We often foresee that this may involve us somehow in conduct on their part that we believe to be objectively wrong—even if we realize that those with whom we cooperate may not in their own consciences perceive it as evil. When possible, we should inform them of the evil and try to dissuade them, but often we know this will have no effect and may even make them more obstinate in their evil intention or result in injury to ourselves, such as losing a needed job. Must we, therefore, refuse to cooperate with them? This can be answered in terms of what is traditionally called the "principle of legitimate cooperation."

Certainly we must refuse to cooperate if we would involve ourselves in *formal* cooperation, that is, agree with, advise, counsel, promote, or condone their objectively unethical actions, because formal cooperation involves us in directly intending the immoral action just as if we were doing it ourselves. If, however, the cooperation is merely *material*, that is, we directly cooperate with the greater good to be done and only indirectly with the evil that we would prevent if we could, then such cooperation is permissible and even obligatory under the following two conditions:

1. that our refusal to cooperate would result in a greater evil or loss of a greater good than if we cooperate.
2. that the cooperation be more remote the greater the evil involved.

In judging the evil involved, even in material cooperation, an important additional consideration is the "scandal" that may be caused, that is, the bad example that others may take from our action because it appears to them that we approve the evil side effect involved and they are thus themselves tempted to commit the evil in the future.

These conditions are needed to insure we are not formally cooperating with moral evil. The closer the cooperation and the greater the evil, the more it requires a serious justifying cause lest one be guilty of formal cooperation. Thus a psychiatrist working in a non-Catholic hospital that performs abortions must consider how closely involved he is in such unethical acts and whether his presence seems to support the "right to choose" policy, since that would cause scandal.

Conclusion

The natural goal of human life, true happiness, is occasioned by integral satisfaction of basic human needs for physical health, security, and moderate material possessions, formation in a good family and the passing on of life, friendship in a community cooperating for the common good, and an understanding of the world of other human persons—all leading toward a loving personal relation to God. Such happiness can be achieved only if one is guided by realistic, prudent decisions that respect the rights of others and are not hampered but facilitated by moderation in one's drives for pleasure and courage in difficulties. Such decisions require us to develop skills or virtues. Christians believe that Jesus perfectly possessed such virtue and gave us both a model and the power of the Holy Spirit in the teachings and sacraments of a community, the Catholic Church, that will ultimately not only restore humanity to happiness but lead them beyond mere human happiness to a share in the eternal happiness of the One God, Father, Son, and Holy Spirit. Christ heals and perfects the character of human persons by faith that clarifies prudence, by love that extends justice to others, and by hope that makes moderation and courage easy. The Catholic health care mission is one of the ministries of this Church and is directed not only to physical but to psychological healing as a component of this true Christian happiness that should be extended to all humanity by love, inspired by hope, and guided by faith. Catholic psychotherapists should follow the Church's moral guidance faithfully and share it with clients, but they may not impose it on them or exploit their trust in the therapist to proselytize the clients.

seven

SHARING IN COMMUNITY

A. Family Ethics

The Human Female and the Human Male

Psychotherapists do not require convincing that personal psychology has to deal not only with individuals but with the families that raised them and those in which they live much of their life. Any attempt to understand fully the natural functions of sexuality and family life leads to many ethical questions that are bitterly debated today. Many of these I have treated in some detail in other publications,[1] and although they are important to psychotherapy, I find it necessary to pass over them in this book, where it suffices to concentrate on the central issue of the family as the natural basis of communal life.[2]

1. See *Justice in the Church: Gender and Participation*, The McGivney Lectures, 1992, Washington, DC: (The Catholic University of America Press, 1996), 125–30; and *The Ashley Reader*, Chapter 14, "Can We Make a Fundamental Option?" 203–22.

2. See my article "A Theological Overview on Recent Research on Sex and Gender," in Mark F. Schwartz, A. S. Moraczewski, and J. A. Monteleone, eds., *Sex and Gender* (St. Louis: Pope John Center, 1983), 1–47; and books, *Justice in the Church: Gender and Participation*, The McGivney Lectures, 1992 (Washington, DC: The Catholic University of America Press, 1996), 125–30; *Health Care Ethics: A Theological Analysis*

Three factors in our culture have called the importance of the traditional family (father, mother, children) into question. First has been the widespread practice of contraception, which is contrary to the traditional teaching of all the Christian churches, as well as to the teaching of recent popes.[3] The practice of contraception has been encouraged by fear of overpopulation and the economic pressure that has resulted from urbanization. On farms a large family is an advantage, but in a city it is often a heavy burden. Second has been the position that the feminist movement has taken, that domestic life necessarily entails oppression of women.[4] Third has been the movement to defend "alternative" ways of sexual expression. Thus today it is difficult to defend the notion that stable, heterosexual, fertile families are natural to the human species. Yet, paradoxically, modern evolutionary theory, sociobiology, and comparative anthropology all support the naturalness of the so-called "nuclear family," and the psychological arguments for it are empirically strong.

First, evolutionary theory and sociobiology make clear why sexual reproduction is advantageous for survival. We learn from the latter that, in most species of animals, the male and female divide the work of reproduction between them and have become adapted physically and psychology to complementary roles. In the case of the human species, although comparative anthropology shows that the cultural diversity so characteristic of the human species is evident also in human reproductive behavior, the *nuclear* family of man, woman, and

---

(co-authored with Kevin D. O'Rourke) (Washington, DC: Georgetown University Press, 1977; 5th rev. ed. 2006), 55–59; and *The Ashley Reader,* Chapter 14, "Can We Make a Fundamental Option? " 203–22.

3. This question is much disputed. World population increased very rapidly in the last couple of centuries but this growth is slowing; half the world has now made the "demographic transition" to a population decline. Yet other experts express pessimistic views about the world population. A good discussion of the various views on this dispute question is at Answers.com, "Overpopulation," last modified 2011, http://www.answers.com/topic/overpopulation-1.

4. See Stephen E. Rhoads, *Taking Sex Differences Seriously* (San Francisco: Encounter Books, 2004).

children is by far the most common way of meeting this human need.

The only real exception is *polygyny* (many wives), but, although it is accepted in many cultures, it is usually confined to a few rich chiefs as a sign of dominance. *Polyandry* (many husbands) is anthropologically rare.[5] It should be noted that cultural variations of family structure almost always support a patriarchy, matriarchy being very rare.[6]

Furthermore the reasons for this prevalence of the nuclear family are sociobiologically evident. The human female has a very long pregnancy and nursing period because of the large, extremely complex brain of the human child. Unlike other animals her menstrual cycle makes her throughout the year ready for sexual intercourse, and this binds the male to her. By his greater average size and strength he is, for his part, adapted to gathering food for her and protecting her and her children from male rivals or other threats. Thus a monogamous relation favors reproduction and proper education of the children, who mature slowly and have much to learn, since humans have only very general instincts and creative and communicative intelligences.

While it is more controversial as to how much of the apparent difference in female and male psychology recognized in all historic cultures is natural, there is increasing evidence that although there is no innate difference in IQ, there are complementary natural differences in the hormonal system, the development of the brain, and certain kinds of behaviors in the two sexes.[7] These gender differences are not so great as to prevent a considerable overlapping between the male and female ranges of physique and psychology greater than in other primates, but the differences are real and congruent with the notion of evolutionary adaptation to monogamous family life.

From this it seems evident enough that the legitimate striving of

5. "Marriage, Forms of," *The Columbia Electronic Encyclopedia*, 6th ed., last modified 2007, http://www.infoplease.com/ce6/society/A0859493.html.

6. See Jaana Holvikivi, "Matriarchy: history or reality?" last modified Apr 25, 2009, http://www.saunalahti.fi/penelope/Feminism/matriarchy.html with bibliography.

7. See Doreen Kimura, "Sex Differences in the Brain," *Scientific American*, May 13, 2002.

women to achieve the same basic rights as men and not to be restricted in their efforts to realize their individual gifts to the fullest is not served by denying these natural differences. Instead, the tendency of men to dominate women, which feminists complain has characterized all known societies and still is not overcome, shows empirically that at least men are physically stronger than women and equipped psychologically to assert their dominance.

Given this hard fact, women, if they are to defend their human rights, must follow quite a different strategy than that advocated by radical feminists. The strategy of the women in Aristophanes' comedy *Lysistrata*, namely, withholding their sexual favors from men in order to force the men to make peace, although advocated by some lesbians, would lead to women's own sexual frustration. The new possibility of meeting women's natural and sometimes urgent desire for children by artificial reproduction is proposed by some; but again women also need male companionship.

Actually such gains as women have made have come about through a united effort to show men that the genders, as complementary, equally need each other and that their common happiness will be possible only if they mutually respect the equal personhood and equal basic rights of the other. The relation between the sexes is inevitably fraught with difficulties because of their natural differences and consequent different experiences and reactions to situations. The difficulties can be overcome only by good communication and the development of the moral virtues by both partners. To treat the relation in terms of "oppression" and "victimization" instead of in terms of mutual understanding and cooperation succeeds only in scape-goating and it only exacerbates disagreements. Problems of marital discord are a specialty within the broader scope of psychotherapy, but they commonly arise as at least secondary factors in most cases with which therapists must deal, either as causes or as effects of mental illness.

The Natural Basis of Marriage

Fundamental to peaceful heterosexual relations is the natural restriction of sex to permanent monogamy enforced by appropriate social standards and rituals. It is a principle of the psychology of habit formation that pleasure reinforces and habituates. The more intense the pleasurable experiences, the more habituating they are, as is evident in chemical addiction. Because erotic pleasure is the most intense of natural physical pleasures (possibly with the exception of abnormal drug experiences), even a single act can significantly contribute to the formation of moral habits. The Church has always considered even a single act of deliberate sexual indulgence (for example, fornication and adultery) to be a mortal sin, since those who with full deliberation sin in this way abandon their commitment to God as their ultimate end and enter on the road of what the Bible calls "idolatry," making physical pleasure their god.

It is generally thought today that masturbation does little harm to those who practice it, and some have even argued that it is natural and beneficial for teenagers because it helps them to "learn about their bodies."[8] Yet *narcissism*, the psychological fixation on oneself that blocks persons from developing the social aspects of human personality, is generally recognized as a psychological defect; masturbation strongly promotes this defect and tends to make the masturbator regard a sexual partner simply as a "thing," a sexual device, rather than a person. Moreover, the ease and secrecy in which self-abuse can be practiced and the intense pleasure derived from it, and then the natural sense of shame and inadequacy the follows on it, sets the pattern of the addictive personality. The addict deals with difficult life situations

8. Fr. Charles Curran, who claimed a right to dissent from non-infallible Church teaching but was removed by John Paul II from his professorship at the Catholic University of America, promoted this view; see his "Masturbation and Objectively Grave Matter," in *A New Look at Christian Morality* (Notre Dame, IN: Fides Press, 1968), 214. Fr. Curran first proposed this opinion at the Catholic Theological Society of America in 1966.

by sensual indulgences that are followed by feelings of shame at the addict's weakness and folly; those feelings are then met by a new bout of indulgence. Masturbation readily takes on this cyclical addictive, depressive, and narcissistic character; hence for therapists to excuse it (or worse, to suggest it) is a grave error.[9] The attempt of certain Catholic "proportionalist" moral theologians to argue that such acts are not mortal sins because they are so common even in the lives of otherwise virtuous persons, or because they are normal stages in adolescent development, is rightly rejected by the Church in its long experience.

The harm of deliberate sexual sin is not physical; nor is it psychological, in the sense of producing neuroses or psychoses, as was thought in the nineteenth century. It is seriously harmful because the use of erotic pleasure for its own sake or to cope with depression or "to relieve sexual tension" produces a vicious, de-personalizing attitude toward sexuality that will make successful marriage much more difficult. True and committed marriage demands that the partners have intercourse not primarily for the pleasure but primarily as expression of fruitful love for a person of the opposite sex with whom one is building or hopes to build a family. This has been the constant teaching of the Church and was fully formulated in Paul VI's 1968 encyclical *Humanae Vitae (HV).*[10] With the concurrence of the bishops it was confirmed in the *Catechism of the Catholic Church,* no. 2366, as the "inseparable connection ... between the unitive significance and the procreative significance which are both inherent to the marriage act (*HV*, n. 12)."

It is true of all physical pleasures that they should not be sought as ends in themselves but as a support to some virtuous action. We should eat to be healthy and thus rightfully take pleasure in moderate eating, because this promotes good digestion and is recreative; as soon as this pleasure becomes an end rather than a support to seek-

9. On this question see John F. Harvey, OSFS (1918–2010), "The Pastoral Problem of Masturbation," last modified 2011, www.couragerc.net/Masturbation.html.

10. Pope Paul IV, "On the Regulation of Birth," last modified 1968, http://www.vatican.va/holy_father/paul_vi/encyclicals/documents/hf_p-vi_enc_25071968_humanae-vitae_en.html.

ing a good end, eating becomes unhealthy gluttony and human freedom is diminished by addiction. Similarly a couple who truly love each other as persons seek a union that is powerfully supported by erotic pleasure, but if a partner becomes a sexual object to be used for pleasure as such, a spiritual division and conflict enter the marriage. Those only are prepared for a good marriage who come to this commitment as virgins or who have overcome sexual vice and acquired a true virtue of chastity. Without this virtue, it is unlikely they can abstain from sex when this is reasonable; while those who have acquired sexual vice through self-indulgence in masturbation, with prostitutes, cohabitation, casual relationships, or other extra-marital eroticism have made true married love difficult. This is also an injustice to their partner and to their future family, for whom the fidelity and permanence of the marriage bond is of great importance.

The Church is accused of proposing a ridiculously ideal and impractical view of sex, but her teaching is based on an age-old experience of human beings as they really are in a fallen world. The Church knows well the great misery caused in human life—and especially for women and children—by male sexual lust, but also the degradation of women through prostitution and adultery. Freud was probably right in claiming that a disordered libido is at the root of most human disorders, including violence, although his views on how to meet such problems are seriously mistaken. If physical pleasure is our god, we are likely to commit any crime to please that idol.

The Inseparability of Sexual Love from Family Life

The inseparably dual, unitive and procreative, character of human sexuality distinguishes it from the purely procreative function of sex in animals. For animals, the good of the species is biologically supreme. The evolutionist Richard Dawkins has emphasized this in his concept of "the selfish gene."[11] According to Dawkins, the individ-

11. Richard Dawkins, *The Selfish Gene*, rev. ed. (New York: Oxford University Press, 1989).

ual animal exists to pass on its genes to the next generation. The human person, however, as we have seen above, is an end in itself, not a means to preserve the species. As a spiritual being, each person survives death as regards her or his soul. Thus procreation, although a major human activity, is not our highest kind of activity, which is to know and love God and the other persons God has created in the formation of a spiritual community. The question of the single life will be discussed more fully in the next chapter.

St. Thomas Aquinas explains that sex is natural for both union and procreation and is legitimately supported by erotic pleasure moderated by reason in order to best serve this twofold goal. *Humanae Vitae* was content simply to state the Principle of Inseparability negatively, not making explicit its more positive formulation. Pope John Paul II has written much, both philosophically and theologically, to clarify this positive relationship.[12] All inter-human relationships must be fundamentally motivated by love. As Aquinas teaches, genuine love seeks both the welfare of the other person and union with the other person, that is, it seeks a community in which a common good is shared. We can apply this principle to the reproductive activity of the human species in contrast to that of other animals by saying that, for us, reproductive activity is subordinate to the higher goal of interpersonal love. For that reason it can, when necessary, be sacrificed for the sake of the higher good by sexual abstinence. Nonetheless, when such sacrifices are not necessary, reproductive activity should be realized in harmony with that higher goal of love and hence must be given its specific character by this subordination.

The subordination of one good to another can either be that of a mere means to an end, or it can be what Aquinas calls a *bonum honestum,* or *per se* good (an end in itself) that is also a means to a higher

12. See Karol Wojtyla (Pope John Paul II), *Love and Responsibility*, trans. H. T. Willetts (New York: Farrar, Straus, Giroux, 1981), and John Paul II, *The Theology of the Body: Love in the Divine Plan*, foreword by John S. Grabowski (Boston: Pauline Books, 1997).

good. Reproduction is not simply a means but a *per se* good, but one that is subordinate to the higher good of the love relation between the two partners. Thus the unitive and reproductive purposes of human sex are related as genus—the higher goal of love that must motivate all human free acts—and species—the sexual, reproductive nature of the human marriage relationship. As the parents' care of their children is a special kind of love, so their love of each other is a special kind of love, the special manifestation of which is the act of sexual union.

The inseparability of the unitive and reproductive purpose of the sexual act does not imply that the couple must intend reproduction in every act, since its unitive purpose is good in itself. This is why sterile couples can morally engage in intercourse and why, when there is sufficient reason to avoid pregnancy, it is legitimate to limit intercourse to the woman's infertile period. What the inseparability of the purposes excludes is the use of contraception or any act of full sexual satisfaction such as mutual masturbation, oral or anal sex, sadomasochism, fetishism, bestiality, etc. that essentially lacks the structure of the natural human reproductive act.

Some have denied the foregoing conclusion on the grounds that to forbid such acts exaggerates the physical character of the act at the expense of its intention; they call this alleged error "physicalism" or "biologism." Yet can it be said that a couple that engages in such acts really intends the natural act of sexual union? Certainly they do not intend it, if their purpose is pleasure without love, as in prostitution. Yet it is argued that a couple can contracept in order to express their love, but why is sexual intercourse expressive of personal love? Doesn't a simple embrace express love? Clearly it is because sex is a natural not merely a culturally invented sign of commitment of persons of opposite sex to each other in a relationship that may involve children and hence a permanent commitment for their sake. In all cultures this significance of sex is recognized as a matter of fact.

Consequently the deliberate separation of this sign from its natural, physical relation to reproduction renders the act disordered, so that it becomes ambiguous whether it is an expression of love or merely the use of the other's body as an object of physical pleasure. Thus, the argument against the morality of contraception does indeed include a "physicalist" element, but only in that this physical sign has a natural significance and hence ought to be used with the intention of expressing love. To claim, as some have done, that a loving intention can be expressed by a contraceptive act is thus to ignore whether such an act is an appropriate sign of such an intention. Actually, contracepting so violates the natural meaning of intercourse as to express a different message, namely, the treatment of the partner as a mere object of sexual pleasure. We can tell a lie with the good intention of making another feel good, yet it remains a lie that, when exposed, injures the relation of trust between two persons.

Partners can perform a contraceptive act with the good intention of "making love," but it remains a disordered act that communicates at best a mixed message that is not unitive but divisive. In our contraceptive culture this effect, perhaps not very evident in individual cases, has become glaringly manifest in the widespread decline of permanent marriages, through "marital infidelity and a general lowering of moral standards" as Paul VI predicted in *Humanae Vitae,* n. 17.

Not only is proper control of the sexual drive learned in the family but also control over the aggressive drive, which itself can serve in a contraceptive culture to defend a Catholic view of the family, love, and sex. Everyone knows that parents have to teach their children not to fight each other and to be patient in waiting for treats. The gentle firmness or "touch love" (employing pedagogical discipline and correction in the name of love, shown by a mother and father and especially by the father who is the physically stronger) is the model in which the child must learn to control anger, endure difficulties without whining, yet be pro-active. In our society, in which the public media constantly glorify violence, even by women, brutality and rage seem admirable. The entire social order, though, depends on the ability of its citizens to keep the peace, yet have the courage to defend that order when necessary. At the core of peace is peace in the security of loving and patient families.

The Well-Being of Children

Fundamental to the well-being of children is the security they feel in their knowledge that both parents are permanently committed to their care. "Love" in the fully human sense of that word is not yet known to a child, who is still largely a self-centered little organism trying to survive. But they experience their helplessness in a difficult world; hence they long for the security provided by the presence of their mother, but also that of their father, because the mother's own sense of security that she communicates to her children is itself strengthened by the father's attentive presence.[13]

Studies of the children of divorce show that the damage the child suffers from this loss of security is commonly greater than that the child suffers by quarrels within the marriage. Important to this sense of security is children's growing awareness that they are linked to their parents by a physical bond (this may have an instinctive basis) and ultimately by the fact that they were generated by a natural act of love. How important this is can be demonstrated by many accounts of the anxiety of adopted children to discover who their "real" parents are, even when their adoptive parents are very protective and loving.[14]

13. "While parents may be devastated or relieved by the divorce, children are invariably frightened and confused by the threat to their security." American Academy of Child and Adolescent Psychiatry, "Children and Divorce," last modified March 2011, http://www.aacap.org/publications/factsfam/divorce.htm. See also Mayo Clinic, "Divorce: Helping Your Child Cope with the Breakup," last modified May 14, 2011, http://www.mayoclinic.com/health/divorce/HO00055. For statistics see "Children of Divorce: All Kinds of Problems," last modified March, 2011, http://www.aacap.org/publications/factsfam/divorce.htm.

14. American Academy of Child and Adolescent Psychiatry, "Children and Divorce," last modified March 2011, http://www.aacap.org/publications/factsfam/divorce.htm.

The mother and father's roles in child-care are both essential, and they are different.[15] Freud at least made us aware of how female children and male children identify with mother and father differently, but must eventually transcend this dependency relationship in order to form wider social relations and enter successfully into their own marriages. The maternal role is most influential in the early years of the child. It seems especially to affect the development of the pleasure drive and the imagination and thus prepare for the development of the virtue of temperance and the virtue of fortitude in its patience aspects and at the intellectual level of intuition. The father's influence increases later and relates especially to the aggressive drive and the evaluative sense, and thus prepares for the virtues of fortitude in its aggressive sense, justice, and prudence. The child with a cold, anxious, or addictive mother is likely to have difficulties of that same type. The child with an absent, weak, or violent father has related problems.

The famous Freudian Oedipus complex is Freud's description of the adolescent's struggle to escape dependence on parents into self-responsible adulthood, and the natural difficulty of this struggle is increased if the complex, complementary parental relationship is abnormal. In current society where cohabitation, divorce, and resort to artificial reproduction are increasing, the insecurity of children will probably continue to increase, because their sense of physical and emotional bonding to their parents is more and more threatened.

The Complementarity of Motherhood and Fatherhood

In the successful family, the nurturing role of the mother and the importance of her permitting the child to acquire autonomy—not to smother it by possessiveness—is too well recognized today to require emphasis. Yet in the past children have suffered much maternal neglect, as in the practice of handing them over to wet-nurses,

15. See Kyle D. Pruett, M.D., *Father Need: Why Father Care Is as Essential as Mother Care for Your Child* (New York: Free Press, 2000).

or to nannies, etc.[16] Today working mothers are likely to hand them over to day-nurseries, with expectable challenges to healthy attachment styles. What is less recognized in our society is the father's role. Feminists urge that fathers act like mothers, so as to relieve the mother for work, but they denounce the evils of "patriarchy." If "patriarchy" is identified with an abuse of the proper male role, I would agree, but not to a denial that the father has a special role different than the mother's. While each family is somewhat different, the child needs the father in order to be prepared to leave the mother's care and meet the problems of the outer "world," "the larger society." It was this sense, I believe, that St. Thomas Aquinas held that the father needs prudence more than the mother. While the mother emphasizes "unconditional acceptance" of the child, the father emphasizes "discipline to meet life's difficulties." The mother is empathetic with the child's emotional state; the father insists that the child abide by objective rules of conduct. The mother moderates the child's pleasure drives by her affection; the father strengthens the child's aggressive drives by encouragement of their efforts.[17] In this way the father is a model for his son's development of a healthy male personality, as the mother is a model for her girl's development of a healthy female personality, while both mothers and fathers serve important roles for their children of the opposite sex, as described in Rhoads's research.[18]

These complementary roles of the parents are cooperative, not opposed. When they become exaggerated so that the mother is indulgent and the father is domineering the balance is upset and the children torn apart. What is most helpful is profound love between the parents that then manifests itself in sacrificial love for the children, and a cooperative effort to help them mature and be prepared to acquire the virtues.

16. See Loyd DeMause, *History of Childhood: The Untold Story of Child Abuse* (New York: Peter Bedrick Books, 1988).

17. See Michael E. Lamb, *The Role of the Father in Child Development,* 5th edition (Hoboken, NJ: Wiley and Sons, 2010); and Paul C. Vitz. "The Importance of Fathers," *The Family in America: A Journal of Public Policy* (2011).

18. See Rhoads, *Taking Sex Differences Seriously.*

B. Social Ethics

We Are Political Animals

As the human race multiplied and spread around the globe, small groups often became isolated. Even today, on the margins of the great cultures, people live in tribal groups that have a very simple economy and a social structure that is hardly more than an extended family. Comparative anthropology has devoted much attention to such tribal societies and their peculiar institutions. Some of the studies have exaggerated the significance of the variant moral standards they exhibit. Humans have experimented, somewhere or another, with almost every type of behavior—for example, cannibalism. It would be realistic to argue that some of these behaviors are aberrations, not evidence of human nature, except as experiments that our intelligence makes possible. In fact, as human cultures enlarge and develop, these cultures tend to become more alike, as is evident in the way the major world religions have rather similar moral standards.[19]

The Common Good of Persons

Aristotle, in one of his most remarkable works, the *Politics,* which beautifully exemplifies his empirical methodology, treats of human life in community as he observed it in the common features of the small Greek states that were in the process of forming the widespread Hellenistic culture from which modern western civilization has emerged. He and Aquinas, who also was experiencing the emergence of medieval culture from feudalism, maintain that there are at least three distinct ethical sciences: that of individual life, of family life, and of social or political life. Aristotle, however, left us only a very brief treatment of family life in Book I of the *Politics,* and Aquinas never gave it detailed treatment. In the writings of recent popes of

19. See Kenan Malik, "Human Nature, Human Differences, and the Human Subject," accessed June 15, 2011, Society for the Study of Human Biology, Symposium, London, Sept 20–22, http://www.kenanmalik.com/papers/sshb_universal.html.

the Catholic Church, especially of John Paul II, it has received much greater attention.

John Paul II has emphasized, from his philosophical perspective, that the family is the basis of the larger society, since the family is necessary for the education of citizens as well as the "school of love" for adults in which, by permanent commitment to each other, they fulfill their sexual needs and fully develop their ability to form relations of trust and empathy with others.[20]

Aristotle said, "Humans are political animals," and then showed that in his time half of the people in Athens were non-citizens, slaves. He was also of the opinion that in most non-Greek, "barbarian" lands, all the people except the king and his court were in effect the king's slaves. He was puzzled by this shocking contrast between human nature as political and the enslavement of most humans at a sub-human level. This seemed inconsistent with his general teleological principle that "nature does nothing in vain," that is, where there is a natural end, there is a natural way to it. The dilemma, as he saw it, was due to the fact that a country cannot rise above the level of barbarism without a liberally educated citizenry that has sufficient leisure.[21] In Greece, the economy was insufficient to permit more than half of its population the leisure to receive such an education, and so the enslavement of the rest was necessary to support the leisure of the contemplative class. Aristotle speculated that perhaps someday machines could be invented to do the slaves' work! The only justification he could suggest for the state of affairs in Athens was that at least the slaves, many of whom had been taken in war, had the advantage of survival and could profit from a certain "hand-me-down" of culture from their leisured masters that was lacking to barbarians.

20. For texts see Ramón García de Haro De Goytisolo et al., *Marriage and the Family in the Documents of the Magisterium,* trans. William E. May (San Francisco: Ignatius Press, 1993).

21. Aristotle, *Politics* I, cc. 4–7, 1253b22 seq.; for the texts and a discussion of this problem see my dissertation, "The Theory of Natural Slavery" (Notre Dame, dissertation, Ann Arbor, MI, 1951).

We ought to look at political issues, as the Protestant theologian Reinhold Niebuhr (1891–1972)[22] exhorted us, with a sober realism. In our actual historical condition, explained theologically by the Fall, even today in our progressively "rights conscious," democratic United States we are very far from a just social order. We actually do have the machines that Aristotle imagined, and they do a great deal of our manual work, but we have not liberally educated a large portion of our people.

It can at least be said for Aquinas, and the Christian worldview generally, that it does not accept the Greek contempt for manual work that in Greek eyes made contemplation impossible for most human beings. The example of the carpenter, Jesus of Nazareth, and the tentmaker, St. Paul, and the whole institution of monasticism with its Benedictine model of *Ora et Labora*, a life of prayer and work with one's hands, presented the possibility of contemplation of divine reality open to all, provided that they first attain to a life of moral "virtue," that is, those practical skills by which the general norms of morality can be applied in a *consistent* manner to concrete particular situations met in actual life. The discipline of manual work and such poverty as suffices for a simple life style can in fact promote the acquisition of such virtue, while the life of lazy indulgence that wealth often promotes is a grave obstacle to good character. Though human freedom makes it possible for even bad persons sometimes to do the right thing, consistently good moral behavior in difficult situations requires virtue.

Since unity of decision is necessary in any community, whether in family or the larger society, there must be an agreement on how if, after consultation and dialogue, a final practical judgment must be made. Aquinas points out, against *anarchistic* (from the Greek for leaderless) theories, that because practical judgments depend on concrete experiences that are never the same for all, and because there are

22. *Moral Man and Immoral Society: A Study of Ethics and Politics* (Westminster, MD: John Knox Press, 2001). There is an online edition.

often several ways of accomplishing an end, none of which is without problems, decision simply by consensus is not practical for common life.[23] Nature has itself provided, therefore, for a certain hierarchical structure in the family. Parents must decide for the children in major matters, and when after consultation the parents disagree, the husband must make the final decision. Hence, while both parents must have the virtue of domestic prudence, this is primarily the husband's responsibility.

In the political order, however, there is no such evident natural designation of communal authority. Consequently, Aristotle points out that three types of constitutions (not necessarily written, but perhaps only customary) are possible for human societies.[24] Final decision for common action for the common good can be entrusted either to one person, to several, or to the whole community. Each system has advantages and disadvantages. *Monarchy* (rule of one, not necessarily hereditary) best serves the unity of decision, but depends on the necessarily limited experience and prudence of the ruler. *Oligarchy* (rule of an elite) has the advantage that the different talents of the elite can balance and moderate each other, but often leads to rivalry and disunity. *Democracy* (*demos* is Greek for people, the rule of all, that is, the majority) has the advantage of freedom and of support for decisions made by the majority, but may neglect the rights of minorities, and because of its lack of unity may easily be tempted to accept or succumb to a tyrannical and demagogic dictator. Any of these three forms of government must rule for the common good, since if they serve only the private interests of the one ruler, of an elite, or of factions in a democracy, they become tyrannies. Hence Aristotle concludes, and Aquinas agrees, that usually the best form of government is the "republic" or mixed form in which there are combined elements of all three simple forms. This advice was followed with notable success by the Founding

23. For Aquinas's arguments on this point, see Yves Simon, *A General Theory of Authority* (Notre Dame, IN: University of Notre Dame Press, 1962).

24. *ST* I-II, q. 105, a. 1.

Fathers of the U.S. Constitution, who established a President for unified action, a congress for more experienced deliberation, and popular vote to elect both the president and the congress.

Modern ethics, especially the social doctrine of the Catholic Church, has also developed the "principle of subsidiarity," which is based on these same principles. It maintains the following:[25]

1. Social decisions should be made as far as possible by those most affected by them and hence most experienced with their effects, that is, the most local possible level of the social hierarchy.
2. Higher levels of social organization, though, must oversee and supplement decisions at the lower level in order to insure the attainment of the common good.
3. These higher levels must not permanently retain such supplementation and regulation but should educate the lower levels to resume their proper responsibility of decision.

The goal of common decision and action in any society must be the *common good,* and this requires obedience according to the virtue of *legal justice* by all members of the society. On the other hand the common good is not merely the good of those in authority, nor of some abstract entity (totalitarianism), but it is precisely the good of *each and all* the members of the society.

How is this possible? Is there not sometimes a contradiction between the private and the common good? Aquinas's answer to this is that the good of the human person consists in both private and common goods.[26] Private goods, such as our clothing, and home, and things we eat and drink, cannot be well shared with others because they are *material* goods that must be divided to be consumed privately. There are, of course, also material goods that are essentially common,

25. See David A. Bosnich, "The Principle of Subsidiarity," accessed June 15, 2011, Acton Institute, *Religion and Liberty* 6.4 (1996).

26. See Charles De Koninck, "In Defense of St. Thomas," *Laval Théologique et Philosophique* 1, 2 (1945): 1–103.

such as the security of the state. Common goods, however, are *primarily* those goods that, precisely because they are *spiritual,* can be shared without division and indeed are best achieved when shared, namely virtue and knowledge. When a teacher shares his or her knowledge with a pupil, neither loses and both gain! The great point of both Aristotle and Aquinas is that, just as the contemplation of truth is the goal of the individual human life, so it is also for any human community.

Aristotle and Aquinas both knew that the goal of government is to promote the virtue and wisdom of its citizens. It should do this, however, according to the principle of subsidiarity. Since the virtue of rulers is prudence, not speculative wisdom, Plato was wrong in asking for a "philosopher king."[27] Rather, government should promote virtue by supporting—but not dictating to—heads of families, schools, and religious centers; it should concern itself not principally with the more private aspects of morality but with those aspects that directly affect human rights.

Freedom of Religion, Conscience, and Speech

The need for authority in any community to make possible common action for the common good arises, as already noted, from the fact that in practical matters the choice of means is prudential. Hence persons of equal intelligence, virtue, and good will can disagree as to what is to be done in particular circumstances. This conflict can be still more serious when their worldviews and value systems differ. Even for secularists who claim not to have a "religion," these differences are *functionally* religious, a notion to be explained more fully in Chapter 8. Historically, therefore, most governments have had an "established" state religion or "public philosophy" and at best merely tolerated minority religions. Nor is the modern democratic notion of

27. *The Republic,* Bk VII. Leo Straus, however, argued that Plato was really arguing that a true philosopher king is an impossible ideal; see Straus's article on Plato in *History of Political Philosophy,* ed. Joseph Cropsey (3rd ed.; Chicago: University of Chicago Press, 1987), 33–89.

the "separation of church and state" an entirely unambiguous solution. This separation is usually coupled with the concepts of freedom of conscience and of speech, but these too are difficult to define, as our United States courts have made very evident.

The Catholic Church was for two terrible centuries under constant persecution by the relatively moderate Roman government, but it then became a state church under Constantine the Great (272–337), the so-called "Constantinian Establishment" that lasted down to modern times.[28] The Church, however, especially the Latin Church in its defense of papal authority, always maintained that in religious matters its authority was superior to that of the state. In England even now the Anglican Church is established, but the United States Constitution, next the French Republic, and now the United Nations of Europe have all adopted the principle of separation of state authority from religion.

In fact, however, as already mentioned, this separation has generally tended to a quasi-establishment of secular humanism as the state functional religion of many modern states and the consequent privatization of other religions. A similar corruption has also occurred in regard to the principle of freedom of speech, which was intended to permit open dialogue so as to arrive at truth and to defeat demagogy and deceit. This is especially evident from in the way that our courts have interpreted it to permit widespread commercialized pornography and much hate-literature. Nevertheless, the Catholic Church in Vatican II in the document *Dignitatis Humanae*, "On Human Dignity" (n. 2) has welcomed the modern democratic separation of church and state:

> This Vatican Council declares that the human person has a right to religious freedom. This freedom means that all men are to be immune from coercion on the part of individuals or of social groups and of any human power, in such wise that no one is to be forced

28. Robert Audi, "The Separation of Church and State and the Obligations of Citizenship," *Philosophy and Public Affairs* 18.3 (Summer 1989): 259–96.

> to act in a manner contrary to his own beliefs, whether privately or publicly, whether alone or in association with others, within due limits. The council further declares that the right to religious freedom has its foundation in the very dignity of the human person as these dignities is known through the revealed word of God and by reason itself. This right of the human person to religious freedom is to be recognized in the constitutional law whereby society is governed and thus it is to become a civil right.[29]

It has, though, specified the following qualification:

> This Vatican Council likewise professes its belief that it is upon the human conscience that these obligations [to embrace the known truth] fall and exert their binding force. The truth cannot impose itself except by virtue of its own truth, as it makes its entrance into the mind at once quietly and with power. Religious freedom, in turn, which men demand as necessary to fulfill their duty to worship God, has to do with immunity from coercion in civil society. Therefore it leaves untouched traditional Catholic doctrine on the moral duty of men and societies toward the true religion and toward the one Church of Christ.[30]

This development in the Church's teaching did not contradict its previous acceptance of the Constantinian establishment because in past circumstances nothing else but subjection to state authority or persecution was available to the Church. The question that remains, however, is whether modern states will really live up to this separation or will in fact, though not in name, *privatize*, that is, rule out of the effective public forum,[31] all religions except Secular Humanism, thus in effect making it functionally the state religion. Consequently

29. Second Vatican Council, *Dignitatis Humanae*, Declaration on Human Freedom, 1965, n. 2.

30. *Dignitatis Humanae*, n. 1.

31. I have argued that this danger is very real and today actual in my *Theologies of the Body: Humanist and Christian*, 2nd ed. (Braintree, MA; Pope John Center, 1995), 51–101, and *Choosing a Worldview and Value System: An Ecumenical Apologetics* (Staten Island, NY: Alba House, 2000), 25–62.

world-views and value systems that are thus privatized must have the courage and seek the necessary resources to get their voices heard in the public forum. Our thinking as Christians must be independent of "political correctness."

The rights of conscience are based on the fact that persons are bound by the natural law to seek true happiness by prudently choosing realistic means to that end. Thus the final criterion of a moral act is its conformity to the conscience of the agent. Jesus said (Mt 7:1-2): "Stop judging, that you may not be judged. For as you judge, so will you be judged, and the measure with which you measure will be measured out to you." We cannot honestly judge the conscience of another, since it cannot be observed by us and we know from our own experience that we sometimes make honest decisions that to others appear immoral. Therefore, we may sometimes honestly dissent from the government's laws or public opinion and it is part of the common good that its citizens be able to follow their consciences.

Yet this "right of civil dissent" has limits, since sometimes an action, which a citizen thinks right, in fact is evidently harmful to others and must be restricted for the sake of the common good. In such a case the individual still must act as they think right and take the consequences of public disapproval and even punishment. Martyrdom for one's conscience is a supremely noble and moral act.

Historically an important issue related to these freedoms was the use of torture to obtain information in the interest of the common good. Many think it is permissible, for example, in order to gain information from terrorists that may save many innocent people. Perhaps the greatest and most often mentioned scandal in the Catholic Church was the use of torture by its Holy Inquisition! What is not understood is that as long as there was an established Church heresy and especially the advocacy of heresy was a crime of treason against *both* the unity of the state and of the Church, consequently it was punished by death by the state. The Inquisition of the Church had no power to punish but reserved to itself the right to judge what was heresy and what was not, since this was a religious question on which the state had no expertise. The Inquisition could, however, use moderate torture in its judicial procedures as did the state, although in the notorious Spanish Inquisition it was used in only about 2% of the cases.[32] This procedure was part of the pagan Roman law, which held that testimony against an accused was not trustworthy unless the accuser maintained it even under torture. The medieval revival of Roman Law in place of the barbarian law previously used under feudalism was on the whole a great advance in the appreciation of legal rights, and for this reason the Church accepted it when it was adopted by the state. Again today in our efforts to stop terrorism our U.S. government is debating whether or not torture to obtain information should be permitted. The *Catechism of the Catholic Church*, however, has now learned from its regretted past mistakes to oppose this in the following statements:

> n. 2297. Kidnapping and hostage taking bring on a reign of terror; by means of threats they subject their victims to intolerable pressures. They are morally wrong. Terrorism threatens, wounds, and kills indiscriminately; it is gravely against justice and charity. Torture which uses physical or moral violence to extract confessions, punish the guilty, frighten opponents, or satisfy hatred is contrary to respect for the person and for human dignity. Except when performed for strictly therapeutic medical reasons, directly intended amputations, mutilations, and sterilizations performed on innocent persons are against the moral law.
>
> 2298. In times past, cruel practices were commonly used by legitimate governments to maintain law and order, often without protest from the Pastors of the Church, who themselves adopted in their own tribunals the prescriptions of Roman law concerning torture. Regrettable as these facts are, the Church always taught the duty of clemency

32. See Thomas F. Madden, "The Truth about the Spanish Inquisition," *Crisis* (October 2003); and also Henry Kamen, *The Spanish Inquisition: A Historical Revision* (New Haven: Yale University Press, 1998).

and mercy. She forbade clerics to shed blood. In recent times it has become evident that these cruel practices were neither necessary for public order, nor in conformity with the legitimate rights of the human person. On the contrary, these practices led to ones even more degrading. It is necessary to work for their abolition. We must pray for the victims and their tormentors.

Sociology, Anthropology, Social Psychology

Since ethics takes its principles from the goals that are given in human nature, it has to be grounded on an anthropology or analysis of human nature. This analysis of human nature is first of all the eminent subject of natural science. Hence ethics depends on natural science as its necessary condition. Aristotle notes, however, that we should look for less certainty in ethics than in natural science because of its greater complexity.[33] Hence ethicists need have only a general knowledge of natural science, although they must be opened to any new scientific information that may improvement ethical analysis. Thus the principles of ethical science are directly evident, although with a merely common sense precision, from human experience that grounds the three autonomous but related disciplines already mentioned, since the problems of individual ethics, the ethics of managing a family, and the ethics of managing a larger community has different specific goals and presents different problems in attaining those goals.

When we speak of "human nature" the term "nature" is only analogous to its use in natural science, since the latter refers only to material things, and natural moral law is only analogous to natural physical law. Thus, while the account of human nature given by natural science suffices to develop a genuine ethic, once it has been concluded that the goal of human life is contemplation and that this requires a kind of knowledge that extends to spiritual realities, then it becomes evident that the completion of ethics whose subject is the human

33. *Nicomachean Ethics* I, 3, 1094 b12–28.

person in its integral perfection must pertain to metaphysics. What metaphysics adds to ethics as such is precisely the appreciation of the human person as spiritual and thus ordered to God and to the community of other spirits.

Unfortunately modern Analytic Philosophy, British Empiricism, and American Pragmatism have neglected human spirituality and are generally content with moral relativism, utilitarianism or "emotive ethics." Catholics too have engaged in a recent controversy over "proportionalism" (similar to utilitarianism, consequentialism, or situationalism) that has, however, been, as already mentioned, officially rejected by the Church as "teleologism" in contrast to a genuinely teleological ethics traditional to Christianity. Only if the spiritual nature of true human happiness is taken fully into account can an adequate human ethics based on reason (without entering into theological considerations based on revelation) be developed.

From the foregoing we can conclude how important it is in interdisciplinary and multicultural dialogue to make use of metaphysics and its comparative study of worldviews to relate natural science and especially the fields of anthropology and psychology to the comparative study of ethical systems. The marked contrast between the secular materialist worldviews and those that understand the human person primarily in spiritual terms must be faced. Furthermore within the spiritual worldviews the marked contrast between the monotheistic perspective of Judaism, Christianity, and Islam on the value of the human person and the often monistic perspectives of Hinduism and Buddhism with their key concept of reincarnation and the relative lack of concern of the Chinese and Japanese cultures about the future life must not be avoided. At the same time the convergence of these various worldviews on many moral norms must also be acknowledged and reinforced by cooperation for peace and social justice.[34]

Today's post-modernism, prophetically anticipated in the nineteenth century by Nietzsche and in the twentieth cleverly proclaimed

34. See my *Choosing a Worldview.*

by Jacques Derrida (1930–3004), can best be understood as the recognition that the Enlightenment and its Secular Humanism, particularly in its Marxist form favored by many European intellectuals, has failed to produce a healthy political order. Yet in the twentieth century, philosophy was centered in political questions, in view of the violent social upheavals and wars of that period. Analytical philosophy dominated Great Britain, beginning with G. E. Moore (1873–1958). It spread to the United States and fused with the pragmatism of John Dewey (1859–1952) and the nominalism of William van Orman Quine (1908–2000). It was at first influenced by the "Vienna Circle" of logical positivists, who were concerned with clarifying the language of science. The Circle was first headed by Rudolf Carnap (1891–1970) and then by Ludwig Wittgenstein (1830–1951), who reduced it to "language games" that have no pragmatic necessity.

These British and American thinkers were generally naturalists (materialists), but also proponents of democratic freedoms against the rise of totalitarianism in Europe. In France thought moved from the structuralism of Claude Lévi-Strauss (1908–2009), which emphasized fixed social patterns, to the existentialism of Jean-Paul Sartre (1905–80). There is also the influential Martin Heidegger (1889–1976) who announced the death of European thought, and gave support to the totalitarian Nazis and then to the postmodernists, such as Jean-François Lyotard (1924–98),[35] who renounced what he called "grand narratives," such as Marxism or any universal system of values, and concluded that communities having different worldviews and value systems must just work out *modi vivendi*, on what basis he did not say.

Other philosophers of the ethical relativist view include Thomas S. Kuhn (1922–96) who employed the notion of the social "paradigm shift" in science independent of real evidence. Jean Baudrillard (1929–2007), who held that we live no longer in a real, historical world but in a world of appearances produced by the media, and Michel Fou-

35. See his *The Postmodern Condition: A Report on Knowledge* (Minneapolis: University of Minnesota Press, 1984).

cault (b. 1926, died of AIDS in 1984), who argued that language does not refer to reality or have meaning but is a method of controlling others and who applied this view notably to psychiatry. Roland Barthes (1915–80), Paul de Man (1919–83, who supported the Nazis), and the "post-modernist" Jacques Derrida were concerned with literature and how "texts" have meaning only by reference to other "texts" and hence must be "deconstructed."

Central to all this varied philosophizing has been the sense that the Enlightenment and the capitalism it had supported had failed and that the hopes for Marxism as a global search for social justice had also spawned Nazism, as well as the perception that science was revealing a humanly meaningless universe. Thus, even in the United States, where political optimism has generally flourished, the pragmatist Richard Rorty (1931–) argues that moral values have no other justification than the common agreement of particular groups as to what these values are.

This post-modern disillusionment can be traced back on the one hand to religious agnosticism or atheism of the Enlightenment and on the other to the totalitarian disasters and wars of the twentieth century (and present terrorism) and to the abuses of modern technology. In both cases, the failure to root ethics in the nature of the human person is manifest. Yet an adequate explanation of many of these social disasters involves the discipline of *social psychology*,[36] which shows how, since we are so deeply social beings, abnormal mental states can spread through groups by communication and suggestion, especially when the group's value system has become conflicted. Because "religion" in the *functional* sense of a worldview and value system is basic to everyone's behavior, mass hysteria such as the European witch craze of the sixteenth and seventeenth centuries, or the

36. G. W. Allport, "The Historical Background of Social Psychology," in *The Handbook of Social Psychology*, ed. G. Lindzey and E. Aronson (New York: McGraw Hill, 1985); also S. Moscovici and I. Markova, *The Making of Modern Social Psychology* (Cambridge, UK: Polity Press, 2006).

anti-Semitism of the twentieth century, or the present terrorism of radical Muslims, is often attributed by secularists to religion in general. In fact such violent phenomena, although they can take on religious garb, often have economic and other causes.[37] As we have seen the use of torture by the Catholic Inquisition was due to the revival of pagan Roman law to replace barbaric law. Hitler was anti-Christian as well as anti-Semitic.[38] Muslim terrorism often results from political motives. It is an important task of social psychology to expose the real motives of such abuses of human dignity.

The modern trend to divorce the "is" from the "ought," facts from values, has given rise to disciplines called "sociology" and "cultural anthropology," disciplines that study human social behavior but claim to take no position on ethical right or wrong. These disciplines legitimately study disruptive social phenomena in order to compare cultures, but it leads to illusions if they do not take into account the needs common to the human species and the socially destructive effect that results from ignoring them. A sociology that would ignore the results of malnutrition, or a declining birth-rate in a society, or the prevalence of AIDS resulting from sexual promiscuity in a country, or growing illiteracy—such a discipline could not claim to be scientific.

Technology and the Environment

Modern politics got special support from the belief that scientific technology, rather than prayer to a merciful deity, could solve human problems. In fact, the technologies are distinguished from the ethical sciences in that the goals studied by the latter are fixed in human nature and are thus *unconditional,* whereas the goals of the technologies

37. See Michael J. Colligan, *Mass Psychogenic Illness: A Social Psychological Analysis* (Hillsdale, NJ: Lawrence Erlbaum Associates, 1982) and http://www.csicop.org/si/2000-05/Robert E. Bartholomew and Erich Goode, "Mass Delusions and Hysterias: Highlights from the Past Millennium," *Skeptical Inquirer,* May/June 2000, http://www.csicop.org/si/2000-05/delusions.html.

38. H. R. Trevor-Roper, *Hitler's Secret Conversations 1941–1944* (New York: Signet, 1961).

are freely chosen. I am ethically obliged to try to keep healthy, but although I am obliged to play ping-pong according to the rules of the game, this is so only if I freely choose to play ping-pong. In a classical view, the technologies are subordinated to the ethical sciences, since unless what they achieve is helpful for a good life they are a waste of time, and if it is harmful (the production of atomic weapons or cigarettes) they are immoral and cannot be properly called "practical." The so-called "technological imperative" to do whatever we have the technological power to do, is obviously bad ethics.

In addition to what has already been said about technology in previous chapters, here it is only necessary to relate the metaphysical notion of "goodness" to what for us today is the pressing problem of *environmentalism*. We human beings could not exist without the remarkably balanced ecology of our earth, and hence we must always be concerned that our use of technological control over the environment preserves these features and alters them only in view of a good life for all humankind.[39] Yet current discussion of environmentalism sometimes loses sight of the fact that our obligation to preserve and perfect the environment is primarily to promote good *human* life, not to preserve the inanimate or subhuman species that constitute this environment. Rocks, trees, whales are ontologically good in themselves, but if the teleological aspect of natural science that has been defended in this book is correct, non-intelligent things find their ultimate perfection in their service of intelligent life. Moreover, sub-human animals do not have intelligent, spiritual life as we have seen human beings do, but at best only present a preparation for the existence of human life.

To hold, as Peter Singer has argued,[40] that animals have "rights" because they can feel pain is mistaken for two reasons. First, and most important, the rights of human beings are not founded on their ability

39. See Allen D. Kanner, Theodore Roszak, and Mary E. Gomes, eds., *Ecopsychology: Restoring the Earth, Healing the Mind* (San FranciscoA: Sierra Club Books, 1995).

40. For the debate over Peter Singer's views, see Dale Jamieson, *Singer and His Critics* (Oxford: Blackwell, 1999).

to feel pain—since even unconscious persons who feel no pain have rights—but on their personhood. Personhood principally depends on intelligence and free will, which humans but not animals possess. Second, it is gratuitous to assert that animal pain is identical with human pain. Studies of human pain show that it consists not only in a physical feeling but also in the fear and anxiety of the sufferer.[41]

Sufferers see either that their pain is a sign that happiness as the goal of life is becoming inaccessible or that it has to be met with a great effort of courage and patience. This major human component in addressing pain is lacking in animals, because they lack true self-consciousness and a perception of an ultimate goal of life. Hence animals have "rights" only in an analogous sense, namely, that they deserve to be treated with respect for the remarkable creatures they are and spared unnecessary injury or suffering. Moreover, cruelty to animals tends to brutalize their human abusers and lead them to abuse other humans. Unless one accepts the notion of the transmigration of souls of Eastern religions, however, we do sub-human creatures no injustice to use them for good human purposes.

We must also keep in mind that the greatest service that the material universe serves for spiritual beings, including human persons, is not just the provision of material needs. As shown in Chapter 2, among spiritual beings only humans require material support, but all spirits, including the pure spirits, need the material universe as the mirror in which they come to a natural knowledge of their First Cause. The Creator has carefully adjusted the universe to the minds of creatures so that it is beautiful and by its beauty attracts intelligent creatures to God in love, as indicated by our word "cosmos," which in the Greek from which it is derived signifies "that which is in good order." Genesis 1:31 declares, "God looked at everything he had made,

41. A standard text is R. Gatchel and D. C. Turk, *Psychological Approaches to Pain Management* (New York: Guilford Publications, 1996); see also International Association for the Study of Pain, "Curriculum on Pain for Students of Psychology," last modified 2011, http://www.iasp-pain.org//AM/Template.cfm?Section=Home.

and he found it very good." Moreover angels, like engineers, serve the Creator in supervising the material creation so that it keeps running, in all its historical contingency.

Consequently, environmentalism must use as its criteria for legitimate changes in the environment not only whether earth's biodiversity will continue to supply our material needs, but also whether such changes will increase the beauty of our *garden* earth that is at once a natural wonder and a work of human art. We cannot, of course, preserve all the species of living things that have existed in the course of evolution; without a rich biodiversity, though, this work of wonder and of art will be greatly diminished,

In our respect for the earth and its beauty we can find much support in all the great religions of the world and in the traditional religions of marginal peoples, since in all of them there are important elements that can contribute to this appreciation.

Professional Ethics

The concept of the learned professions, including psychology, psychiatry, and psychotherapy, as very important factors in providing a system of social ethics goes back to the "Hippocratic Oath" taken by Greek physicians.[42] Its extensive development, however, began in the medieval universities that prepared physicians, lawyers, the clergy, and teachers.

Today other professions have been added and the older ones subdivided. It is common for professionals to form organizations to supervise the responsible conduct of their members, to set professional standards of competency, and to formulate codes of ethics. In recent years there has been a great development of what was formerly called "medical ethics" and is now called "bioethics." This is true also of psychiatry, but we should not, therefore, conclude that psychologists are

42. See L. Edelstein, *The Hippocratic Oath* (Chicago: Ares Publishers, 1979), and Steven H. Miles, *The Hippocratic Oath and the Ethics of Medicine* (New York: Oxford University Press, 2004).

professional ethical counselors. It is the thesis of the present book that the task of mental health professionals is to free those they treat from disordered feelings that prevent them from making prudent moral decisions.

Conclusion

The natural goal of human life, true happiness, is fulfillment of the basic human needs for physical health, security, and moderate material possessions, formation in a good family, the passing on of life and friendship, cooperating for the common good, and seeking a true understanding of oneself and of God. Such happiness can be achieved only if one's personal, family, and community life are guided by realistic, prudent decisions that respect the rights of others and are not hampered but facilitated by moderation in one's drives for pleasure and by courage in difficulties. To make consistently good decisions requires the development of skills or virtues and the formation of helpful social and governmental structures of authority, respectful of subsidiarity.

Christians believe that Jesus Christ perfectly possessed such virtues and gave us a model to imitate. Furthermore, He and the Father have sent the Holy Spirit, whose power underlies the teachings and sacraments of a community, the Catholic Church, and who will ultimately not only restore humanity to happiness but lead them beyond mere human happiness to a share in the eternal happiness found in the Beatific Vision of God, Father, Son, and Holy Spirit. Christ heals and perfects the character of human persons by faith that clarifies prudence, hope that makes moderation and courage possible and even easy, and love that includes justice but extends beyond it through mercy.

eight

SEEKING GOD

The Human Need for a "Religion"

Freud wrote *The Future of an Illusion* to prove that religion is based on the Oedipus complex and the super-ego and is essentially a neurosis.[1] Later, in *Moses and Monotheism*,[2] he modified this to say somewhat more positively, as Jürgen Braungardt writes:

> Freud interprets the formation of religions in terms of their function in this conflict between nature and culture, or between the ego and the drive. Religions are remarkable compromise formations: they allow the human being to admit its extraordinary vulnerability and at the same time, to retain a sense of superiority in relation to the surrounding reality. The price for the compromise is the submission to an "illusion." Religious dogmas are not the results of experience or thinking, but they are refined fantasies, wish-fulfillments in response

1. *The Future of an Illusion*, with "A Brief Life" by Peter Gay, reissue edition (New York: W. W. Norton, 1989; original 1927); cf. Paul C. Vitz, *Sigmund Freud's Christian Unconscious* (Grand Rapids, MI: W. B. Eerdmans, 1993), who shows that Freud struggled with his own religious problems all his life.

2. *Moses and Monotheism* (New York: Vintage, 1955, original 1939).

to the most basic needs of humankind. The strength of the illusion is therefore reciprocal to the strength of the need.[3]

The element of truth in Freud's view is that in some religions—particularly Judaism and Christianity, which Freud had in mind—the best analogy for our relation to God, as Jesus said, is "Abba, Father" (Mk 14:36; Rm 8:15; Gal 4:6; Isa 63:16). How his view would apply to monistic religions in which the goddess is the object of faith is not so clear. In any case his view is based on his reductionist materialism, which as I showed in Chapter 2 is disproved by the foundational scientific demonstration of the existence of the First Cause, a demonstration that is entirely independent of fanciful illusion.

We must recognize that religious illusions are common features of mental illness, but to conclude from this fact that religion is a mental illusion is bad logic. It is not surprising that, because religion is a person's worldview and value system, which is basic to all free decisions and therefore sets the relative importance of a person's life goals, it necessarily is involved when a person's freedom is inhibited by mental illness. The schizophrenic who hears voices may very well have the illusion that God or the devil is telling him to perform bizarre acts, but it is not his religious faith but his sick imagination that is their cause.[4] On the contrary, religious faith may help the person in their struggle to come to a truer self-understanding and seek to regain mental and physical health.[5]

Agnosticism about religion, or even atheism, is a common feature of psychology and psychotherapy as they are taught in today's universities.[6] In the "functional" sense, used by experts in compara-

3. See Jürgen Braungardt, "Freud on Religion," last modified 2002, http://www.braungardt.com/Essays/Freud's%20view%20of%20Religion.htm

4. *Catechism of the Catholic Church*, no. 1673.

5. See Louis Dupré, "The Wounded Self: The Religious Meaning of Mental Suffering," accessed June 15, 2011, http://www.religion-online.org/showarticle.asp?title=1826

6. See Paul C. Vitz, *Psychology As Religion: The Cult of Self-Worship*, 2d ed. (Grand Rapids, MI: Eerdmans, 1994); Vitz, *Faith of the Fatherless: The Psychology of Atheism* (Dallas, TX: Spence, 2000).

tive religion, rather than in the ordinary "content" sense, we all have to have a "religion."[7] The content of the different world religions is so varied though that it does not serve well to call them all "religions"; Buddhism for example is not based on a belief in God, and many religions are monistic, identifying God with the world. It is instead their *function* in human life that makes meaningful comparison possible. We all have to make decisions and commitments and hence must have some *value system* and also a *worldview* by which that value system is validated.[8] Thus atheist and agnostic secularists, who are "anti-religious" as regards the content of the traditional religions, are nevertheless themselves committed to the functional religion of secular humanism that has grown up since the Enlightenment and is today becoming global. Most therapists, therefore, have been subjected, at least at the level of super-ego, to this anti-religious religion.

Psychotherapy may free a client to clarify or even to reconsider the worldview and value system or religion to which the client is committed, but it ought not leave the client without some reasonable system of values, since without such a system clients cannot make free decisions. Christian therapists, if they rightly understand the consequences of their own religious commitment, can enable others to recognize and clarify the value system to which they are committed or to which they would prefer to be committed once they are thinking realistically. They should, however, leave the client free to choose their system of values, unless it is obvious that the client's commitment was not really free but symptomatic of mental illness. As Jesus began to preach, "When his relatives heard of this they set out to seize him, for they said, 'He is out of his mind'" (Mk 3:20). Since, however, Jesus showed such profound wisdom and serenity and worked true miracles, the Pharisees said, "He is possessed by Beelzebul," and "By

7. See Robert D. Baird, *Category Formation and the History of Religions* (The Hague: Mouton, 1971).

8. See my *Choosing a Worldview and Value System: An Ecumentical Apologetics* (Staten Island, NY: Alba House, 2000).

the prince of demons he drives out demons" (Mk 3:22). Throughout history geniuses have been called "crazy." The psychotherapist Thomas Szasz became famous for his book *The Myth of Mental Illness*,[9] in which he contended that distinction between mental health and illness is mainly cultural. Yet, as I have argued through this book, critical reasoning that is empirically based can distinguish reality from illusion and prejudice.

Mental health, ethical goodness, and religious credibility are not merely arbitrary notions. As we saw in Chapters 6 and 7, it is common today to talk about ethical "values," a term derived from economics, rather than, as in traditional ethics, about "goods." The danger of this newer terminology is that it suggests that moral laws only state *ideals* that can never be perfectly realized in actual human life. In Chapter 6, I argued to the contrary, that a sound teleological ethics must be based on an anthropology that is *empirically* verifiable. Christian ethics, therefore, is based on the historical realization of perfect human virtue by Jesus Christ and his Mother, which is closely copied by the Christian saints. Since "grace perfects nature," from what we know historically, apart from revelation, of these models, their lives provide an empirical basis for a natural ethics. Hence the revealed ethics of faith can also be a support and refinement to an empirical ethics of reason and be supported by it.

Our need for a set of values cannot be simply a matter of individual commitment, as the existentialists claimed. For, as I argued in the last chapter, we are profoundly social beings, and so in order to live a set of values we must find a community of like-minded persons who will support us and share values with us. That is why the Church is central to the Christian religion and why even secular humanists seek to dominate the culture of which they are apart, as we see them today striving to dominate the public media.

9. Thomas Szasz, *The Myth of Mental Illness: Foundations of a Theory of Personal Conduct*, revised ed. (New York: Harper and Row, 1984).

Life after Death

An ethics directed exclusively to the moral problems of the present life considered apart from the historical situation of humanity is very incomplete. As we saw in Chapters 1 and 5, Aristotle demonstrated in his *De Anima* that natural science demonstrates that the human intelligence is immaterial. In his extant works, however, he did not tackle the question of the fate of this spiritual soul after the death of its material body. Indeed, it is very difficult to reconcile the survival of the soul after death with Aristotle's principle that "nature does nothing in vain." In his anthropology and epistemology, according to which intellectual knowledge depends on the bodily senses, death of the body seems to put an end to the possibility of our attaining our natural end, namely, true happiness in which the supreme good is intellectual contemplation.

For Aquinas, as a Christian theologian, this difficulty was ultimately answered by the revealed doctrine of resurrection of the body. But even if this is granted, the question of the state of separated souls prior to the resurrection remains a problem. Hence some Protestant theologians, such as Oscar Cullman (1902–99)[10] have argued for "soul sleep" and the re-creation of the souls of the dead at the resurrection. Aquinas, however, thought that metaphysics, since it deals with the analogy between material and immaterial Being, assures us that the soul survives and retains an intrinsic relation to the body it has lost but requires to constitute a complete human person. Hence St. Thomas was convinced that the separated soul continues to contemplate itself, the universe, and God in a manner that resembles that of the pure spirits.[11] This is possible because it no longer acts as a form of the matter of the body that in bodily life limited the proper and di-

10. See Carol Zaleski, "In Defense of Immortality," *First Things* 105 (August/September 2000): 36–42. Cullman was a Lutheran, and Luther had for a while held for soul sleep, but eventually denounced it.

11. *ST* I, q. 89, aa. 1–8; Suppl., q. 70, aa.1–2.

rect object of its intelligence to the essence of material things. In its separated condition, though, the human soul's self-consciousness of its own spiritual acts (and hence of the spirituality of its intelligence and of the self for which it is a property) ceases to be indirect and becomes direct by "immediate information," just as it is for pure spirits. Aquinas, using a term of St. Augustine's, speaks of this mode of knowledge as a "divine illumination," but he intends by this the *natural* participation of the angels in divine knowledge through the innate ideas given them in their creation as part of their very natures.

Yet, since Aquinas denied that human souls have such innate ideas, it was necessary for him to posit that God gives to humans souls at death, in addition to those abstract concepts they have learned during their bodily lives, those ideas of concrete singulars that they need to know before they get their bodies back in the resurrection. Those virtuous souls, therefore, who at death are committed, along with other good spirits, to the true natural end of the contemplation of God will continue this contemplation after death and even more perfectly than in this life and thus will attain a true natural happiness.

Yet for the dead, natural happiness remains an imperfect happiness. They lack their complete body-soul personhood, and their natural happiness is also limited by their finite natures. Perfect beatitude, Aquinas shows,[12] is possible only through intimate participation in the life of God; and to this beatitude creatures have no natural right, although the Christian Gospel assures them this gift can and should be attained by the unmerited grace of God that transcends creaturely limitations.[13]

12. This is the extended argument in the first five questions of *Summa theologiae* I-II.

13. *ST* I, q. 89, aa. 1–8. It was on this basis that Aquinas also proposed the famous "limbo" (threshold) theory that unbaptized children, innocent of personal sin, yet deprived by original sin of the grace they would have inherited from the first parents of the human race, would enjoy only a state of natural happiness. In 2007 the International theological commission published a study entitled "The Hope of Salvation for Infants Who Die without Being Baptized" (http://www.vatican.va/roman_curia/congregations/cfaith/cti_documents/rc_con_cfaith_doc_20070419_un-baptised-infants_en.html).

Thus metaphysics provides some account of the state of separated souls that permits us to say that the *natural* goal of human life is the contemplation of God and that creation is most perfectly attained after death by those who have lived earthly life virtuously. Aquinas agrees with Plato and the Hindu religions, which also posit this goal and believe it to be a state of enlightenment attained after death. Yet Aquinas, as we have seen, would not agree with them that this enlightenment is identification with the Absolute, as Hindu *Vedanta* holds, or the cessation of the individual in Nirvana, as Buddhism holds.[14]

For Aquinas, as a Christian, the achievement of this goal of life with God must be made in a single lifetime, since for him the human soul has only existed since its creation in the womb, whereas for reincarnation religions the soul has existed from eternity. Some Thomists have pointed out, though Aquinas never speaks of it, that his view raises the question, unanswerable with certitude by reason, whether it is part of the *natural order* or whether it is by a special provision of his providence, that God will resurrect all human bodies so that human beings can again be complete persons.

The Order of Grace

For Christians the Creator freely produced the world, including its spiritual beings, out of nothing and ordered his creation so that these creatures could reach their true ends. But God has also freely chosen, apart from any demand of the nature of human beings, to

---

It concluded "that there are theological and liturgical reasons to hope that infants who die without baptism may be saved and brought into eternal happiness, even if there is not an explicit teaching on this question found in Revelation."

14. Regarding Hindu belief, see "The Heart of Hinduism: Atman: the Soul, the Real Self," last modified 2004, http://hinduism.iskcon.com/concepts/101.htm, with quotes. Regarding Buddhism, see Richard Hayes, "Madhyamaka," in *Stanford Encyclopedia of Philosophy*, accessed December 1, 2012 (last revision November 6, 2010), http://plato.stanford.edu/entries/madhyamaka/.

invite them into the divine community of the Father, Son, and Holy Spirit, whose very existence in the One God is beyond the capacities of natural human knowledge and can be known only through God's revelation made by *grace*.

This term "grace" is often used, in describing the *bahkti* devotions to a particular god in Hinduism or to the Buddhas of Mahayana Buddhism, to indicate that, by the invocation of these divine beings, those who might otherwise be unable to attain enlightenment by asceticism and concentrated meditation can do so. While this analogy with the Christian term "grace" is important for ecumenical dialogue, there is a profound difference between two notions of "grace."

For the Christian "grace" is not merely the help of superior spiritual beings to achieve that enlightenment which it is the natural destiny of the human spirit to pursue. Instead it is a *transforming* action of God by which a being is elevated from its natural condition, in which it is teleologically ordered to a purely natural goal, to a "participation in the divine nature" (2 Pt 1:4). Monistic or non-dualistic systems such as Hinduism or Buddhism exclude "grace" in this sense, as, for those religions, the human spirit is from all eternity identical with the Absolute. In the Christian understanding, however, this union with God in the intimacy of the community of Trinity is based on nothing in human nature that necessitates it; rather, it comes about entirely through God's generosity, yet it does not result in a loss of the human creaturely reality as distinct from its Creator. Rather, the union is completed in an interpersonal I-Thou relationship by being elevated to a state of being infinitely beyond what is by nature due to a creature.

Some, like the Catholic theologian Henri de Lubac, SJ,[15] have argued that Aquinas meant to say that in fact there is only one goal for

15. See his *Surnaturel: études historiques* (Paris: Aubier, 1946) and in English, *The Mystery of the Supernatural* (New York: Crossroad, 1998). In response to his critiques, he also published a more nuanced statement: *A Brief Catechesis on Nature and Grace* (San Francisco: Ignatius Press, 1984).

human life, the supernatural one provided by grace. Then de Lubac, in order to maintain, as Catholic orthodoxy requires,[16] that our supernatural ordination is utterly gratuitous, had to claim that this was gratuity was sufficiently saved simply by asserting that, while the teleology of the human person is entirely supernatural, it cannot attain this goal except by the grace of God.[17]

Moreover, for Aquinas, as an Aristotelian, de Lubac's notion—that we human persons have no natural end—would amount to saying that we have no *nature*, since without its own proper final cause no substantial nature is possible. This real duality of goals for the human person, maintained by Thomists faithful to Aquinas's text, does not entail (as de Lubac seems to think) that the supernatural goal in relation to the natural goal is a sort of second story on top of a first story of the human structure, which merely parallels and duplicates the first story. Rather, grace transforms and elevates while preserving and perfecting nature according to the famous dictum of Aquinas, "grace perfects nature."[18]

Therefore, besides the natural virtues necessary to attain the telos intrinsic to human nature, we need, in order to attain union with God as One God in Three Persons, supernatural or "infused" virtues.[19] Some of these are moral virtues that simply elevate the corresponding natural moral virtues, but some are "theological"—namely faith, hope, and Christian love—and these directly unite the baptized to God in his inner life as Father, Son, and Holy Spirit. Thus Aquinas says that natural happiness, though it is proportionate to human nature, is still an imperfect happiness, whereas the *beatific vision* of eternal life, in which God is known as He actually exists and is loved un-

16. *Catechism of the Catholic Church*, nn. 1996–2011.

17. *ST* I-II, q. 51, a. 4.

18. *ST* I, q. 1, a. 8 ad 2; q. 2, a. 2 ad 1.

19. *ST* I-II q. 51, a. 4. Here Aquinas argues that there can exist at the same time a natural virtue proportionate to the natural end of an individual and a corresponding infused virtue proportionate to that individual's supernatural end.

reservedly, is perfect happiness that excludes not only every evil of this life but any human limitation.[20] It cannot be earned by any merely human effort, but is a gift that can be finally possessed by those who *by grace* cooperate *with* grace.

Obviously, in the realm of spiritual substances, whose study is proper to metaphysics, goodness and badness exist and are known by us analogously from our own human experience. Human ethical good, just described, includes spiritual values far more important to human happiness than material ones. It is because human beings have freedom that they can make good and evil choices and can acquire virtues and vices that make their lives consistently good or vicious.

What Is "God" Like?

In Chapter 2, "A Mediating Foundation for Psychology" I showed (a) that the more specific conclusions of natural science can logically be constructed on general foundations that themselves rest on the assured evidence of our senses; and (b) that these foundations must include empirical proof that the existence and changes of our physical world have a First Cause that is Unchanging Existence Itself. Such a First Cause is what is generally meant by the term "God." Because many of today's scientists illogically ignore or even deny this foundational truth, the present state of science, magnificent as it is, floats on a mathematical cloud. The concept of this transcendent God, who as certainly exists as do any of the realities studied by science, remains blank until we fill in the blank by the work of metaphysics and theology.

Because the audience for whom this book is primarily written comprises Christian psychologists and psychotherapists, I have assumed that for them the God who is First Cause of all that exists is not a blank but is known to them from the believing community to which they have committed themselves as faithful members. Now in

20. *ST* I-II, q. 5, a. 5 c.

this chapter I want to consider the relation of reason and faith more explicitly.

The Christian faith itself insists that faith is not based merely on some "feeling" but that reason can prove the existence of God as First Cause as a basic element in the preparation for faith. Because we are rational beings, we humans cannot reasonably believe in a God unless we can first know God's existence by reason, and if our faith were not reasonable it would be a delusion. Pope John Paul II in his encyclical "Faith and Reason" (*Fides et Ratio*) reaffirmed this truth of faith defined by Vatican I and confirmed by Vatican II on the basis of many biblical texts, but especially the words of St. Paul: "Ever since the creation of the world, his [God's] invisible attributes of eternal power and divinity have been able to be understood and perceived in what he has made" (Rm 1:20).[21]

To discuss Aquinas's famous "Five Ways" of demonstrating God's existence from "what he has made" and the Divine nature as we can know it through the First Cause's empirical effects,[22] and then to answer in detail the never-ending efforts of some who, wishing to escape this truth, want to find flaws in these arguments—such discussion is beyond the scope of this book. These proofs in outline, however, are in fact quite simple and can be understood, at least intuitively, by anyone of ordinary intelligence; yet, as St. Paul goes on to explain (Rm 1:21–23), after sin entered their lives, human persons became "vain in their reasoning, and their senseless minds were darkened. While claiming to be wise, they became fools and exchanged the glory of the immortal God for the likeness of an image of mortal man or of birds or of four-legged animals or snakes."

21. First Vatican Council, *Dogmatic Constitution on the Catholic Faith*, Chap. 4, "On Faith and Reason": Denzinger 1800 (3020). *The Encyclicals of John Paul II*, ed. and trans. J. Michael Miller: *Fides et Ratio* c. IV, nn. 36–48 (Huntington, IN, Our Sunday Visitor; 2nd edition 2001), 833–914; Second Vatican Council, *Dei verbum*, 1965, n. 6 in *Vatican Council II*, Vol. 1: *The Conciliar and Postconciliar Documents*, by Austin Flannery (Northport, NY: Costello Publishing Company, 1975).

22. *ST* I, qq. 2–26.

As already discussed in Chapter 2, Aquinas bases his first proof, which he says is the most evident of his Five Ways, on the most fundamental fact of our human experience, namely, that everything that we observe with our senses undergoes change. Indeed, it is known to us only because it changes us in the very process of our observing it, and we change it. Thus I know I exist because I can feel my warm, heavy, easily pained body as I move about. No discovery of modern science will ever disprove this basic fact, since all science is based on the sense observation of a changing world.

Yet I also experience that nothing simply changes without being changed by something else. To change is to acquire a new actuality, and the thing that changes does not have that new actuality before it changes, so it cannot give that new actuality to itself.

Some have argued that, according to Newton's laws of motion, once a body is in motion it keeps on moving without any further cause. While that is puzzling, it remains a fact that bodies do not start moving until they are pushed or drawn by other bodies. Others have argued that living things move themselves, and animals obviously do, but not unless these organisms have a constant input of food and, for all but the simplest animals, air to provide the energy without which they would become inert and die. Thus it remains true that when we observe change, especially the most obvious kind of change, *motion,* it must have a cause other than the object being changed. Thus the universe is made up of things that are caused by other things that in turn are caused and thus could not be causes until first they themselves were caused. These lines of causation cannot be circular, since that would again entail being self-caused, which is impossible.

Nor can any line of causation be infinitely long, since then again there would be no first cause and the action of this whole line of causes and effects would be uncaused and thus unable to produce the effect of change that we in fact observe. For a scientist to explain the world by the Big Bang and then to say, as some have done, that the Big Bang "just happened" is contradictory, since it was a change in matter, and science is based on the Principle of Causality, that nothing material can change itself.[23] The First Cause, however, did not "happen" or change, since it is Pure Immaterial Existence and therefore it is not contradictory to say it has no cause, that is, that it is uncaused.

This proof of a Prime Mover or Uncaused Cause is thus a case of the argument given in Chapter 2 for the fact that the unity of every material system depends on a principal or "prime" mover, as the life of the human body depends on the soul. Yet the argument may be extended beyond such a principal mover *intrinsic* to a material system, to a *transcendent and hence non-material or spiritual* mover that is unmoved and uncaused. Although we never observe any uncaused cause in this universe, this argument shows that the universe as whole, since it is in the process of change, must itself be caused by an Unmoved Mover, which transcends the universe as its Creator or First Uncaused Cause. What the advance of modern science has made more evident to us than it was to the ancients and medievals is how pervasive in our universe is change.

As we also saw earlier, Aristotle hypothesized that the heavens never change except for their cyclical motion and have existed for all eternity. Such a steady-state universe must also be cyclical; in that case, the Big Bang whose effects we observe must have been preceded by and will end in a Big Crunch, and this endless cycle goes on forever. The generally accepted hypothesis in current modern cosmology, however, is that the universe began about 13 billion years ago with the Big Bang and will expand till dies in the Big Freeze, when nothing further will happen. For either hypothesis, since everything we observe changes, there must exist an ultimate Being that causes these changes

23. See Paul Davies, "What Happened Before the Big Bang?" http://www.beliefnet.com/News/Science-Religion/2001/01/What-Happened-Before-The-Big-Bang.aspx. Davies answers the problem hesitantly with Stephen Hawking's theory that time, like space, may be "finite but unbounded"; but what is in question is not time but motion, since time is only a measure of motion. Whereas motion can be in finite cycles and it is not evident, as Aristotle thought, that an infinity of circulations is possible, even if in fact this does not remove the necessity of an immobile First Cause.

but does not itself change, a First Cause. For its part, modern science can never refute this argument, since it rests only on the fact of change in our universe and the law of cause and effect; both of these truths are basic to science, and if they are denied, all modern science collapses.

Aquinas states this First Way of arguing to God's existence in terms of the most evident fact of motion. His Second and Third Ways reframe this First Way by taking as the observed effect not the motion but the *action* of one body changing another (Second Way) or the *contingency* (dependence) of the motion of a body and its cause (Third Way). Thus all the changes we observe in this world are *contingent*, that is, it is possible that any one of them would not have happened, since it had to be caused, and its cause might not have acted.

The Fourth and Fifth Ways, also, presuppose the First, but they are based on kinds of causality other than the *efficient* causality involved in the first three ways. The Fourth is base on *formal* causality or order; it is what is today called the Design Argument. To construct something complex requires not only some force or forces (efficient causality) but also some *information* that guides the application of these forces to organize matter in some particular pattern.

Now as was shown in Chapters 3 and 4, our universe is made up of an immense range of things from the simplest to the most complex (the human brain, as far as we know). Although this universe as a whole with its vast desert spaces and scattered galaxies of stars seems to have a low order of complexity, science has shown that if it were less big or old or otherwise ordered, then life could not have emerged in it. When we see a range of objects of different orders of unified complexity, we know that they must be dependent for their information on some cause that has at least all the information found in any of them, and this has to be the First Cause. Modern science, again, can never refute this argument, since to do so would be to say that there is no order in the universe at all. The very purpose of science is to establish natural laws that explain what we observe, and such laws express some kind of order, not mere chance.

The Fifth Way, which presupposes the other ways, is based on teleology or final causality, that is, on the fact that efficient causes produce change that is not merely random but regular and that leads to order in the universe. Thus change must be pre-determined to act in a regular way so as to produce these uniformities that exhibit regularity, stability, and order. This is the very notion of natural law that science exists to discover. Strangely, today some scientists have been driven by the problem of evolution to declare that order and intelligence have arisen in the universe by sheer *chance*.[24] "Chance," however, is impossible without the existence of natural laws, since a chance event is the interference of one line of determined natural causality with another. The Big Bang theory has led others to say, "Well it just happened!" That is to give up on the possibility of a rational understanding of the world and is the death of science.

In response to such positions of scientists, post-modern philosophers are today arguing that science is no better than poetry and is generally a rhetoric of domination.[25] The existentialist philosopher Jean-Paul Sartre assumed that the world *was* absurd and further concluded that God must not exist.[26] Hence, Sartre claimed that every individual must create his or her own meaning to life.

24. Walter Gilberti, "On the death of paleontologist Stephen Jay Gould," last modified July 1, 2002, http://www.wsws.org/articles/2002/jul2002/goul-j01.shtml, a World Socialist, quotes Gould as saying: "This means—and we must face the implication squarely—that the origin of Homo sapiens, as a tiny twig on an improbable branch of a contingent limb on a fortunate tree, lies well below the boundary [the boundary between law and contingency, WG].... Homo sapiens, I fear is a 'thing so small' in a vast universe, a wildly improbable evolutionary event well within the realm of contingency." Gilberti shows that Gould did not deny general evolutionary laws such as "natural selection," but only that they could predict the actual results of evolution. Gould was bitterly attacked by other evolutionists for admitting secondary factors for evolution other than natural selection; see his answer to these critics, in "Darwinian Fundamentalism," *New York Review of Books*, vol. 44.10, June 12, 1997.

25. See Peter Childs, *Postmodernism, Literary Theory: A Guide for the Perplexed* (New York: Continuum Press, January 2011).

26. Sartre thought God's existence was contradictory to human freedom, whereas Aquinas holds that it is God who enables us to be free. See Thomas Flynn, "Sartre" in

Post-modernists, however, logically point out that it is hopeless for humans to try to create meaning in human living if the whole universe is meaningless (which they, like Sartre, also consider it to be). To create anything, we human persons have to use our own intelligences and wills, and we must work with other natural forces that have the power to produce order, a power they would not have in a meaningless universe. If all these natural forces act by pure chance, our efforts to create order will have only random results. Any psychotherapist would diagnose this post-modern philosophical position in a client as a symptom of a suicidal major depression or the incoherence of the schizophrenic. It is the "culture of death" as John Paul II called it.[27] And so it is up to Christians to save modern science from despair, as the medieval Christians saved Greek ancient science, by being willing to face the fact that God exists and without God nothing would exist.

Do Spiritual Creatures Exist?

Modern science manifests God's existence even when modern scientific training is afraid to admit it. Further, we saw in Chapter 5 that human behavior manifests that the human soul—with its powers of abstract, intelligent thought and free will—is not explicable simply by

Stanford Encyclopedia of Philosophy, accessed December 1, 2012 (last revision December 5), 2011, http://plato.stanford.edu/entries/sartre/.

27. "[Today] we are confronted by an even larger reality, which can be described as a veritable structure of sin. This reality is characterized by the emergence of a culture which denies solidarity and in many cases takes the form of a veritable "culture of death". This culture is actively fostered by powerful cultural, economic and political currents which encourage an idea of society excessively concerned with efficiency. Looking at the situation from this point of view, it is possible to speak in a certain sense of a war of the powerful against the weak: a life which would require greater acceptance, love and care is considered useless, or held to be an intolerable burden, and is therefore rejected in one way or another." John Paul II, *Evangelium Vitae* ("The Gospel of Life"), n. 12, last modified 1995, http://www.vatican.va/holy_father/john_paul_ii/encyclicals/documents/hf_jpii_enc_25031995_evangelium-vitae_en.html.

the brain, which is only its instrument, although a necessary one. The arguments given there for this spirituality of the human soul, supported by the limitations of any possible kind of "artificial intelligence" that we intelligent persons may invent or improve, are actually applications of the argument just given for the existence of a spiritual God.

The human intelligence is the true prime mover of the human body (using the brain as its primary instrument), since by acts of free will, which in their freedom transcend the determinism of natural law (as well as chance, and quantum indeterminism), human intelligence can produce order in the world. Yet God created our intelligences and, as First Cause, activates them. From this it follows that the First Cause itself is infinitely intelligent since He makes us intelligent and free, and his intelligence and freedom are necessary and unlimited.

As was shown in Chapter 3, scientists today are quite willing to suppose that there is intelligent life in the universe elsewhere than on our earth. SETI (Search for Extraterrestrial Intelligence Institute) of the University of California has kept sending out radio signals since 1979, hoping to receive return signals from such intelligences, but to date has had no success. These researchers seem not to have considered whether such intelligences might be pure, disembodied spirits, as Christianity and most religions believe. Is there any evidence for the existence of such spirits created by God as part of the universe and in his service? It can be reasonably argued that the existence of such spirits is manifested by the causal structure of the universe. If we generalize the argument, and replace its outdated astronomy with the modern data given in Chapter 3 about our universe as a unified system, we get the following line of reasoning.

Modern science holds that there is only one kind of matter in the universe and that it is subject to alteration as well as motion. Thus, as already explained in Chapter 3, the question of whether the universe began at a certain time in the past becomes open and the modern cosmological theory of the evolution of the university from a "singularity" (the Big Bang) replaces the steady-state universe of Aristotle and Hoyle-Bondi. According to modern theory, some unified natural force in the original plasma of the singularity caused it to expand and very quickly differentiate into its present four fundamental natural forces (gravity, electromagnetism, and the weak and strong nuclear forces internal to atoms). Quantum theory also removes rigid determinism in the universe and leaves room for true chance. Thus it is impossible to predict the future of the universe in any detailed way, although the Second Law of Thermodynamics and its continuing spatial expansion seem to make inevitable a final state of the material world in which matter is so spread out and entropy so maximized that no change will take place except in the form of random quantum "fluctuations."

Therefore, nothing in modern physics disproves—indeed, it all seems to support—the view that it is because our universe contains alterable matter that events in it are subject to true chance. Hence, since chance is the result of the interference of one line of causality with another, our universe must also contain more than one relatively independent line of causality going back to certain physical prime movers endowed with natural powers given them by the First Cause, God.

Furthermore, since the spirituality of the embodied human soul can be demonstrated as shown in Chapter 5, it can be demonstrated that each of these lines of causality in the material universe, whatever their physical prime movers, must also be moved by intelligences, as Aristotle in his formulation of the argument supposed the planets were moved. Since it is obvious that it is not human intelligence that controls the whole universe and its evolution, therefore either extraterrestrial embodied intelligences or disembodied ones must exist as the causes of these independent lines of causality in the universe. Yet, if these are extraterrestrial *embodied* intelligences they would, like ourselves, depend on natural physical forces and hence could not be the causes of the existence of such basic natural forces in the universe. Therefore, *we must conclude that natural science demonstrates that the universe contains, at least, as many pure spirits as there are fundamental forces in the universe.*

The Wider Spiritual Community

Pure, created spirits are also free, and it is reasonable to suppose that, although most have chosen their own good and that of the universe, some—like human beings—have chosen evil. In the Jewish and Christian Scriptures they are called "Satan and his demons" and "Iblis, the Adversary and his evil jinni" in the Qu'ran. In most cultures it is believed that there are both good and evil spirits, although their existence is variously explained. It is not clear in Zoroastrian, Manichaean, or Gnostic dualism whether spirits are by nature good or evil only by their own free choice or whether they were created evil. In some religions, even good spirits can become malevolent if not properly propitiated. In Christianity and less explicitly in other monotheistic cultures it is believed that the angelic spirits were all created good, but from the beginning of their existence some chose evil and hence wage constant warfare against God's plans for the good of creation. God tolerates these evil spirits in order to test human beings (see the Book of Job, and also Jesus' own temptation by Satan in the desert, Mt 4:1–11 and parallels) so that humans may acquire greater virtue. At the Last Judgment these demons will be forever subdued. Evil spirits can never repent, but human sinners by the grace of God can do so.[28] After death, however, human souls free of the body are like the angels and hence have a fixed destiny, although they may not reached their final reward without first undergoing a process of spiritual purification (purgatory) by God.[29]

28. According to Aquinas, *ST* I, q. 64, a. 2, humans can repent because the variability of the bodily senses that are the instruments of our intellects makes possible changes in judgment and hence in our freely willed moral decisions; in pure spirits, this variability of judgment is impossible.

29. On purgatory see the *Catechism of the Catholic Church*, nn. 1031, 1472.

If it is objected that these different lines of physical causality could all be caused by the First Cause, it can be answered that they are *ultimately* caused by the First Cause, but if there were not intermediate, created, pure spirits as prime movers that are part of the universe, the universe would not be a complete and stable system. A metaphysical model of reality that ascribes all causality to the First Cause and gives no genuine autonomy to secondary causes is contradictory to the true existence of a universe and would reduce our phenomenal world to a mere dream of the Absolute of Advaita Hinduism or The Void of Buddhism or the ineffable One of Neo-Platonism.[30] The very possibility of a realistic natural science would thereby be eliminated.

Thus an adequate defense of a realistic natural science requires that it be open to the existence both of God as First Cause and to pure spirits as part of the universe. This conclusion is also supported by the fact of evolution that modern science has established. Such deterministic theories of cosmic evolution as the Greek Orphic religion of the "primeval egg,"[31] or St. Augustine's *rationes seminales,*[32] and *élan vital* of Henri Bergson (1859–1941) and Pierre Teilhard de Chardin, S. J. (1881–1955),[33] or Whitehead's "creativity," or even Stuart Kaufmann's "self-organization"[34] and other *autopoietic* (self-causing) theories fail to explain how something can give itself what it does not already have.

30. On Hinduism, see Ninian Smart, *World Philosophies* (London; Routledge, 1999). On Buddhism, see Bijoy H. Boruah, "Atman in Sunyata and the Sunyata of Atman: An attempt to reconcile the alleged difference between Buddhism and Advaita Vedanta on the nature of the Self," http://www.katinkahesselink.net/tibet/atmsun.htm#een. For Neo-Platonism, see Plotinus, *The Enneads*, V, 10. Stephen McKenna and B. S. Sage translation, last modified 2009, http://classics.mit.edu/Plotinus/enneads.html.

31. See Samuel Aun Weor, *Gnostic Magic of the Runes* (New York: Glorian, 2008).

32. See Michael J. McKeough, *The Meaning of the rationes seminales in St. Augustine* (Washington, DC, 1926).

33. Henri, Bergson, *Creative Evolution*, authorized translation by Arthur Mitchell, with a foreword by Irwin Edman (New York: Modern Library, 1944); Pierre Teilhard de Chardin, SJ, *The Phenomenon of Man* (New York: Harper and Row, 1959).

34. *At Home in the Universe: The Search for the Laws of Self-Organization and Complexity* (New York: Oxford University Press, 1995).

Complex substances contain extensive information, but inanimate matter as we know it in the elements and their constitutive particles has a comparatively very small amount of information. A living embryo develops from a single cell to a mature animal because it has an intrinsic genetic code that contains the complex information necessary to guide the differentiation and inter-relation of its parts. Nothing we know about the matter of which our universe is composed indicates that such information is naturally intrinsic to it. It is assumed in the Big Bang theory that the original "singularity" or the plasma that first originated from it were programmed with the laws of quantum mechanics, but those provide only general and probable predictions.

Not only is the universe as we now observe it a true system, but in at least one region of it the human body exists as prepared matter for the reception of spiritual souls from the Creator who can alone produce spiritual entities *ex nihilo.* These spiritual souls have free will and independent action. Hence, although it seems certain that the universe has evolved, it is not possible to assign an adequate cause for its evolution. How could it culminate, as it has, in human bodies ready for spiritual ensoulment by the spiritual First Cause, unless included in that system are pure intelligences having all the necessary information to guide this extremely complicated and chancy process? Although by studying the natural process of evolution we embodied spirits may someday be able to produce organic life and guide its evolution, we did not guide the evolution of our own species. Nor is it likely that extra-terrestrial embodied intelligences, if they exist, guided our human evolution, since they too would have evolved and at a great distance from us would have produced us.[35]

Thus the cause of biological evolution in our universe cannot be reduced to the interaction of material causes whose history necessar-

35. The science fiction writer Arthur C. Clarke, in his *2001: A Space Odyssey* (New York: Penguin/Roc, 2000; original 1968—the basis of Stanley Kubrick's famous film), imagines that terrestrial evolution is caused by a black monolith on the moon placed there by former terrestrials, who have themselves already evolved into intelligences with no other bodies but "space." Why not pure spirits?

ily involves so much chance; it must rather be ascribed to that part of the universe that is a community of pure spirits. Hence modern science, although it hesitates to draw this conclusion—which supports the intuitive belief in pure spirits found in all cultures, even in our own, as the current popular interest in angels shows—certainly cannot disprove their existence, but rather gives increasing support to it as it tries to understand the history of the cosmos.

The obvious objection to the foregoing line of argument is that it can lead to all kinds of fantasizing superstition. Hence the Catholic Church has strictly forbidden its members to participate in the invocation of spirits and in other forms of occultism. The following points should be kept in mind by psychotherapists.

First, angels, good or bad, cannot act directly on the human intelligence or will. The comic excuse "The devil made me do it" is always false. Yet spiritual intelligences can act on the physical world and hence on the human senses and on the brain, promoting helpful images or dangerous ones.

Second, the *Catechism of the Catholic Church* (n. 336) teaches:

> From its beginning until death, human life is surrounded by their [the good angels] care and intercession [Cf. Mt. 18:10; Lk 16:22; Ps 34:7; 91:10–13; Job 33:23–24; Zech 1:12; Tob 12:12}. "Beside each believer stands an angel as protector and shepherd leading him to life." [St. Basil]. Already here on earth the Christian life shares by faith in the blessed company of angel and men united in God.

This assurance, which does not contradict our own responsibilities to act reasonably, can be of real help in the pressing anxieties and depressions that beset modern life, and can be invoked by a therapist's dealing with Christian clients. On the other hand, the reality of demonic temptation should not be denied, as modern psychiatrists mistakenly tend to do.[36]

36. In the past, fear of the demonic has led to violent approaches to witchcraft. Lyndal Roper, *Witch Craze: Terror and Fantasy in Baroque Germany* (New Haven: Yale University Press, 2006) shows that the death toll was not nine million, as has often

The Dignity of Human Persons

The account we have given in these chapters of our universe and its relation to God, an account based on reason and modern science, seems to show that the human person ranks in the middle of the whole "chain of being" that stretches from quarks to God. That means that while we transcend the material universe of atoms, molecules, plants, and brute animals, we (perhaps along with not yet discovered embodied persons on other planets) rank lowest in the vast range of created intelligences so powerful that they need no bodies to think, but through their innate ideas know much more than we ever can (as Plato and Descartes mistakenly supposed we humans do). It might seem, therefore, that materialists who claim that science shows that intelligence is nothing but the work of a material brain, have a higher opinion of human dignity than we do, since we humans are more intelligent than any other material beings of whose existence we know. Yet even if there is extraterrestrial life on other planets, the brains of such creatures cannot be very much better than ours, since the complexity of our brains seems to be close to the limits of any material organ. Thus secular humanism, the worldview and value system that more and more dominates modern culture, exalts human persons as the masters of the world. In that case, we alone can, as Jean-Paul Sartre (1904–80) and the existentialists declared,[37] give meaning and value to the world by our human artistic, technological, and social creativity. Secular humanism, by placing its faith in man, functions for modern culture as a substitute for any religion that has faith in God.

Ancient religions and those of less technologically advanced cultures that still survive did not rank humans very high in the scale of

---

been stated, but about 100,000. See also Wolfgang Behringer, *Witches and Witch-Hunts: A Global History* (Cambridge, England: Polity Press, 2004), who shows such panics over witchcraft have appeared all over the world in history. Also H. R. Trevor-Roper, *The European Witch-Craze of the Sixteenth and Seventeenth Centuries and Other Essays* (New York: HarperCollins College Division, 1969).

37. See Thomas Flynn, "Sartre" in *Stanford Encyclopedia of Philosophy.*

being, but for reasons different from those of secular humanism's low evaluation of humanity. The animism characteristic of many simple cultures pictures humans as surrounded by more powerful spirits and the souls of ancestors who must be appeased by various rituals. The mythology of the great ancient civilizations depicted the gods as jealous of humans, whom Prometheus created and to whom he gave fire. The gods exploited humans as slaves or, in the case of women, mistresses. In these religions there is often a supreme, "creator" god, such as Zeus for the Greeks, or the Mother Fertility goddesses among the Mesopotamians, but these gods themselves emerged from chaos and were subject to fate, lust, and quarreling. The high gods of Africa are often benevolent, yet, disgusted with humanity, they have retired to the heavens leaving humans to struggle with lesser spirits.

Out of these earlier cultures religious reformers arose in many centers—such as Buddha and Shankara in India, Confucius in China, Socrates, Plato, and Aristotle among the Greeks—who all believed in an ultimate Spiritual Reality to be attained by a virtuous life and profound contemplation. Yet none of these reformers came to a clear notion of God as an absolutely transcendent and free Creator of all contingent things out of nothing (*ex nihilo*). The Hindus understood the human soul as a spark of the Divine that is reincarnated in body after body until it returns to the Absolute and is absorbed into it. Plato and the Neo-Platonists had similar views. For Buddhism, also, the human soul is subject to reincarnation, but this is only an illusory existence, so that when this illusion is dispelled the human person disintegrates into the ineffable void called Nirvana. In all these religions, the human body-person is in a fallen state and will ultimately be lost again in the Absolute that alone truly exists.[38]

The only religious reformers who clearly recognized God as transcendent Creator were Moses and the Hebrew prophets. Judaism is genuinely *monotheistic*, in contrast to other older world religions that

38. For a good review of world religions, see Ninian Smart, *World Philosophies*.

were *monistic*, reducing all reality to some "One" of which all other things are merely parts; but, for the Jews, God has given his creatures true being and dignity in themselves, although by their own free will they can injure that being and besmirch their dignity through sin and in fact have done so. This unique Judaic monotheism underlies Christianity and Islam. Hence in these three monotheistic religions human persons are recognized as having a genuine dignity.

Secular humanism and the monistic religions often characterize the monotheists as "dualists" because monotheists do not find a unity in which Creator and creatures are united. This accusation, however, is misleading. God is Absolute Unity, but has also given to his universe a unity that is genuine yet contingent and dependent on his absolute unity. Moreover, although God transcends the universe, he is not exterior to it. Precisely because God is First Cause of the universe he is immanent to it. "God closer to me," as St. Augustine said, "than I am to myself."[39] God is within all things giving them being, movement, and life and yet exists utterly independently of them.

Among the three monotheistic religions, moreover, Christianity goes a step further, because it declares that in God there are Three Divine Persons, absolutely equal to each other and sharing one single Being. The Second of these, the Son, has obeyed the Father by becoming incarnate, a human person like us "in all but sin." In doing so the Incarnate Word, Son of God, Jesus Christ, revealed to us the inner nature of God as Father, Son, and Holy Spirit, and sends the Holy Spirit on his redeemed human community, the Church, which will share the eternal life of God as one community, yet a community in which all persons, human, angelic, and divine, will retain their unique existences. Judaism by refusing to recognize Jesus as the Christ, and Islam by reverencing him but only as a human being, are unable to understand this communal unification in which God is "All and in All, yet above All." Thus, alone of all historic religions, that of the Catholic Church

39. *Confessions* III, 6, 11.

under the successor of St. Peter reflects that inclusive unity of God in a way that the Eastern Orthodox and Protestant Churches are unable to do, and thus sums up the true elements of all religions. Catholicism even sums up the strengths of secular humanism, the religion of man, because it teaches the harmony of reason and faith and encourages humankind to develop its control over nature in stewardship to God. Thus Jesus is true God and true man, and the New Adam for whom our garden universe will be recreated and glorified, and Mary, Mother of God, who gave Jesus his human nature, will reign with him as the New Eve. Nature is thus restored and elevated by God's grace to intimate community with God.

Christian Vocation

As God the Father called Jesus Christ to the task of redeeming the world, so Christians are called to share in that same task. This calling or "vocation" is first of all a share in Christ's priesthood, by which creation is returned in sacrifice to its Creator. By baptism all Christians share in this "general priesthood." In view of the coming of God's eternal Kingdom on earth, every Christian has to discern how this fundamental vocation given by God in baptism is to be realized in a particular "vocation" in personal life. We live at a particular time in history, in a particular place and culture, with particular social relationships. Moreover we are, by reason of our different bodies, individuals, and since our spiritual souls are correlative forms of our bodies, this individuality makes each human soul unique.

To carry out this task we must grow in the virtues or skills of meeting life's problems discussed in Chapter 6. These virtues are both the four cardinal virtues and their auxiliary virtues that perfect our natural powers and also the graced virtues that transform these natural powers, especially the theological virtues of faith, hope, and love, We need these transforming graced virtues so that we can seek not only our natural goal of contemplating and loving God by reason, but also so that we can seek our ultimate super-natural goal of union with the Trinity in immortal life.

In a schematic way every Christian, to attain perfection in this life, must past through three spiritual stages.[40] If we do not complete this process in this life, we will have to finish it after death, in purgatory, before we are ready for God's intimate presence.

The first of these stages is the work of *purification,* by which the beginner is freed from mortal sin and fully deliberate venial sins. The second stage is traditionally called that of *illumination,* in which the mature Christian develops all the virtues in harmony. The third and final stage is the *unitive,* in which the theological virtues and the gifts of the Holy Spirit come into full play. The "Dark Night of the Soul" divides the first of these ways from the second. The "Dark Night of the Spirit" divides second from the last. These metaphorical terms can be translated psychologically, by saying that in the first dark night, the Christian learns not to depend excessively on pious feelings, sentimentality, and "experiences" at the level of the external and internal senses (the "Soul"). In the second dark night, the Christian learns not to depend excessively on intellectual understanding, but on faith, hope, and charity (the "Spirit").

The seven gifts of the Holy Spirit (wisdom, knowledge, understanding, counsel, fortitude, piety, and fear of the Lord) operate in all Christians, but, as the spiritual way is traveled, increase in their effective guidance of the Christian's free decisions and prayer. They are ways in which Christians rely on the grace of God and his guidance more than on their natural powers. The dark nights consist in suffering that, like hard exercise or surgery for the body, is painful but is also healing, life-giving, and empowering. In the darkness of faith the Christian takes up the Cross of Christ. It is not the proper task of a

40. Reginald Garrigou-Lagrange, OP, *The Three Ages of the Interior Life*, 2 vols. trans. M. Timothea Doyle, OP (reprint: Rockford, IL: Tan Books, 1999); and Juan G. Arintero, OP, *Mystical Evolution*, trans. Jordan Aumann, OP (reprint: Rockford, IL: Tan Books, 1978); and my own *Spiritual Direction in the Dominican Tradition* (New York: Paulist Press, 1995).

psychotherapist to diagnose these processes in the life of a Christian; it is the task of a spiritual director. Yet since, as just shown, advance in the spiritual life requires psychological changes, the spiritual director should sometimes refer those he directs to a psychotherapist and vice versa.

The Vocation to Marriage

According to St. Thomas Aquinas (*Summa theologiae* I, q. 99, a. 2, ad 3), commenting on the first chapters of Genesis and on the fact that God has provided that human males and females are born in approximately the same numbers, the Creator originally intended all human persons to marry. This was not only to multiply the human race but also to provide married couples with companionship and teach them how to love unselfishly so that they might attain human perfection and teach it to their children. Even after sin had disturbed the harmony of this unifying and fruitful relationship so that the "war of the sexes" began to be a miserable feature of the human fallen condition, most persons still have a vocation to marriage.

Yet Aquinas also, following the counsel of St. Paul (1 Cor 7:32–35), held that while it is natural for all humans to marry and have a family, nevertheless, in the present fallen and sinful human condition, domestic life is often a hindrance to the achievement of the highest element in happiness, namely, contemplation of the supreme truth.[41] Hence it was not necessary for all to choose marriage, but some could freely choose celibacy, provided that some marry so as to maintain the species and form its new members (as was discussed in Chapter 7).

Also it is not contrary to human nature to choose never to exercise one's sexual power and to remain celibate, if this will be of service to some important human goal.[42] Nevertheless, if our race had not

41. In his *Commentary on Aristotle's Nicomachean Ethics* Bk X, lect. 10, and *Summa theologiae* I-II, q. 3, aa. 6–8.

42. On priestly celibacy see Stefan Heid, *Celibacy in the Early Church: The Begin-*

fallen into sin, it would not have been necessary for anyone to sacrifice sexual fulfillment to some other goal. Our actual tragically disordered human world, in which some have to die in war to protect the rights of others and in which some cannot find a suitable spouse, can only be explained by a historic misuse of human freedom that the Bible explains as "original sin."

What, in a world that had not fallen, would have been the relation between sexual fulfillment and the superior good of unitive love? Some of the early Church Fathers (for example, St. Gregory of Nyssa in his *De Hominis Opificio*), puzzled by this question and influenced by the dualism of Plato, who exalted the spiritual soul at the expense of the material body, thought there would have been no sex in Eden. God, they supposed, would have enlarged the human race by directly creating the human body just as he now creates each human spiritual soul for a body prepared by the sexual action of its parents. St. Augustine, often accused of being neurotically anti-sex, was not entirely free of this Platonic dualism, but he saw clearly that sex as such is given us by God to be rightly used, and thus even if Adam and Eve had not sinned, they would have had sex for the begetting of children. Today our great pope John Paul II has in many writings made clearer than ever the nobility and beauty of marriage, which Christ made a sacrament of his own love for his people, the Church. Thus although there will no longer be sexual union in eternal life, the love of the couple, and the love between them and their children, will last forever in a deeper, more perfect union.

The Vocation to the Single Life

Just as the call to marriage is natural to human personhood, so it is natural for us all to be called to at least temporary celibacy and, in eternal life, to a permanent state free of erotic activity. All human per-

nings of a Discipline of Obligatory Continence for Clerics in East and West, trans. Michael J. Miller (San Francisco: Ignatius Press, 2000).

sons, male and female, are morally bound to remain virgin until marriage and celibate in widowhood or when separated from their marriage partner, or, if they choose, as chaste single persons. The chaste single life does not require, as some claim, a "special charism" but simply the grace of Christian baptism, prayer, and the use of the sacraments.

From the beginning of the Catholic Church, some women and men, in imitation of the virgin Jesus, his mother Mary and her husband Joseph, and St. Paul, and according to tradition, the apostles after Pentecost, chose celibacy "for the sake of the kingdom." Although not all historians agree, a strong case can be made that in the Early Church the bishops, priests, and deacons, although chosen chiefly from married men who had governed their families well, were required on ordination to separate from their wives and to live as celibates. This remains the law of the Catholic Church for priesthood in its Latin Rites, for two fundamental reasons: (1) the priest's primary role is to symbolize Jesus in leadership of the Christian community, and Jesus renounced marriage for the sake of his mission; (2) to ask someone to fulfill both this demanding task and that of a father of a family is excessive and will too often lead to neglect of both duties.

In the period immediately following the Constantinian Establishment, the lax practice of many Catholics led to the formal establishment of the monastic institution, beginning with the desert hermits; somewhat later it took on a community character. From that time on, the "religious life" in the sense of the choice of some men and some women to consecrate themselves to God through obedience, chastity, and poverty became an important institution in the Church.

Religious life has taken a number of forms suited to particular historical circumstances, and most religious congregations have seen a growth, then a decline, and finally extinction. The hermitic life is now rather rare but is still practiced. More common is the monastic life, in the Eastern Church principally under the Rule of St. Basil, in the Latin Church chiefly under the Rule of St. Benedict. The life of Canons, initiated by St. Augustine, differed from that of monks in emphasizing the priestly ministry, while the monks were commonly laypersons. The thirteenth century saw the rise of the Mendicant Friars, especially the Order of Friars Minor, founded by St. Francis of Assisi, and the Order of Preachers, founded by St. Dominic. Like the canons, these friars, though contemplatives like the monks, also engaged in active ministry, but they differed from both canons and monks in being international orders not centered in independent monasteries.

In the Counter-Reformation period, the Society of Jesus developed a new form of religious order that was active in nature and no longer practiced the monastic liturgy and the distinctive manner of dress of the older orders. This pattern was then taken up by a variety of religious communities, commonly called not "orders" (because their vows were more easily dispensed), but congregations. Recently, still new forms of consecrated life are developing in the Church, such as Opus Dei and the Focolari.

Holiness and Mental Illness

All Christians are called to holiness in Christ, but does this mean that all holy Christians are mentally healthy? No, any more than all saints are physically healthy. As we have seen, mental health is rooted in the body, in nervous and hormonal dysfunction, and especially in a defective habituation of the internal senses and feelings to which nervous and hormonal dysfunction can dispose the sufferer. Yet, as long as a person is mentally capable of some realistic thinking and some free decisions, he or she can advance in virtues and become holy. In the past, hagiography has often covered over the evidence of mental illness in certain saints, but with modern psychology we are beginning to recognize that, because saints are human like all of us, they can suffer from neuroses and even psychoses.

For example, it is well known that the holy and wise Doctor of the Church, the great moral theologian of the eighteenth century and founder of the Redemptorist Order, St. Alphonsus Ligouri, suffered all his life from extreme scrupulosity.[43] Some biographers think that Dominican St. Catherine of Siena, also a Doctor of the Church, and a great mystic, suffered from *anorexia nervosa* brought on by too much fasting.[44] Another Dominican mystic, Blessed Heinrich Suso, has given us a very clear description of a major depression that he suffered. It left him sitting for days in his cell unable to pray or study; he eventually recovered by "getting up and sweeping my cell," that is, by physical exercise.[45]

No doubt good Christians, by striving to lead a reasonable and moral life, can contribute to the healing of whatever mental problems they suffer from causes for which they were not responsible or are no longer responsible. Moral living makes for good health, but good people still need physicians, and so they also may need psychotherapists. As for therapists themselves, Jesus with the Samaritan woman at the well (Jn 4 is a model. He first won her confidence by asking her for a drink of water, although this would unthinkable for a Jew, since the Jews and Samaritans were enemies. That request emphasized the common dignity and mutual respect that must be the foundation of the relation of therapist and client. She comes to trust him because, when she reacts with suspicion that he might be making sexual advances (natural to her, in view of her own experience—five previous husbands and a current boyfriend), he suggests she bring her hus-

43. See J. W. Ciarrocchi, *The Doubting Disease: Help for Scrupulosity and Religious Compulsions* (Mahwah, NJ: Paulist Press, 1995); and W. Van Ornum, *A Thousand Frightening Fantasies: Understanding and Healing Scrupulosity and Obsessive Compulsive Disorder* (New York: Crossroad, 1997).

44. Rudolph M. Bell, *Holy Anorexia*, epilogue by William N. Davis (Chicago: University of Chicago Press, 1987); Caroline Walker Bynum, *Holy Feast and Holy Fast: The Religious Significance of Food to Medieval Women* (Berkeley, CA: University of California Press, 1988); Walter Vandereycken and Ron Van Deth, *From Fasting Saints to Anorexic Girls: The History of Self-Starvation* (New York: New York University Press, 1994).

45 Henry Suso, *The Life of the Servant*, trans. James M. Clark (London: James Clarke, 1952).

band to the meeting as a safeguard. The fact that he understands her leads her to begin opening up to him. He then begins to help her see the need she has for "living water," freedom from her blindness and sense of inferiority and guilt that no doubt arise from the unresolved wounds of her life. The therapist, by his sympathy and understanding, awakens hope of freedom in the client. But the Samaritan woman at first resists and tries to argue with Jesus on an abstract level. Gently he calls her attention to the real facts that she is, in a conventional way as a Samaritan, denying. Finally she begins to listen; then she makes a decision to act and, when she calls others to hear him, says: "May this be really the Messiah?" shows her freedom, her ability now to confront the puzzles of reality.

Therapists cannot look into the depths of their clients' souls as Jesus could, and therefore they need to pray for enlightenment by the Holy Spirit so as to use their scientific therapeutic knowledge and personal experiences to attain some degree of true insight. It is essential, moreover, that psychotherapists recognize the limits of their healing power. Although inevitably needing to address ethical issues, they are not expert ethicists and generally ought to leave difficult ethical advising to other counselors. Nor are they spiritual directors per se, even though inevitably needing to address spiritual issues. So generally they ought to leave difficult theological matters and certain spiritual practices to other lay ministers and the sacraments to priests. They must be concerned with enabling the person to transcend and be free of fantasies and feelings,that prevent them from seeing themselves as they really are. While aiming at their true end, they will seek to help the person to accept their own dignity and defects, and with hope to begin to see themselves as they really are in the community and the world as it really exists.

Is the Catholic Faith Trustworthy?

Before leaving this chapter, this question must be asked, although here it can be answered only very briefly.[46] The Catholic Church does not ask anyone to accept its faith contrary to their conscience or their reason. Some rationalists, like Immanuel Kant, claim that we should live only by what we can see to be true by our own reason, but that would make human life impossible. "Faith is the realization of what is hoped for and evidence of things not seen" (Heb 10:1). Each of us has only limited knowledge, and we have to trust others, such as doctors, psychotherapists, pharmacists, etc. in matters of life and death. To do so, however, without first being sure that the expert we trust has licenses to practice and a good reputation to show they are trustworthy is to risk our health and even our lives.

When we trust another to give us information they have but we do not, we do so not on *internal* evidence (because that is precisely what we lack), but on *external* signs (credentials) of their honest and expertise on the matter in questions. Jesus did not ask others to believe what he spoke in the name of God (Lk 7:18–23) but pointed to his miracles, his fulfillment of the ancient prophecies, the truth of his teaching, and finally his bodily resurrection:

> The disciples of John told him about all these things. John summoned two of his disciples and sent them to the Lord to ask, "Are you the one who is to come, or should we look for another?" When the men came to him, they said, "John the Baptist has sent us to you to ask, 'Are you the one who is to come, or should we look for another?'" At that time he cured many of their diseases, sufferings, and evil spirits; he also granted sight to many who were blind. And he said to them in reply, "Go and tell John what you have seen and heard: the blind regain their sight, the lame walk, lepers are cleansed, the deaf hear, the dead are raised, the poor have the good news proclaimed to them. And blessed is the one who takes no offense at me." (Lk 7:18–23)

46. I have treated it more fully in my *Choosing a Worldview and Value System.*

Many today, on supposedly scientific grounds, refuse to recognize miracles, but this deterministic notion—that the world would collapse if scientific laws were frustrated—cannot be reconciled with quantum mechanics, which admits indeterminism, or evolutionary theory, which admits chance. Nor does the argument of David Hume (1711–76) hold that because miracles are improbable we should always deny their historicity.[47] God is free to produce events that cannot be explained by natural law and yet are not chance because they communicate a recognizable message. From a natural law point of view, the letters on this page are random, yet you can read them and recognize what I mean to say. Thus the Pharisees who saw Jesus' miracles and refused to acknowledge them as such were dishonest.

There is, however, the obvious problem for us that all these things happened 2,000 years ago. The historical reliability of the Gospels can be defended, but modernist critics have carefully built their attacks on the Bible's reporting as propaganda. Recent theologians have therefore developed their apologetics (or rather what they prefer to call "foundational theology") for the Christian faith on "religious experience." Thus Karl Rahner, SJ (1904–84) and Edward Schillebeeckx, OP (1914–2009), who were influential on Vatican II, attempted in somewhat different ways to show the Catholic faith is trustworthy because it more adequately accounts for the deepest of our life experiences than does any other worldview or system of values. While this approach is appreciated by many today who are disillusioned by the conflict of "expert" claims and the shifting clamor of the public media, it suffers from its *subjectivity* in comparison to the critical objectivity in which modern historical scholarship and science have developed.

Already faced with this question of historicity, Vatican I declared:[48]

47. *An Enquiry Concerning Human Understanding*, L. A. Selby Bigge, ed. (Oxford: Clarendon Press, 1902), 114–16. Cited by Paul Halsall, "David Hume: On Miracles," Modern History Sourcebook, last modified Aug 2007, http://www.fordham.edu/halsall/mod/hume-miracles.html.

48. Ecumenical Council Vatican I, *Dogmatic Constitution on the Catholic Faith,*

> *So that* we could fulfill our duty of embracing the true faith and of persevering unwaveringly in it, God, through his only begotten Son, founded the Church, and he endowed his institution with clear notes to the end that she might be recognized by all as the guardian and teacher of the revealed word. To the Catholic Church alone belong all those things, so many and so marvelous, which have been divinely ordained to make for the manifest credibility of the Christian faith. What is more, the church herself by reason of her astonishing *propagation,* her outstanding *holiness* and her inexhaustible fertility in every kind of goodness, by her catholic *unity* and her unconquerable *stability*, is a kind of great and perpetual motive of credibility and an incontrovertible evidence of her own divine mission.

These "marks of the Church," usually named as, in the Creed, "one, holy, catholic, and apostolic," are present realities that can be known to anyone who becomes acquainted with the Church in its present condition and considers it with an open mind. The ancient quarrels and mistaken attacks of heretics and schismatics and present scandals dim this evidence but do not hide it, as is evidenced in the many conversions of learned scholars and in the continued growth of the Church. It may be that the sins of Catholics and the delay of reforms may, as in the past, greatly weaken the Church and its growth in the future, but the signs of holiness, catholicity, and apostolicity will remain. Catholic psychotherapists, therefore, should not hesitate to critically examine the attacks they may hear from colleagues against the Church and seek their honest answers from reliable theologians. They should not simply seek a *modus vivendi* between their faith and its critics. It is true that most Catholics receive their faith from their believing families, infant baptism, and their catechism. Nothing is more natural. Yet as they mature they must seek a mature and reasoned faith. Only such a reasoned faith will free them to be true healers.

---

session 3 (24 April 1870), chapter 3, nn.10–12, accessed on December 1, 2012, http://www.ewtn.com/library/councils/v1.htm

Conclusion

The existence of a personal God as the first cause of all other things, including especially personal beings such as we humans are, is not a truth extrinsic to natural science but a part of its foundational principles, although today this fact is neglected in scientific education. Indeed, the denial of this truth is also at the root of the widespread mental illness, as well as physical illnesses, of yesterday's and today's culture. Our culture denies or ignores this truth because it is blinded by fantasies, feelings, and falsehoods that urgently need to be healed. Psychotherapy, although it cannot provide that ultimate spiritual healing, can be of important service to the process, by beginning the client's freedom to think realistically and hopefully. The Christian therapist should seek to achieve a reasoned faith and the skills that the natural and Christian virtues can alone supply.

nine

HEALING FOR FREEDOM

What Is Mental Health?

Oddly enough, medical education often neglects explicit discussion of just what it means to be a "healthy person." It is taken for granted that the physician will from experience come to recognize the difference between what is normal and what is not, in spite of the fact that completely healthy persons are rare indeed and are not likely to be in his clinic. A similar failure to define normality is common in the discussion of psychotherapy, but how can we heal persons psychologically unless we have a sound view of the goal of healing?

As shown earlier, psychotherapy is directed at the borderline of animal and human psychology and hence at the borderline between natural scientific and metaphysical understanding of the human person. It is a practical application of what natural science has so far discovered about the healthy functioning of the material but living human senses and affectivities located in bodily organs and especially the brain. But these bodily functions are the instruments of the spiritual intellect and will that has to use this body to perform its uniquely transcendent functions of abstract, essential thought and free, practical decision. Thus the proper goal of psychotherapy is to heal the animal aspect of human psychology (the part that we share with other animals) so that it can normally serve the whole human person. Only when this delicate balance is maintained is the person psychologically healthy. The wise psychotherapist will not step over the line into the properly ethical and religious levels of human personality but will refer these to experts in ethics and spirituality. Reference to the ethical and the religious will be seen in the light of therapeutic goals.

Persons who need psychotherapy are, for some reason, having difficulty in thinking and feeling in a healthy way: they suffer from some mental aberration, which means that they are not *normally free in making realistic life decisions*. Through the level of external and internal sensation, human cognition rises to the level of the intellectual. In the process, human beings are able to distinguish the real from the mental, the true from the false, the realistically helpful from the harmful, the universal and essential from the particular and accidental. This is a process aimed at becoming free to make realistic life decisions.

Thus psychotherapy deals primarily with unreasonable habits of feeling and evaluation acquired by the secondary sense called the *evaluative* sense (*vis cogitativa*) discussed in Chapter 4. Today the terms "imagination" and "fantasy" are often used to include both what Aquinas calls the imagination and the evaluative sense. This is a mistake, because the images of the imagination omit both the chronology of their origin that pertains to the sense memory, and also any reference of whether an image is of an object useful to or useless or harmful to the subject. It is the evaluative sense that estimates this relation between the person and the object known and thus perceives the object as desirable or undesirable. Since what the therapist is interested in is precisely the defective desires and fears of the client, it is the defective habituation of the evaluative sense that is significant for therapy.

Yet since the knowledge of relations is possible only at the intellectual level, because we sense the physical objects but not the relations between them, how can the evaluative sense perceive a relation of fittingness or unfittingness of an object to the needs of the person who senses that object? The answer to this puzzle seems to be that relations of similarity been particular objects is accessible to the senses, but that relation as such, in the sense of a universal concept of a relation, can be known only intellectually. Thus even a chimpanzee can recognize that it has as many fingers on one hand as on the other, but this is not the same as the abstract mathematical equation that 5 = 5, since this abstract notion of "equality" can be applied to many, many different kinds of objects, while the similarity of the chimp's one hand to another cannot be applied to anything but those two hands.

If we grant, as argued in Chapter 5 that the human soul and its intelligence and will are spiritual powers, they cannot be made defective by the material body, although they can be rendered inoperative by its defects. Hence mental illness cannot be a defect in the human intelligence or free will, but only in the material body that serves this spiritual soul. The human intellect in this life cannot operate without its instruments of the bodily primary and secondary senses. It directly requires some image (*phantasma*) provided by the internal senses in order to achieve an intellectual insight (intuition, *intellectus*, "simple comprehension" of a concept, second act of the mind). Such an insight differs from an image in that the image is always particular or individual, but the intellectual concept is a universal that can apply to many particulars.

The one concept can apply to many individuals identically because real objects, although they differ individually, nevertheless have many aspects that can be essentially identical, for example, all mammals breast-feed their young. Nominalism erroneously denies the real basis for this and therefore denies any essential difference between animal knowing and human knowing. Yet, as I have previously argued, this fails to explain the human freedom behaviorally manifest in the creativity and diversity of human cultures and languages. Moreover, it is contradicted by the success of modern science in discovering universal natural laws.

Still more fundamental for sound science is the fact that intellectual insights are not only universal but are so precisely because they abstract the essences of objects, which are stable and identical for as long as the objects exist, from their more superficial aspects, which can change. Yet human intelligence seldom attains the specific essence of any object immediately. It has to begin with some very generic insight that is gradually made more and more specific by further sense examination and analysis of the object. Indeed, we never come to an exhaustive essential knowledge of anything, not even of our own selves.

This process of more and more, but never complete, exploration of the essences of things is achieved by examining their properties that flow from the essence as their root cause and manifest it as effects manifest their cause. For example, a dog owner gradually comes to understand what is special to dogs as compared to cats and other animals, by observing canine anatomy and behavior, and in a similar way a chemist comes to understand what is special to water (H_2O) as compared to other chemical substances.

As we better know the properties of a certain species of things, we seek for the most fundamental property that no other kind of object possesses, and then by relating all the properties and coming to some notion of what unifies them, we attain essential knowledge. Thus we know that all members of the human species are distinct from Neanderthals or chimpanzees by noting our properties of language and culture. We can make such a distinction because of our most important ability, namely, to think abstractly. Thus we can give an essential definition of *homo sapiens* as a "rational animal," and we might be even more explicit and say "A human person is an animal that can think abstractly and make free decisions."

It must also be kept in mind that in order to arrive at *essential* knowledge of something we must first have an *existential* knowledge of it. As shown in Chapter 2, the first question we must ask in thinking about something is whether it exists, since unless it now exists or at least has existed in the past, we have no way of being sure that what we are thinking even possibly is or has been real, since our hypothetical definition may be in fact internally contradictory. For example, I can talk about "a square circle" but I cannot even imagine such a thing, and indeed it is meaningless.

Thus our thinking normally begins from some real object, whose reality we know either directly—by observing it with our own senses—or indirectly—by proving that it must exist because it causes other objects, known to exist, that we can observe; or we must believe it exists on the word of some trustworthy person who has either observed it, reasoned to it from its effects, or is passing on to us a tradition from trustworthy persons going back to some original observer, or reasoned from observations. Aberrant thinking, though, contains contradictions, notions that are *not* real. Have not we all experienced such contradictory imagery in our dreams, in drunkenness, in daydreaming, in joking conversation, or when for a moment we were mentally confused? The type of human behavior that we recognize as somehow psychotic or neurotic, moreover, exhibits some defect in this capacity to think abstractly and choose freely. This means that the brains of such persons are not forming the images required for normal abstract thought in an effective manner.

While an image inherently is neither pleasing nor displeasing, but value-neutral, yet many, perhaps most images when presented in sensation stimulate either a positive or a negative affect (feeling) within us, so that we tend to move toward or away from the object presented, to seek pleasant images and avoid unpleasant ones. Thus feelings or emotions play a large role in the movement of one image after another ("the stream of consciousness"). It appears that mental aberrations are somehow a blockage or unhealthy diversion of the normal flow of our imagination and evaluative sense and hence of our intelligence that has to use these images to think in an abstract, essential, and existential manner.

From the preceding chapters it should be evident how much development and formation by family and society in a particular culture or a multicultural society is required for any human person to become fully mature. Such formation can fail in two ways: it may be inadequate so that the person fails to achieve full maturity, or it can actually wound and distort personality so as to raise serious obstacles to this achievement. When it is recognized that a person seems to be a victim of some mental defect or illness, the first step in healing or, if this is not possible, to improvement, is correct diagnosis of the defect and its causes. If this is a serious biological abnormality, due to genetic causes, birth defect, or subsequent trauma, the available medical means—surgical, or pharmaceutical, or proper physical exercise—should be used to restore normal functioning, or at least to improve functioning. The danger here is that physicians are often tempted to stop at this level of medical therapy, even when the condition also involves learned behavior patterns that are aberrant and which require psychotherapy.

When this is the case the psychotherapist must be involved in the diagnosis and, when therapy begins, must create situations in which the client becomes free to reveal their fantasies. The therapist can then suggest interpretations of some fantasies that seem especially significant but should avoid imposing those interpretations on the patient. Unless clients learn to reflect freely on their own memories, such interpretation is of little value. Empirical research on the effectiveness of the various current modes of therapy have, as shown in Chapter 1, indicated that psychoanalytic therapy is comparatively less effective than other therapies and generally takes too long to be very practical. I have raised questions also about its theoretical soundness. This does not mean, however, that psychoanalysts are always poor therapists, since empirical research has also shown that all forms of psychotherapy depend for their effectiveness principally on the skill of the therapist in establishing a helpful relation with the client, and many therapists trained in psychoanalytic techniques have these skills and are in actual practice eclectic.[1]

1. See Greg Mulhauser, "Evaluating Therapeutic Effectiveness in Counseling and Psychotherapy," http://counsellingresource.com/types/effectiveness.html.

Cognitive therapy has been empirically shown to be the most reliable and effective of methods for treating depression.[2] This makes sense in view of the model of personhood we have described, since the technique helps a person who has formed various habits or schemas in their use of their memory, imagination and evaluative senses that are excessively negative, and has turned their attention away from more positive imagery. Consequently, the person continually stimulates negative bodily changes and experiences constant negative emotions or feelings. These habits of their stream of consciousness must be replaced by more normal habits.

Types of Mental Illness

Currently psychological diagnosis is generally based on the *Diagnostic and Statistical Manual* (DSM-IV, with Text Revision, 2000) published by the American Psychiatric Association (it is to be updated in 2013). Diagnosis is located along five possible axes:

Axis I: Clinical disorders, including major mental disorders and learning disorders, depression, anxiety disorders, bipolar disorder, ADHD, autism spectrum disorders, anorexia nervosa, bulimia nervosa, and schizophrenia.

Axis II: Personality disorders and intellectual disabilities including: paranoid personality disorder, schizoid personality disorder, schizotypal personality disorder, borderline personality disorder, antisocial personality disorder, narcissistic personality disorder, histrionic personality disorder, avoidant personality disorder, dependent personality disorder, obsessive-compulsive personality disorder, and intellectual disabilities.

Axis III: Acute medical conditions and physical disorders that include brain injuries and other medical/physical disorders

2. See *Medical News Today*, 5 April 2005, "Cognitive Therapy as Good as Antidepressants, Effects Last Longer."

which may aggravate existing diseases or may present symptoms similar to those of other disorders.

Axis IV: Psychosocial and environmental factors contributing to the disorder.

Axis V: Assessment of the client's global functioning from 1 to 100 in severity. In this list, the condition rated lowest—and therefore highest in degree of impairment—are (a) persons in persistent danger of severely hurting themselves or others or unable to maintain personal hygiene (1–10); (b) those in some danger of hurting themselves or occasionally failing to maintain personal hygiene (11–20); and (c) those suffering from delusions or hallucinations or serious impairment in judgment or inability to function. Of these it is evident that some of these disorders are probably rooted in malfunction of the nervous or hormonal systems, and these necessitate medical treatment as well as psychotherapy.

How do these major types of mental disorders relate to the view of human personhood presented in previous chapters? Since mental illness is at the sensory level of human personality, not directly at the spiritual level, these mental illnesses will be understood only with further consideration of primary and secondary sense cognition and the affective states or emotions that sense cognition arouses.

The secondary senses—imagination and the evaluative sense—play a major part in therapy, for several reasons. First of all, as Freud emphasized, dreams and fantasies often express desires and fears whose direct recognition is too painful for the neurotic to face. The psychoanalyst, therefore, needs to be expert in the interpretation of such metaphors and symbols, so as to enable the neurotic to gain courage to recall and face repressed traumas. Yet an overreliance on such interpretation has been responsible for a great deal of the criticism of psychoanalysis, since such interpretations, including Freud's own, often seem arbitrary and imposed on the client. Nevertheless, as the discipline of semiotics makes clear, human thinking is profoundly metaphorical.

St. Thomas Aquinas recognized the importance of such symbolism in his theory of analogy, which has been further developed by his followers.[3] Human language and the imagery to which it constantly refers are far from adequate to the complexity of human thought. Consequently, we may have to use a word that originally designated some simple object of sense experience in a great variety of different yet related senses. In this process, a word arouses a number of related or associated images that may be quite different for different speakers or hearers because of their diverse experiences. This is true in communication between two or more persons and raises many problems of interpretation, but it is also true to a lesser but significant degree for an individual's own thinking. Our imagination at any given moment is in rapid motion from one image to another associated or contrasted image, and the links between these images are highly conditioned by that person's history. In ordinary practical life this mobility of fantasy makes it necessary for us to focus our attention on certain images and force others into the background of consciousness where, however, they still tend to color our thinking.

Thus it is not necessary to resort to Freud's theory of repression to understand that the overt, easily verbalized content of our imagination is only a small part of this background noise. In the process of "free association" used by psychoanalysts and the "brain-storming" sessions often now used for the sake of "creative" thinking, the client is encouraged to give full rein to this association of images and memories, in the hope that his repressed desires and fears will emerge. The network of associated images stored in our memory is far too rich for it all to be immediately accessible to recall or to verbal expression and can be discovered only by permitting one image to lead others into consciousness.

Breaking addictive patterns of imagination and thought and acquiring new and better ones involves two factors. First, habits are

3. See Ralph McInerny, *Aquinas and Analogy*, reprint (Washington, DC: The Catholic University of America Press, 1998).

changed by exercise and this is explained by the operant conditioning advocated by behavioristic theories. Second, clients can be helped to transcend the fixated attention on their stream of consciousness so as to criticize it intellectually in relation to reality. At first this is impossible or at least very difficult for the depressed person, but, as the area of their freedom of will is expanded and as they receive support and encouragement from the therapist, the neurotic is more able to think at the intellectual level rather than to be lost in preoccupation with negative imagery. Here also drug therapy and physical therapy may help the neurotic to become more energetic and extroverted and less inclined to isolate himself or herself from normal life and communication.

The opposite problem of euphoria in persons suffering from bipolar disorder requires the opposite of these methods of stimulation to quiet the person down. The human intelligence becomes confused when the stream of consciousness becomes too rapid and disordered by excitement.[4] The cyclic character of the bipolar condition is probably due to the fact that the euphoric phase exhausts the victim, who then subsides into depression—just as most of us experience to a minor degree a cycle of moods from intense work to tired rest. It is generally recognized, moreover, that the bi-polar patient is fundamentally depressed.

The clinical evidence Freud offered for his notion of the "death wish" is in part better explained simply as the limit of our human capacity to engage in life; for example, experience shows that we must rest at normal intervals in order to recover our strength and desire for life. In modern life many people suffer from overwork and a failure to find satisfactory ways of recreation. This failure also is the basis of chemical and other addictions that are harmful ways of trying to attain rest and recreation. Psychotherapists often lament that what

4. See National Institute of Mental Health, "Bipolar Disorder," 2002, http://www.nimh.nih.gov/health/publications/bipolar-disorder/complete-index.shtml.

is called "border-line personality disorder" (so named because it borders on psychosis) is one of the most difficult mental illnesses to treat. Women are its most common victims and it is characterized by extreme emotionality that exhausts the victim's energies.[5]

A major element in most mental illnesses is anxiety or fear. Aquinas shows that this feeling is the result of situations in which aggression, one of our two basic drives, is blocked by our inability to escape or overcome something that is painful and harmful to us. Life is full of barriers that must be surmounted and often, as we attempt to hurdle them, we find that we cannot make it and we fall. If, however, we do not have a healthy fear of real danger, for example, concerning the risks involved in drug use or other hazardous practices, we will more easily fall prey to their allure. Fear is a necessary and helpful element in our life.

A person who has the virtue of fortitude, which strengthens the aggressive drive, is able to meet difficulties with courage and, when frustrated (by an injustice for example), may at first be angry and then decide to be patient and endure the pain until a realistic solution can be found. Yet persons who have fortitude may also be in a morbid psychological state in which they are not free to deal with difficulties realistically. In such a condition the resultant anger may be turned inward and possibly cause depression and even self-destructive, suicidal behavior.[6]

Obsessive-compulsive disorder is a persistent state of excessive anxiety, whose roots may be genetic, or a hormonal imbalance, or neurotic habituations.[7] The lowering of the physiological aspects of such anxiety by medication is often advisable. One form of this disorder is scrupulosity, which makes it extremely difficult for obsessive-compulsive clients to decide whether they have been guilty of mis-

5. See "Borderline Personality Disorder," http://www.stanford.edu/~corelli/borderline.html.

6. Karl Menninger, *Man against Himself* (New York: Harcourt Brace, 1938).

7. See Internet Mental Health, "Obsessive-Compulsive Disorder," http://www.mentalhealth.com/dis/p20-an05.html.

conduct, or whether the ordinary decisions that face them may be harmful or sinful. This condition can progress until the person is unable to carry on his or her regular activities and sinks into depression. An important feature of scrupulosity is that sufferers seek relief by communicating their doubts to someone they trust, who will make their decisions for them. Yet this temporary relief only serves to reinforce their morbid pattern of fear and guilt from which they suffer so much. This condition also can be treated by sensitization techniques, but the sufferer is likely to refuse to engage in these unless he also has the support of someone whose *moral* judgment he trusts. Therefore it is often helpful for the therapist to team up with the scrupulous person's priestly confessor or pastor, who can encourage confidence in the therapist's methods.

The behavioristic technique of "desensitization," in which the obsessive-compulsive person is deliberately placed in the situation that provokes excessive fear but is sustained by the support and encouragement of the therapist, is often successful. As scrupulous persons experience the reality of situations they fear and realize that they do not actually lead to the feared consequences, their habit is broken and replaced with a more courageous attitude.

Individual Histories

Although we all belong to one species, human persons are highly individuated. They cannot be hierarchically ranked though, as can angels,[8] because they excel in different respects in complex ways. Every human being reflects some unique aspect of God that no other person can supply to the totality of the universe.[9] So "eccentric" is each

8. Aquinas showed that humans are quasi-species approximating the angels, who are each specifically different. The angels form a clear hierarchy according to the number of ideas innate to each angel, the highest having the fewest and most powerful ideas. See *ST* I, q. 50, a. 4 c.

9. *ST* I, q. 47, aa.1–3.

one of us that some psychologists have argued that mental "illness" is largely a social construct, since what is aberrant behavior in one culture is not so considered in another culture.[10] This notion is, however, very exaggerated, since it is plain enough that some psychotic states prevent individuals from realizing the human potential. To say that the catatonic schizophrenic is a healthy human being is absurd. We must allow, however, that some who can do well in one cultural environment are functionally inadequate in other cultures.

Individual differences in intelligence are obvious. Modern theory, however does not reduce all these to the so-called IQ or "intelligence quotient," but considers what we commonly regard as intelligence as "multifactorial."[11] Some persons, for example, may rate high in memory, but poor in reasoning, and others rate vice-versa.

The unity of the human person results from its ensoulment by a direct creative act of God when a suitable human body has been prepared for this soul by the natural forces of evolution and human reproduction, which are also God's creation. Thus it is reasonable to suppose that in general those who have more finely tuned brains are given proportionally more powerful intelligences by God.[12] Yet it is also possible that accidents in the course of life may injure the brain of a person whose soul would tend to make her or him highly intelligent. Thus the anencephalic infant or the genius in a persistent vegetative state are both functionally unable to think at all and will never be able to think, yet both may have highly intelligent souls.

It remains true, however, that some entirely healthy persons have better brains and more insightful intelligences than others who have inferior intellectual ability but yet are also healthy persons. Human dignity does not depend on the degree of our intelligence. All hu-

10. This was the thesis of the much-discussed book of the psychiatrist Dr. Thomas Szasz, *The Myth of Mental Illness: Foundations of a Theory of Personal Conduct*, rev. ed. (New York: Harper Collins, 1984).

11. See Stephen Jay Gould, *The Mismeasure of Man* (New York: Norton, 1981).

12. St. Thomas Aquinas thought that because touch is the basic sense, persons having sensitive skin are more intelligent; *ST* I, q. 76, a. 5 c.

man beings deserve respect, but those who are morally (not always intellectually) more perfect, the saints, deserve special honor and are models for less perfect persons.

From ancient times, a fourfold classification of opposed personality types was recognized between the melancholic (pessimistic) and the sanguine (optimistic) personality and between the mercurial (active) and the lethargic (passive) personalities and their various combinations.[13] Carl Gustav Jung proposed his own four dimensions of personality somewhat similar to the ancient ones: whether we are energized (a) by sensing or (b) by intuition, and whether we react in decision by (c) extroversion or by (d) introversion.[14] This categorization is used in the familiar Myers-Briggs Personality Indicator, MBPI. These, however, are only general categories, since every human person—and this includes twins—is individuated by a special combination of genes and a unique life history. What must not be forgotten, however, is that because we have spiritual intelligence and will that transcend material limitations, these differences cannot ultimately determine who we are. Our aim in life includes becoming capable of making free and responsible decisions. The goal of psychotherapy is to bring healing in this capacity.

Neuroses and Psychoses

A mental aberration or disorder is an impairment of the ability of the person to make free decisions because of an inability to perceive reality. On the one hand, a disorder that seriously disrupts the victim's contact with reality is often called a *psychosis;* on the other, a *neurosis*, although it causes the victim to think unrealistically about some matters, leaves the victim able in most matters to think realistically.

13. See "Personality Types," http://www.ptypes.com/temperaments.html

14. C. G. Jung and H. G. Baynes, *Psychological Types, or, The Psychology of Individuation* (London: K. Paul Trench, Trubner, 1923); vol. 6 in *Collected Works* (London: Routledge & Kegan Paul, 1953–67).

Although this distinction would seem to be a matter of degree, it is important, since psychotherapy is possible only when the victim has some degree of freedom and can at times and to a degree exercise that freedom. There can be no freedom when persons are unconscious (even though they may be able to dream) or when they are deeply drunk or drug impaired, and it is limited when they suffer from dementia such as in Alzheimer's disease, or from schizophrenia, paranoia, or in the extremes of mood disorders, such as major depression or bipolar disorder.

The role of medical therapy, therefore, is directed to overcoming barriers to free decision making so that psychotherapy can take place. Neuroses, on the other hand, leave a normal degree of freedom for the individual in some areas of life, but make it painful or even impossible for the victim to make realistic decisions and act on them in certain other areas of life. In normal life we all form certain habitual ways of acting that permit our attention and energies to be directed to making decisions about new life problems. These routine responses to ordinary situations are below the level of the intelligence and free will that mark out human behavior from that of other animals; these routines are like animal instincts, generically innate but specified by learning experiences. When I drive a car, most of the time I am only quasi-conscious of my routine actions, although if some special problem arises in the road before me, I suddenly become wide awake to it and deliberately choose what move to make next.

It is not surprising, therefore, that we can acquire bad habits as well as good ones, and that this learning of habits begins in the womb. As good habits predispose to the formation of virtues in which our freedom is expressed for our own good and that of others, so bad habits progressively distort human behavior and predispose to vices. Virtues and vices, however, are more than mere habits, since they enable us to use our intelligence freely to solve new problems and set new goals. Thus we can distinguish a neurosis from a vice, by saying that neurosis is a distorted habit of behavior at a psychological level below that of intelligence and freedom, which, however, limits and distorts intelligent and free behavior.

From the analysis of human intelligence given in previous chapters it should be evident that a person cannot make free decisions unless the sense of touch provides the intellect with the information required for it to know "being," that is, that there is a real world of which the person is a part. All human intellectual conception demands that what is abstractly conceived as a universal essence really exists or once existed as the cause of some effect that we here and now know exists.

Thus it is probable that abnormality in the sensation of touch, caused by some injury to the structure or function of the body, underlies some mental aberrations. The clearest case of this is schizophrenia, since it is often remarked that victims seem "out of touch" with reality, unable to distinguish between their "voices" or other mental images and real objects.[15] The lack of affect manifested in their faces and gestures also seems to express this, since "feelings" are sensations of rather finely tuned bodily changes. Victims of schizophrenia also find it difficult to remain on the drugs because, while these quiet their disordered imagination and "voices" and thus enable them to think somewhat more coherently, these also tend to increase this kind of affective numbness. The fact that the thinking of schizophrenics is so incoherent also shows that the Principle of Identity—our intellectual awareness that "being is not non-being"—is necessary to all logical thinking, because something cannot both be and not be real in the same way at the same time.

What is more puzzling is that schizophrenics, as well as other types of the mentally disturbed, can also be paranoid, although paranoids often seem to be very logical in their reasoning as they construct their accounts of the plotting of others against them. This paranoid logic,

15. "Schizophrenia.com," http://www.schizophrenia.com/. Copyright 1996–2009. Schizophrenia.com. provides a variety of information on this subject, much of it from victims of the disorder.

however, rests on assumptions that are contrary to reality, and this fact reveals that the victim's contact with reality is only partial.

The mood disorders, as in states of euphoria or depression, are also related to the sense of touch in that the level of bodily functions and the feelings of bodily changes that accompany them are extremely activated or inhibited. We all experience such moods; for example, when we are tired we tend to be depressed, when rested we tend to be activated. This does not mean, however, that euphoria and depression are simply caused by these physiological states, since cognitive states can stimulate or tire the body. Probably there is often a cyclical causation in which physiological abnormality is increased by mental experiences and vice versa. I once knew a bipolar woman who, when she became physically tired and dehydrated, suddenly became wildly euphoric and then lapsed into deep depression and passivity.

What, if any, are the roles of the senses besides touch in mental aberration? Taste and smell are related mainly to the pleasure or displeasure that supports the biological drive for food, although smell is also related to sexual stimulation. Sight and hearing are the senses through which most of our information is obtained—sight being the most directly informative and hearing, for humans, the social sense by which we principally communicate with others, although sight also communicates, especially through facial expressions and through gestures. As touch is the existential sense by which we distinguish the real from the mental world, so sight and hearing are the essentialist senses that supply us with the information to answer the question "What is it?" They help us clearly to distinguish one kind of thing from another.

How are external sense illusions possible, in view of the basic epistemology defended through this book, according to which the information received from our primary senses is objectively trustworthy? Optical and other illusions exist, but they either pertain to the secondary senses rather than primary senses or are due to abnormal conditions of observation. Thus error in cognition at the level of primary sensation is generally merely negative—that is, a person may be color-blind or tone-deaf and hence unable to discriminate certain differences—but what we *positively* see or hear is not illusory.

It is important to make this point, because one of the most influential errors in the history of human thinking was the denial by Galileo and Locke that the qualities we perceive by sight and hearing are real.[16] Because of the growing use of mathematical models in science, from the time of Galileo on, like-minded scientists tended to think that what they called the "primary qualities" such as the size and shape of objects that could be mathematically abstracted were objectively real, whereas the "secondary qualities" such as color and sound were merely subjective products of the human senses. They overlooked the fact that we know the size and shape of objects only through the colors we directly see, so that if these so-called secondary qualities are not real, our knowledge of the primary qualities is also called into question.

Positive sensory error becomes possible, however, at the level of perception in the four internal senses whose organs are in the brain. We can think we remember something that in fact we have only imagined.[17] The imagination, precisely because it is the power of separating images from the state in which they were first received from the external senses and recombining them in various ways, is even more likely to confuse the real with the mental, as is obvious in our dreams and daydreams. The common sense that synthesizes information coming from the different senses seems less liable to error, but some persons confuse colors and sounds (*synesthesia*).[18]

The internal sense that is the most important for our topic is the

16. Galileo Galilei, *The Assayer*, n. 196, http://www.philosophy.leeds.ac.uk/GMR/hmp/texts/modern/galileo/assayer.html. See chapter 8 and 10 of John Locke, *Essay Concerning Human Understanding*, http://socserv.mcmaster.ca/econ/ugcm/3ll3/locke/Essay.htm.

17. See Wikipedia, "False Memory syndrome (FMS)," en.wikipedia.org/wiki/False_memory_syndrome, revised 2 September 2012. The topic has recently become controversial because of disputed sex abuse cases.

18. See Patricia L. Duffy, *Blue Cats and Chartreuse Kittens: How Synesthetes Color Their Worlds*, reprint (New York: Owl Books/ Henry Holt, 2002).

evaluative sense, discussed in Chapter 4, which corresponds in humans to animal instinct. It is the sense that evaluates sensed objects positively or negatively as good or bad for the survival and normal functioning of the organism. Although sub-human animals can learn from experience and can even be trained by humans to do remarkable tasks, animal learning is very limited compared with the human capacity to learn, that is, to specify in countless ways the few and very general instincts that are natural to our species. Obviously this instinctual flexibility makes us liable to learn error as well as truth, and the various schemas of neurotic behavior mentioned above are examples of such false learning.

What Freud called the super-ego is actually the evaluative sense, which has been conditioned by our parents or peers, like an animal's conditioned instinct, to consider certain ways of acting good or bad.[19] Our common super-ego is what is often called our "raising," "background," or "culture." Such socially learned values may or may not be realistic, so that as we mature we need to review such habits and perhaps change them to correspond to our experience or to sources of information that have proved trustworthy in our experience. For the Christian, this means in particular conformity to God's guidance provided through his Church. Thus a married couple, who have accepted present-day cultural standards and practiced contraception, when they learn that the Church teaches that contraception harms, not helps, marital love and family welfare, may rightly follow that guidance, even as they follow their physician's advice about the prescriptions they take. While the young Christian in obeying the Church may be simply following it at the super-ego level, i.e., the evaluative sense level, the mature Christian does so at the level of intelligence and freedom out of a faith conviction.

Neuroses do not ordinarily seem to reflect physiological disturbances, yet they are connected with the sense of touch. Pleasure and

19. Priscilla Roth, "The Superego," http://www.freud.org.uk/education/topic/ 10575/ subtopic/40017/.

pain and the feeling of "comfort" are primarily (not exclusively) matters of touch; we feel our body's needs are being satisfied in pleasure and that our body is being injured when we are pained. As we saw in Chapter 5, an analysis of affectivity shows that our biological drives, primarily either for pleasure or aggression, are as such unconscious, but they produce bodily changes which when they become conscious we call "emotions" or "feelings" in the body, and these pertain to the sense of touch. To feel angry is to have certain bodily sensations associated with the biological drive of aggression.

Emotions, as such, are normal and necessary for human freedom, since, just as we cannot form abstract intellectual concepts without appropriate images, we cannot make a decision and carry it out without the support of appropriate affective drives. Thus emotions can enhance freedom, but, if they are excessive or defective, they can also restrict freedom. When they are sufficiently violent they can make it impossible for us, at least temporarily and with regard to certain situations, to think straight or to make rational, free decisions.

As was explained in a previous chapter, Freudian psychoanalysis is based on the conviction that the fundamental cause of mental problems is to be found in the biological drive for physical (i.e., bodily touch) pleasure, which he named "libido," and a second biological drive, the "death wish," which his followers now tend to explain as aggression in the service of the libido. Thus the male animal attacks his rival so that he can enjoy his mate. This is a true, but seriously incomplete, account of the human person, whose happiness is indeed supported by pleasure and aggression. However, happiness more properly involves knowledge of the truth and freedom to love what is known to be truly good. Freud, moreover, did not really acknowledge human freedom, since he had a nineteenth-century, mechanistic and deterministic view of science. Consequently, in his 1929 *Civilization and Its Discontents*,[20] he pictured the individual as hopelessly caught in

20. See excerpt translated by Joan Riviere, http://www.writing.upenn.edu/~ afilreis/50s/freud-civ.html Revised 31-May-2007/.

a society in which human survival is possible, yet which requires its members to suppress their biological drives for the good of society, a suppression that is painful and often results in neuroses and even psychoses. The goal of psychotherapy is thus to "adjust" patients to social respectability while enabling them to satisfy their drives sufficiently that they do not self-destruct—a definition of the goal of therapy that, as shown above, is still accepted by the American Psychiatric Association.

In a more adequate account of the human person, psychological health is the condition in which persons can freely and realistically choose the means necessary for them to arrive at their specifically human goal, which is to live in the community of persons who share true love and wisdom. In our historic condition, however, sin has placed many obstacles in the straight path to happiness that the Creator intended we should have. First of all, our natural environment has been polluted and wasted and its improvement neglected or abused. As God says to Adam (Gn 3:17–19): "Cursed be the ground because of you! In toil shall you eat its yield all the days of your life. Thorns and thistles shall it bring forth to you, as you eat of the plants of the field. By the sweat of your face shall you get bread to eat, Until you return to the ground, from which you were taken; For you are dirt, and to dirt you shall return."

Nurture vs. Nature

Modern biology shows us that the environmental and social conditions produced by their human misuse have also caused the human genome to be in many ways defective in different individuals and hereditary lines. Inevitably, therefore, humans suffer from birth defects, low I.Q., and a host of nervous and hormonal shortcomings that render them subject to mental defect and illness. Thus we come into this world not only with individual differences, which are good and enriching for the community, but with a variety of defects that, among other disorders, make it difficult for our biological drives to operate in a balanced manner and to produce an integrated affective life, and as a result our greatest gifts—those of intelligence and freedom to live well—are restricted.[21]

In the natural order, as argued in Chapter 7, the human monogamous and permanently committed family provides children with an emotional situation that should permit them step-by-step to develop a healthy, integrated emotional life. While this cannot correct genetic defects, it may provide an environment in which the natural healing powers of the human organism can do a great deal to correct and compensate for these defects. Many human families, however, are dysfunctional and operate in a culture that does not provide adequate help in recovery.[22]

Freud thought that very early traumatic incidents in the child's development produce patterns of action by which the growing child seeks to cope with difficult life decisions in ways that are unrealistic and hence ultimately self-defeating. These traumas, because they are painful and thus against the libido drive, are instinctively forgotten (suppressed by the censor), and they form the unconscious, but the

21. *Catechism of the Catholic Church,* no. 404: "How did the sin of Adam become the sin of all his descendants? The whole human race is in Adam 'as one body of one man.' (Thomas Aquinas, *De Malo* 4,1.) By this 'unity of the human race' all men are implicated in Adam's sin, as all are implicated in Christ's justice. Still, the transmission of original sin is a mystery that we cannot fully understand. But we do know by Revelation that Adam had received original holiness and justice not for himself alone, but for all human nature. By yielding to the tempter, Adam and Eve committed a *personal sin,* but this sin affected the *human nature* that they would then transmit *in a fallen state.* (Cf. Council of Trent: DS 1511–1512.) It is a sin which will be transmitted by propagation to all mankind, that is, by the transmission of a human nature deprived of original holiness and justice. And that is why original sin is called 'sin' only in an analogical sense: it is a sin 'contracted' and not 'committed'—a state and not an act."

22. See Sheryl A. Benton and Dorinda J. Lambert, "Dysfunctional Families: Recognizing and Overcoming Their Effects," http://www.ksu.edu/counseling/topics/relationships/dysfunc.html Counseling Services (Manhatten, KS: Counseling Services of Kansas State University, 1997), last updated July 23, 2012.

disordered patterns of action they have generated persist as neurotic symptoms. The child's social adjustment begins in the family and takes the form of the super-ego that governs the child's overt behavior. Gradually, however, as the child begins to develop a conscious ego, the growing person is able to distinguish between the parental and societal commands of its super-ego and to take a degree of realistic control over its own decisions as to how to satisfy its libido, to protect itself, and control its aggression. Psychotherapy seeks, by free association, to recall the traumatic incidents that have distorted the person's behavior as neuroses.The therapist, playing the role of a loving, satisfaction-giving parent (transference), enables neurotics to learn a more realistic way of obtaining needed satisfactions within the limits of their social situation (adaptation).

The most dubious element in Freud's model (besides its deterministic mechanism) is found in the concept of the unconscious and the suppression of memory of trauma. Although it is true that it is sometimes painful to recall traumatic incidents, they are forgotten not only because they are suppressed but much more often simply through the normal process of putting our attention on the present, as we must do to live. Hence the past, whether pleasant or painful, is gradually more and more difficult to recall.

A much more plausible explanation of causal effect of traumatic incidents on future neurotic behavior is that provided by the behaviorists. They have shown experimentally that animals learn habits through conditioning, by intense pleasure or pain, and they seek to repeat the pleasurable events and avoid the painful ones. Similarly, if a child suffers a traumatic event but does not cope realistically with that event, but instead obtains at least partial relief by behavior that is inadequate or inappropriate, he or she may become habituated to dealing with similar situations in later life in the same inappropriate way, even when the original trauma is long forgotten. The only way to correct this bad habit is through the sort of reconditioning learning that behaviorism has taught us to use (operant conditioning). Freud claimed that once the traumatic event was raised from the unconscious id to the conscious ego by the therapeutic process, it would be overcome, but empirical studies of the success of psychoanalytic techniques have not confirmed this. Consequently the trend now in psychotherapy is to avoid the lengthy periods of treatment required by psychoanalysis and to go directly to correcting the harmful habits of behavior by learning new and better coping behaviors. Of course, seeking some insight as to the origins of bad habits is not thereby precluded. Such insight can be useful for a more profound self-understanding, but it is not usually necessary for the cure of neurosis.[23]

So-called "cognitive" therapy is essentially a process of breaking neurotic habits and replacing them with normal ones. Its techniques take into account the character of human learning and thus help the neurotic first to recognize and acknowledge the lack of evidence for the truth of their practical thinking and choosing and, then, to have the courage to face reality and behave reasonably.

Hence Freud's notions of id, ego, censor, and super-ego all require reinterpretation. The unconscious is simply certain habits, good and bad, whose origin in learning experiences is now difficult to recall from the memory. The ego is the conscious mind composed of external and internal sensation and intellection and various levels of attention and integration.[24] The censor is the normal process of gradual forgetfulness

23. "Clinical Decision-Making: Short vs. Long-term Therapy," http://www.columbia.edu/cu/csswp/journal/newswin90/therapy.html.

24. In an article published some time ago, "A Psychological Model with a Spiritual Dimension," *Pastoral Psychology* (May 1972): 31–40, I argued that a distinction should be made between what Aquinas called the *ratio superior* and the *ratio inferior*. The latter is our intelligence as it is habituated to dealing with ordinary practical life; the former comes into play in more profound meditation and decision-making and especially in what is today called "creativity." Mystical writers insist from experience that it is in this "apex of the soul" that we make fervent acts of faith, hope, and love. This *ratio superior*, however, is not a faculty distinct from the intelligence and its *ratio inferior*, but a different mode of the intelligence's operation. In spite of the similarity of the names, it should not be confused with the super-ego, which is in the id or animal area of psychological functioning.

of experiences to which we no longer give attention, whether this refusal to think about them is an evasion of painful facts or simply the need to give attention to other more profitable matters than brooding over the past. The super-ego (poorly named, since it is really part of the id) is the collection of habits of regarding certain behaviors as good or bad, acquired not from our own experience or analysis but by a passive submission to parental, peer, or other social pressures.

Cognitive therapists speak of habitual patterns that have a neurotic or unrealistic character as "schemas"—for example, habits of feeling rejected or of withdrawing from personal relationships, of excessive dependence or co-dependence, of emotional deprivation, of subjugation, of abandonment, etc. Such reactions in themselves are not unreasonable for anyone in certain difficult situations, but they become neurotic when they become habits of meeting situations to which they are not realistic responses. Chemical and other addictions are of the same nature as these schemas, except that they may be reinforced by physiological changes in the addict.

Clearly the defective habits that I have discussed relate to the three main personality disorders previously listed. The eccentric personality exhibited in persons inclined to paranoia and schizophrenia develops out of great feelings of insecurity and detachment from reality. The dramatic personality type is encouraged by experiences of social isolation and neglect that drive the victim, who is social by nature, to demand attention and, at the same time, to feel no responsibility for others, since others show no care for the victim; such a person may even be tempted toward self-destruction. The anxious personality develops out of sense of fear and guilt that the victim can never live up to the expectations of others.

Theological Reflections

For some psychiatrists and psychological counselors, the goal of therapy is to relieve the client of psychological conditions that "regularly cause distress, or interfere with social effectiveness." No doubt these problems are what usually lead a client to seek therapy, but do they define mental illness? And are these two criteria of mental illness adequate? Are there not people who seem happy and socially effective who, like the person with an unrecognized genetic defect or with diabetes, are in fact in serious trouble? Their illness is even more harmful because they do not recognize how ill they are. And as for the secularist culture in which we live today, how healthy is it? May not some people who seem well adjusted to it be adjusted precisely because they share its illusions?

The foregoing account of all these mental sufferings and the obstacles they place in the way of human persons attaining their goal of eternal life with God in Christ and the Holy Spirit can utterly discourage us. In any year some 22.1 percent of Americans ages 18 and older suffer from a mental disorder—about 44.3 million persons. Moreover, four of the ten leading causes of disability are mental disorders: major depression, bipolar disorder, schizophrenia, and obsessive-compulsive disorder.[25] Mental illness is a major feature of the human condition, and Christian faith tells us it was never the Creator's intention but has been acquired by the human race's own sins, the innocent suffering from the sins of the guilty and the guilty dragging down the innocent with themselves.

Yet Jesus Christ is our Savior and also our Physician. Through his Holy Spirit he has inspired researchers, even such an atheist as Sigmund Freud, to try to understand and find therapy for mental illnesses, and he has called countless physicians, psychotherapists, and counselors to treat sufferers patiently and gently, but with "tough love." The Christian virtue of hope and the power of prayer should inspire us all to overcome the environmental, social, and family injustices that are at the root of so much of this suffering. We must be confident that, as we grow in understanding of the mystery of human

25. These statistics are taken from a recent publication of the National Institute for Mental Health, www.nimh.nih.gov, July 29, 2010.

personhood and our eternal destiny with God, the cloud of mental darkness and confusion will be lifted and humanity will be emancipated to think clearly about God's real world and to make free decisions that will lead us all to the Father, Son, and Holy Spirit.

From earliest times it has been recognized that, just as many persons are physically crippled in a variety of ways, so also many persons are mentally ill. A fundamental distinction must be made, however, between illnesses due to natural causes, those due to possession by demons, and those of a moral character, the vices. In much of history, however, mental disorder resulting from natural causes (lunacy) was often attributed to demonic possession, and the Christian worldview not only acknowledges this as a possibility but affirms it as a fact. It was Jesus' power "to cast out demons" (Mk 3:20–30) that he conferred on his apostles and the Church (Mk 16:17). Yet the New Testament also recognizes the difference between natural illnesses and demonic possession: "They brought to him [Jesus] all who were sick with various diseases and racked with pain, those who were possessed, lunatics, and paralytics, and he cured them" (Mt 4:24). Today when more is known about mental illness, the Church, as pointed out in Chapter 8, is very cautious about exorcisms of those allegedly possessed. Private "prayers of deliverance" are permitted, but these are not properly called exorcisms. According to St. Thomas Aquinas, angels, good and bad, cannot move the intelligence or will of other spirits or of human persons and hence cannot directly cause them to sin. However, just as the human spiritual soul has power over its body, so spirits can use natural forces to cause physical changes. Thus they can move physical objects, produce apparitions, and affect the bodies and senses of human beings. Thus demonic possession is possible and we should not lose sight of the fact that there may be a demonic element in mental aberrations, so that prayer can also be an important element in therapy.

The *Catechism of the Catholic Church,* # 1673 says:

> When the Church asks publicly and authoritatively in the name of Jesus Christ that a person or object be protected against the power of

the Evil One and withdrawn from his dominion, it is called *exorcism*. Jesus performed exorcisms and from him the Church has received the power and office of exorcizing. In a simple form, exorcism is performed at the celebration of Baptism. The solemn exorcism, called "a major exorcism," can be performed only by a priest and with the permission of the bishop. The priest must proceed with prudence, strictly observing the rules established by the Church. Exorcism is directed at the expulsion of demons or to the liberation from demonic possession through the spiritual authority, which Jesus entrusted to his Church. Illness, especially psychological illness, is a very different matter; treating this is the concern of medical science. Therefore, before an exorcism is performed, it is important to ascertain that one is dealing with the presence of the Evil One, and not an illness.

The fact that today it seems difficult to identify authentic cases of demonic possession in our scientific culture does not prove that those many cases related in the New Testament were not authentic. Today cases are more often reported by missionaries in less advanced cultures than are reported in advanced cultures.[26] Nevertheless, it should be obvious that, since Satan's purpose in such possessions is to terrify persons who believe in spirits and to gain power over them, his strategy would be to do this in a spectacular manner in simple cultures, whereas in cultures dominated by modern secularism, which denies the existence of spiritual beings, it is hardly to Satan's advantage to prove his existence to doubters.

In our culture the spirit world is treated as a matter of fantasy and half-belief that can become obsessive in anxious and deranged per-

26. On a trip to Nigeria I discussed this with Catholics who were performing "deliverances," chiefly of women, but I was not convinced by their reports that these "possessions" were more than mass hysteria. Yet I have also heard in the United States a well-educated psychologist claim that she herself had been delivered from depression and fits of self-mutilation through charismatic deliverances; she recounted that her Brazilian parents (members of a Satanist cult) had dedicated her as a child to the devil! By the very nature of demonic deceit, it seems almost impossible to apply controlled research methods to authenticate such accounts.

sons. A psychotherapist need not suspect demonic possession simply because a patient claims to be possessed, but only when phenomena occur that do not seem to be explicable medically, in which case the priest appointed by the local bishop to examine such cases (or, if the diocese has no such official, the local bishop himself) should be consulted.

Psychotherapists, therefore, must remain sincerely open to the inescapable question of the world views and value systems of their clients and also of their own. The right choice of these cannot be settled by modern psychotherapeutic theorizing or modern psychology, because they are more fundamental issues and pertain to metaphysics and theology.

Conclusion

This book has argued that the goal of psychotherapy is to enable persons to overcome obstacles arising principally from the malfunctioning of their secondary senses and affective drives at the border where these serve human intelligence and free will. We have placed the human person in the context of the evolving physical world, as we know it through science; but we have raised cautions about confusions in current scientific thinking. In this evolutionary context, this book has described the human body, its senses, and its drives and related them as instruments to the human spirit that unifies and guides that body and relates the person to reality through reason and a reasonable faith in God's guidance.

In examining these questions this book has tried to synthesize the current results of twenty-first-century science in a critical manner, while at the same time following the divine guidance given us through the Catholic Church. Yet most of the information and analysis it provides is independent of the Catholic faith and is addressed to all.

INDEX

ALSO FROM THE IPS PRESS

The John Henry Cardinal Newman Lectures
EDITED BY CRAIG STEVEN TITUS

1. *The Person and the Polis: Faith and Values within the Secular State* (2007)
2. *On Wings of Faith and Reason: The Christian Difference in Culture and Science* (2008)
3. *Christianity and the West: Interaction and Impact in Art and Culture* (2009)
4. *The Psychology of Character and Virtue* (2009)
5. *Philosophical Psychology* (2009)

Monograph Series

1. Fergus Kerr, *"Work on Oneself": Wittgenstein's Philosophical Psychology* (2008)
2. Kenneth L. Schmitz, *Person and Psyche* (2009)
3. Kevin L. Flannery, SJ, *Christian and Moral Action* (2012)